`Upoho Uka Nui O Kekokia
(Scotland's Great Highland Bagpipe)

The Story
of Bagpipes,
Bagpipers, and
Bagpipe Bands
in Hawai`i
with Accounts
of
King Kalakaua's
Visit to Scotland

Hardy Spoehr

AUTHOR:	Hardy Spoehr
EDITOR:	Gayle Bonham
DESIGN & LAYOUT :	Donald Kroitzsh

Copyright ©2004 by Hardy Spoehr. All rights reserved under International and Pan-American copyright conventions. No part of this publication may be reproduced, stored in a retrieval system or transmitted, in any form, or by any means, electronic, mechanical, recorded, photocopied, or otherwise, without the prior written permission of the copyright owner, except by a reviewer who may quote brief passages in a review.

Printed in the United States of America

A portion of the proceeds from this publication goes to support bagpipe instruction in Hawai`i

Published by:
Ki`ilea Publishing Company
1833 Vancouver Place
Honolulu, Hawai`i 96822
(808) 944-8601

Prepared by:
Five Corners Press
Plymouth, Vermont 05056 USA

`Upoho Uka Nui `O Kekokia
Scotland's Great Highland Bagpipe
ISBN: 0-9762968-0-2   US$24.^{95}

Bagpipes In Paradise – Pipe Major A. J. Frappia Plays For Visitors On The Beach At Waikiki (1980s)

This publication is dedicated to all the bagpiping instructors in Hawai`i who throughout time have shared their knowledge freely with those with the burning desire to master the instrument. This list begins with Agnes Wallace and Lawrence Coleman and continues today with Dan Quinn and Tina Berger Yap.

A Plea for Help:

As with most histories, this one has a number of stories yet to be told. We ask you, the reader, if you have any interesting information about bagpiping in Hawai`i, including any additional information about early Honolulu pipers such as R. McDonald Murray (1902), Fraser/Frazer (1907), Stewart (1908), Burns (1927), and William McDougall (1921), please contact the author at:

> Celtic Pipes and Drums of Hawai`i
> PO Box 30093
> Honolulu, Hawaii 96820-0093

Table Of Contents

Introduction ix

Chapter 1
The Bagpipe — An Instrument Of Calling 1
The Pipes And Highland Society 21
The Pipes And The Military 37

Chapter 2
First Encounters 59
   A. Hawaiians Traveling The World
   B. Bagpipes Arrive In Hawai`i

Chapter 3
Social Acceptance Achieved 95
   A. Celebrations And Parades 95
      (1) Burns Night 96
      (2) St. Patrick's Day 113
      (3) Highland Games/festival 119
   B. Pipe Bands And Pipers 121
      (1) Pipe Bands 121
      (2) Noted Local Pipers 148

Band Photographs 157
Royal Scots 159
Honolulu Pipes And Drums 163
Shamrock Pipe Band 175
Celtic Pipes And Drums Of Hawai`i 179
Hawaiian Thistle Pipe Band 193
Marines Own Highlanders 197
Maui Celtic Pipes And Drums 201

Bibliographical Notes 205

Illustrations And Photographs 247

Appendix 1 — King David Kalakaua's Trip To Scotland (1881)
Scotland Itinerary 271
Newspaper Accounts Of The Trip
   Edinburgh Courant 279
   Glasgow Herald 295
   The Bailie 313
   Pacific Commercial Advertiser 317

APPENDIX 2 — Newspaper Account Of Piper Macintyre Playing For Kamehameha III (1845)
The Polynesian 331
APPENDIX 3
Pipe Majors And Drum Majors Of Hawai`i's Pipe Bands 335
APPENDIX 4
Prince Alfred's March – Farquharson's Tune For
The Duke Of Edinburgh 341

`Upoho Uka Nui `O Kekokia – 𝄞 – vii

Saved By A Bagpipe (1896)

A Highland bagpiper was one evening going from a village to a neighbouring town, having only collected a few coppers after playing all day. On his way he asked a boy to show him the nearest way to the town which he wished to reach. The boy told him to go across some fields, which he pointed out to him, and which would bring him to a road leading directly to the town. After the bagpiper had got to the middle of the second field, he noticed a bull coming full speed towards him. He had heard some animals liked music, so he took out his bagpipe and began playing. The bull stopped as soon as he heard the music, and seemed much pleased, but at each attempt of the man to escape, the bull's anger returned. It became evident that he must either play all night, or be gored by the bull; but, presently, help came in the shape of the farmer with his dog, who drove the bull off, and so rescued the poor bagpiper from his dangerous position.

viii – 𝄞 – Scotland's Great Highland Bagpipe

A YOUNG HUMANITARIAN.

"Oh, Mamma, Mamma, couldn't you interfere? There's a horrid Man squeezing something under his Arm, and he IS hurting it so!"

The Bagpipes; An Uncommon Instrument (1887)

INTRODUCTION

The history of bagpiping in Hawai`i offers a great vantage point from which to glean bits and pieces of Hawai`i's unique and fascinating history. It is a story of music, but it is more than that. It is an account of human inter-relationships and cultural adaptation.

Hawai`i's noted band maestro, Henry Berger, writing in 1885, voiced the dilemma of all who write about music they love: *It is rather a hard task to write about music – hard to begin at the right place and hard to know where and when to stop.*[1] For those who love and play the music of the Great Highland Bagpipe that task is daunting towards the impossible so this author asks forgiveness at the start of this story if it either provides too much and closes the eyelids, or not enough and leaves the brain undernourished.

The story of music in Hawai`i offers a wonderful eyeglass from which to view the influx of one culture into another and the eventual acceptance and emergence of what was foreign becoming "localized" and taking on its own unique qualities. Just as the Hawaiian flag proudly exhibits the Union Jack within its design, and Hawai`i's national anthem, *Hawai`i Pono`i*, was written by King Kalakaua after hearing Britain's *God Save the King*, and the beloved tune *Hawai`i Aloha*, a song arranged by the Rev. Lorenzo Lyons, is that of *I Left It All with Jesus*, a traditional Scottish hymn written by James McGranahan (1840-1907); so, too, has bagpiping transitioned from a foreign music played by visitors to Hawai`i to a local music played by those who call Hawai`i home.

After a brief general discussion of the bagpipe, this story reviews three major facets about bagpipes in Hawai`i; first, some conjecture about when Hawaiians could have first heard the sounds of the bagpipe; second, a review of the historical record of bagpipe playing in Hawai`i; and, finally, a brief discussion of how bagpipers and bagpipe bands have developed and continue to develop in Hawai`i today (through 2003).

Throughout the text there are numerous quotations from original sources. In most instances original spellings of words have been kept in order to keep the 'color' of original quotations despite the fact that they may be considered incorrect according to today's standards.

Interspersed throughout this story are illustrations and photographs which attempt to portray not only a historical image but also an emotional feeling for the Great Highland Bagpipes and those that have played and continue to play them. Historical anecdotes are also provided as NOTEs within the text. Expanded reference sections on written, engraved, and photographic resources related to this publication are found at the end of the text which, hopefully, will spark continued research by others.

This story could not have been told without the support and help of numerous individuals who contributed their mana`o. Any success this account achieves in capturing this unique story is due to the help and support of pipers, family members of pipers, those who are the guardians of historical resources, and those who simply love bagpipes and bagpipe music.

Included on this list are pipers and drummers Lawrence Coleman(O`ahu, Hawai`i), Stuart Cowan(O`ahu, Hawai`i), David Furumoto(Madison, Wisconsin), David Siegel(Karmiel, Israel), Barbara Macaulay(Hayden, Idaho), Alexander Causey(O`ahu, Hawai`i), Kanoe Miller (O`ahu, Hawai`i), Dr. Rob Knudson(Santa Fe, New Mexico), Hamish (Jim) Douglas-Burgess(Maui, Hawai`i), Andrew Wright(Dunblane, Scotland), and the late A. J Frappia and Dr. John Sheedy who all shared their rich knowledge and life experiences to make this book possible.

A big 'thank you' goes to family members of past Hawai`i pipers who shared their memories and photos openly with the author including the families of Donald Mackay including his granddaughter Carolyn Mackay in Thousand Oaks, California and family member Carole Commeford of Kailua, O`ahu; Aggie Wallace including Anna Ross, Ian and Debra Ross, Heather Ross, and Leigh Ann Davis of Honolulu; Shelley Cost Chaffee of California who shared her experiences with and photos of her father Maui piper Robert

Cost; and Roy Forbes of Hilo, Hawai`i who shared his family history and provided photos of his father Robert Forbes and uncle William Forbes of Hilo.

 In researching this project, the author is greatly indebted to multitudes who have provided encouragement, guidance and historical documentation including Barbara Dunn and Karen Sinn at the Hawaiian Historical Society and Marilyn Reppun of the Hawai`i Mission Childrens Society Library; to Mary Stacey Judd, formerly at the Punahou School Archives; to Luella Kurkjian and her fine staff at the Hawai`i State Archives; to Linda Laurence and DeSoto Brown at the Bishop Museum Archives-Library; to Aletha Kaohi, Chris Faye, and the staffs at the Kaua`i Museum and Kaua`i Historical Society; to Ian Howarth, Secretary to the Black Watch Retirees Association; to DeeDee Acosta and Michelle Itomura, UH Libraries, Hamilton Library, University of Hawai`i, Honolulu, Hawai`i, and Mr. Chris Payne of The British Library, London, England, for assisting with procuring copies of Scottish newspaper accounts of Kalakaua's visit; to Tim Hughes of Tim Hughes Associates (London) for researching British ship records in London; to the many who researched their respective collections for written records and photographic resources related to this publication including Lt. Col.(Retd) Stephen J. Lindsey, Regional Headquarters, The Black Watch, Balhousie Castle, Perth, Scotland; John Ambler, Photographic Librarian, Royal Marines Museum, Hampshire, England; Brian Liddy, Curator of Collections Access, National Museum of Photography, Film and Television, Bradford, England; Carol Maclaren, History and Glasgow Room, The Mitchell Library, Glasgow, Scotland; Anna Petersen, Hocken Library, Dunedin, New Zealand; Stephen Courtney, Curator of Photographs, Royal Naval Museum, Portsmouth, Hampshire, England; R.G. Todd and Imogen Gibbon, Historic Photographs and Ship Plans Section, and Liza Verity, Information Specialist, National Maritime Museum, Greenwich, London, England; Olwen Morgan, Royal New Zealand Naval Museum, Auckland, New Zealand; Michael St. John, Curator, Department of Manuscripts, the British Library, London, England; Rachael M. Rowe, Smuts Librarian in South Asian and Commonwealth Studies, University of Cambridge, England; to John Walker and his friends Michael and Carol Knight and her sister Beverly Biddlecombe of Norfolk, England for sharing their information on J.F. Farquharson, Piper to the Duke of Edinburgh; and to Mrs. Jill Kelsey, Deputy Registrar, and Miss. Frances Dimond of the Royal Archives, Windsor Castle, Berkshire, England for searching their records for Hawai`i material.

And, finally, to ku`u hoaloha `ohana Rubellite Kawena Johnson for her help with the Hawaiian language; to Tom Layton at the Wallace A. Gerbode Foundation and Kelvin Taketa at the Hawai`i Community Foundation, for without their support this publication would not have been possible; to Gayle Bonham who undertook the editing and reviewing of this publication; to Don Kroitzsh who performed miracles with the material provided and who designed the layout of this publication; and to my family for allowing me to explore the wonderful world of bagpipes – mahalo. To all of you —

`A`ohe pilo uku...mahalo kakou

Chapter 1
The Bagpipe — An Instrument Of Calling

Bagpipes are one of the world's oldest reed instruments. There are depictions in sculpture of early Romans playing some form of bagpipe more than two thousand years ago.[1] Bagpipes also are one of the more-widely dispersed instruments in the world, traditionally being played from the British Isles in the west, to the Scandinavia in the north, and to the Caucasus Mountains, Afghanistan, and Pakistan in the east. Bagpipes, also, come in all shapes and sizes.[2] Those things which all bagpipes have in common include a reed chanter from which distinct notes are made and an air bag which provides the air reservoir for 'exciting' the reed to produce sound. In addition, bagpipes may have any number of 'drones' with additional reeds which produce additional 'background' sound for the chanter. The drone reeds, generally, are single-tongued while the reed for the chanter is double-tongued.

This story focuses on the bagpipe which evolved in Scotland and is known as the Great Highland Bagpipe, in Gaelic, *piob mhor*, or in Hawaiian,`*upoho uka nui*. The Scottish bagpipe is characterized by its one large bass drone and two tenor drones all tuned to the low hand A on the chanter. The tenor drones are tuned to one octave below low A on the music scale and the bass drone is tuned to two octaves below low A, thereby giving the instrument its harmonious sound. Reeds traditionally have been made from Spanish cane, however, now there are a number of chanter and drone reeds made of synthetic materials.

The chanter and blowpipe are two additional appendages to the instrument; all of which, including the three drones, protrude from an air bag made of hide or, more recently, gortex which serves as the air reservoir for producing the instrument's continuous sound. The chanter is the instrument's 'tune-maker' and possesses eight finger holes from high A to low G, (an octave and one note including High A, High G, F, E, D, C, B, Low A, Low G).

2 – 🎼 – Scotland's Great Highland Bagpipe

Types Of Bagpipes

Great Highland Bagpipe Scale:

Great Highland Bagpipe:

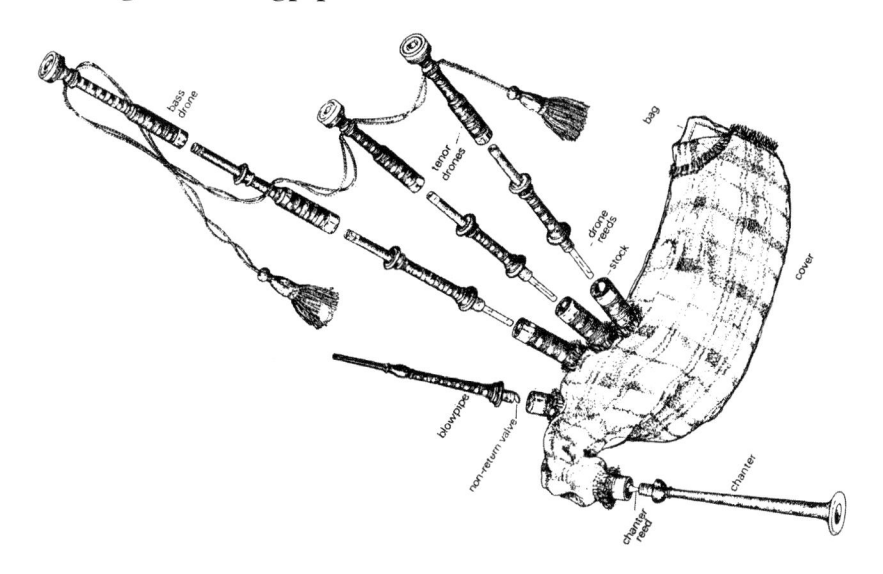

Some of the technical aspects of the instrument are that it is tuned to the key of B♭ (467 cps) though originally it was tuned to a pitch of A (440 cps), that it operates at a 'loudness' level of 85 decibels, and that synthetic materials are now being used in the manufacture of bagpipes with some success.

Culturally, the Great Highland Bagpipe evolved in Scotland and continues to maintain a tradition which extends back more than five hundred years. While today's most favored wood for pipe-making is African blackwood, ebony and rosewood have been used in the past. The instrument's classical music called *piobaireachd* continues to grow in popularity each year as does interest in the

A Roman Bagpiper By J. Gilbert (1861)

complete oral language associated with the teaching of *piobaireachd* called *canntaireachd*.[3]

No one is sure when the Great Highland Bagpipe first appeared in Scotland. What is known, however, is that playing this pipe reached a high level of sophistication in the mid-sixteenth century. At that time, history records the emergence of the family MacCrimmon in Skye or, perhaps, Glenorchy. From where this family first came is not known, but it is acknowledged by historians that this family dominated the style of bagpipe playing and set the standards for instruction for more than two hundred years.[4] While tradition has the MacCrimmons originally emerging from the north-west area on the Isle of Skye, a recent discovery in the papers of the Campbells of Glenorchy notes a MacCrimmon piper (Malcolme pypar Makchrwmen) in the household of Colin Campbell of Glenorchy in 1574.[5]

Later in this era, many of the old Highland chiefs had their own pipers whose job it was to celebrate various events of their respective chief's clan with piping. Each piper would prominently display his chief's banner on his large drone. This custom is still followed by the Scottish Regiments today.

> NOTE: The Queen's Piper. The British Monarchy has adopted the custom the appointing an official piper to the Monarchy. In 1843, Queen Victoria visited Lord Breadalbane and was so taken by his piper that she initiated the practice and appointed Angus Mackay to her Household as her official piper. This practice continues today. These pipers have included:
>
> <u>Queen Victoria (1837-1901)</u>:
>   Angus Mackay (1843-1854)
>   William Ross (1854-1891)
>   William Lays (2nd piper) (1871-1876)
>   James McHardy (2nd piper) (1878-1881)
>   James Campbell (2nd piper) (1881-1891)
>
> <u>King Edward VII (1901-1910)</u>:
>   James Campbell (1901-1910)

<u>King George V (1910-1936)</u>:
   Henry Forsyth (1910-1936)
   John MacDonald (honorary) (1935-1936)

<u>King Edward VIII (1936)</u>:
   Henry Forsyth (1936)
   James MacDonald (1936)

<u>King George VI (1936-1952)</u>:
   Henry Forsyth (1936-1941)
   John MacDonald (honorary) (1936-1952)
   Alex MacDonald (1945-1952)

<u>Queen Elizabeth II (1952-present)</u>:
   Alex MacDonald (1952-1965)
   John MacDonald (honorary) (1952-1953)
   Andrew Pitkeathly (1966-1973)
   David Caird (1973-1980)
   Brian MacRae (1980-1995)
   Gordon Webster (1995-1998)
   Jim Motherwell (1998-present)

A day in the life of the piper who holds the title as piper in the Office of the Sovereign's Piper was recently described in *Piping Times*:[6]

Every weekday at 9am his (the piper) day begins playing in the open air beneath the Queen's apartments. The pipe major is responsible for selecting and arranging suitable pieces for these sessions. He generally follows tradition by marching up and down four times. This ritual takes place every morning when the Queen is in residence at Buckingham Palace, the Palace of Holyroodhouse, Edinburgh, or at Balmoral Castle in the Highlands.....

A normal day at Buckingham Palace means other duties.... After playing at 9am, he must be ready at 11am to escort the Queen from her private apartments to her reception room. He then works with the Equerry and Page controlling the entry and exit of the Queen's guests for the day. These can include Government ministers, Ambassadors, and visiting Heads of State.

At state banquets the pipe major is responsible for the forming up, entry and exit of the 12 pipers who play round the table after the meal. These banquets can take place in London or at British Embassies abroad. The Queen's Piper often travels with her on foreign visits.

> After dinner at Balmoral, Holyroodhouse and Windsor he plays a selection which includes either a medley or a march, strathspay and reel. This happens nightly Monday to Saturday at the Queen's table. Sometimes there will be only three or four guests at dinner.
>
> The royal stay at Balmoral is 11 weeks long. P/M Motherwell must therefore play 15 minutes in the morning and six minutes at night, every day except Sunday, and is not allowed to repeat a tune all week.

Throughout the 17th and 18th centuries, the bagpipes' history is interwoven with British-Scottish relations. In 1653 when Oliver Cromwell became 'Lord Protector' of England, he declared that anyone found playing the bagpipe would be banished to Barbados. In 1746, after the English defeated the remnants of the Scottish clans at the Battle of Culloden, George II issued the Act of Proscription which prohibited Highlanders from bearing arms, wearing the kilt, or speaking the Gaelic language. The playing of the bagpipe is sometimes coupled with the restrictions associated with this act for in 1746, James Reid of York was accused of being in possession of arms under this act when, in fact, all he was carrying was a set of bagpipes. The judge found him guilty after ruling the bagpipe an 'instrument of war,' and he was hanged in November, 1746.[7]

Because of this and the fact that individuals could no longer maintain any semblance of livelihood in the private sector by piping, the instrument lost much of its popularity. This began to change in 1757, when the British Army ironically became a bastion for pipers and the continuation of piping instruction and playing.

In the early 17th century, Sir John Hepburn raised the first Scottish Regiment in the British Army which later became known as the *Royal Scots*. In 1633, a piper from Clan Mackay is noted as having joined the Regiment. This is the first recorded instance of a piper serving in the British Army.[7]

From this point on, as various Highland Regiments were formed by the British, pipers were brought into the army by their 'benefactor' officers, first as solo pipers and later as bands of pipers as responsibilities moved from performing solo command tunes to providing music for marching and for concerts.

The Queen At Balmoral
Waking Her Majesty –The Queen's Piper (1882)

Soon, piping became a British Army tradition. In 1760 the 42nd Highlanders, known as the 'Black Watch,' marched out of Perth with their pipers playing 'The High Road to Gairloch.'[9] In North America, the bagpipes were heard for the first time when the 42nd Highlanders marched on the French at Fort Ticonderoga during the French and Indian Wars in 1758.

> NOTE: Bagpipes At The Battle Of Ticonderoga. Ticonderoga is the Mohawk Indian word for 'meeting of the waters' and was the name given to the fort which guards Lake Champlain where it meets Lake George in New York State. In 1758, against this beautiful backdrop, is the legend of Major Duncan Campbell. It begins in Scotland twenty years before the battle. Campbell had a vision of a dead ancestor who had quarreled with him. The ghost warned Campbell they would both meet again at a place called Ticonderoga. Troubled by this warning Campbell searched for this place without success. Eventually he joined the Black Watch, rose to the rank of Major and was sent to fight in America. The day before the attack on the French held fort on Lake Champlain, Campbell asked an Indian scout what this beautiful place was called. "Ticonderoga" said the scout. Campbell froze for he knew the following day would be his last, and it was.[10]

A short time later in the 1770s, the 42nd Highlanders' pipes were heard again throughout the American colonies during the Revolutionary War.

However, the pipes were not always used as an instrument of war. In 1848, the 79th Highlanders on route from Gibraltar to Quebec "became fog-bound in the St. Lawrence River. To ward off a possible collision, the pipers and drummers were ordered to play together on deck."[11]

Yet, despite this popularity in the British Army, pipers often had to be disguised on muster rolls as drummers for there was no official ranking for pipers in the army.

> NOTE: Bagpipes At The Alamo. Individual pipers who left the military service and set off for new frontiers played a major role in spreading the sounds of bagpipes throughout the

10 – 𝄞 – Scotland's Great Highland Bagpipe

Pipers and Pipe Majors — British Military Regiments

`Upoho Uka Nui `O Kekokia – 11

Pipers and Pipe Majors — British Military Regiments

12 – Scotland's Great Highland Bagpipe

Pipers, Royal Highlanders, The Black Watch.

Pipers 2nd Black Watch, South African Kit.

"AN ATHOLE HIGHLANDER."

Pipers and Pipe Majors — British Military Regiments

world. One such person was John McGregor who emigrated with his bagpipes from Aberfeldy, Scotland to America after the Napoleonic Wars around 1815. He eventually settled in Nacogdoches, Texas near the Louisiana boundary and in February,1836, he joined Lieutenant Col. William Travis, Jim Bowie, Col. David Crockett and about 150 others at the Alamo in San Antonio. At the age of 28, he held the rank of 2nd sergeant with Captain Carey's artillery company. As Mexican General Santa Anna's army moved to surround the Alamo, one historical record notes:

Bowie, though desperately ill, did his best to encourage the men. He had his cot brought out...urged them to keep fighting, whatever happened. Crockett turned on the tested charm that had never failed him yet. His favorite device during these dark days was to stage a musical duel between himself and John McGregor. The Colonel had found an old fiddle somewhere, and he would challenge McGregor to get out his bagpipes to see who could make the most noise. The two of them took turns, while the men laughed and whooped and forgot for a while the feeling of being alone.[11]

John McGregor died at the battle of the Alamo.[12]

It was not until 1854 and the Crimean War that the British Army finally recognized piping as an official duty within its ranks. Each of the Highland regiments was allowed a Pipe Major and five pipers, an allotment which continued to World War II. It was not until 1918, however, some 60 years later, that this same privilege was afforded the Scottish Lowland regiments. Each of these regiments developed their own unique uniforms which carried over to their pipers and, eventually, to their pipe bands.

By 1859, five years after institutionalizing bagpipers within the army structure, pipes and drums had replaced fifes and drums as the major instruments of the British regiments. Most of the regiments had more than their allotted five pipers. In fact, it was not uncommon for some regiments to field pipe bands of more than thirty pipers. The extra pipers generally had their instruments and full-dress uniforms provided by the officers of the regiment.[13]

NOTE: Scottish Regiments In The British Army. Many of today's bagpiping traditions have been preserved through the Scottish Regiments in the British Army. Over time, a number of these regiments have been combined but today there are eight active Scottish Regiments in the British Army as the Cameronians chose to disband rather than amalgamate with another regiment.[14] These regiments, their earliest roots, and their amalgamations include:

The Royal Scots (1633)
    The Royal Regiment
    1st Regiment

The Scots Guards (1642)

The Royal Scots Dragoon Guards (1678)
    Carabiniers
    Royal Scots Greys

The Royal Highland Fusiliers (1678)
    Highland Light Infantry
    Royal Scots Fusiliers
    Princess Margaret's Own Glasgow and Ayrshire Regiment
    21st, 71st, and 74th Regiments

The King's Own Scottish Borderers (1689)
    King's Own Borderers
    25th Regiment

The Cameronians (1689) – DISBANDED in 1968
    Scottish Rifles
    26th and 90th Regiments

The Black Watch (1725)
    The Royal Highlanders
    42nd and 73rd Regiments

The Queen's Own Highlanders (1778)
    Seaforth Highlanders
    Queen's Own Highlanders
    Cameron Highlanders
    Seaforth and Camerons
    Gordon Highlanders
    72nd, 75th, 78th, 79th, and 92nd Regiments

The Argyll and Sutherland Highlanders (1794)
    Argyllshire Highlanders
    Sutherland Highlanders
    Sutherland and Argyll Highlanders
    Princess Louise's
    91st and 93rd Regiments

Drums have always been in close proximity to bagpipes. Their use by the British Army predates that of bagpipes and were used to keep cadence and to give commands. In the early years, the drums were usually placed in the front of marching units to enable all to hear. When bagpipes were introduced into the marching unit, there developed on-going squabbles as to who would be up front in the military formation – the drums or the pipes. This dispute continued for many years until in the 1870s Queen Victoria stepped in and decreed that "The pipes must lead." In consolation for this acknowledgement, the "de facto" leader of the pipe band was made the leader of the drum section – the Drum Major. This continues to be the case in pipe bands today.[15]

> NOTE: Drummers and Drumming. Without drummers, bagpipe bands would not be what they are today. Drummers are often referred to as the "musicians" in the band. Most bagpipe bands include three types of drums, all of which are necessary for a complete pipe band; the bass drum, the snare drum, and the tenor drum. Of the three, the bass drum is essential for it "keeps the beat" both in playing tunes and when the band is on the march. The other tenor and snare drums add flourish and enhance the pipe band's sound and spectacle. Tenor drummers also are renown for their abilities of twirling drumsticks. It is not by chance that the leader of the pipe band in formation on the march is the Drum Major.
>
> The reason for the early preeminence of the drum stems from an English military tradition more than five hundred years old. Originally, 18th century British Army units (and later American units) marched to the fife and drum or simply to the drum. The bagpipe evolved in the Scottish units and was later introduced into marching units with the drum in the 19th century. On 18th century British Navy vessels along with a detachment of Royal Marines, it was not unusual for a drummer to be assigned to signal commands. Captain Cook had Marine drummers assigned to all of his ships:[16]
>
> 1st Voyage (1768-1771):
>   H.M.S. *Endeavour* – Thomas Rossilter
>
> 2nd Voyage (1772-1775):
>   H.M.S. *Resolution* – Philip Brotherson
>   H.M.S. *Adventure* – John Lane
>
> 3rd Voyage (1776-1780):
>   H.M.S. *Resolution* – Michael Portmouth
>   H.M.S. *Discovery* – Jeremiah Hooloway (Holloway)
>
> This tradition of using drums as a communication's medium continues to survive in pipe bands today and is the principle reason why the Drum Major serves as the band's director when it is on the march.
>
> In Hawai`i, the Kingdom of Hawai`i's Royal Household Guard used drummers in its ranks to keep cadence in

16 – 𝄞 – Scotland's Great Highland Bagpipe

Drummers — British Military Regiments

`Upoho Uka Nui `O Kekokia – 17

The Kingdom Of Hawai`i's Queen's Royal Household Guards Under The Command Of Captain Sam Nowlein (1890)
(Note Drums)

marching and to signal commands just as the English did. The drums were placed in front to ensure all could hear the appropriate beats and signals.

The tradition of British Army pipers continued throughout the late nineteenth and twentieth centuries and remains today. British Army pipers in World War I and World War II often led the charge with nothing more than their dedication to purpose and tradition protecting them. They were an inspiration to their units, but they had one of the higher casualty rates for both World Wars within the British Army.[17]

> NOTE: Bagpipes At Normandy. During the D-Day Landing in Normandy on June 6, 1945, a number of pipers were involved but only one man in the invasion force is recorded as wearing a kilt and bravely playing the pipes – Pvt. Bill Millin of the 1st Commando Brigade of the Royal Marines. He landed at Sword Beach instrument in hand playing "Highland Laddie." Millin served as Brigadier Lord Lovet's personal piper.[18] In 2000, Millin donated his pipes and his uniform to the National War Museum located in Edinburgh Castle.

Today, despite the consolidation of many of the Scottish regiments, pipers continue to play a vital role in the military life of the British Army. Also, other armies modeled on the British experience such as those of Australia, Canada, New Zealand, and Jordan, all have pipers associated with their military units. Their importance remains unchallenged.

Maintaining the piping tradition in the British Army has been the primary responsibility of the Army School of Piping founded in 1910 and endowed in 1919 by the Piobaireachd Society as a memorial to World War I pipers. The home of the Army School had been Edinburgh Castle until recently when the school was moved to modern facilities outside the castle's gates. Its students and graduates not only have included the Pipe Majors and pipers in the British military but also many of the Pipe Majors and pipers in military services from countries around the world.

In the United States military, the Air Force, Army, and Marines all have bagpipers within their ranks who are called upon from time to time to play for special occasions. The Air Force, Army, and Marines, also, have organized pipe bands which perform at official functions as well.

Winston Churchill once observed:

Regiments have been known to march to their deaths led by bagpipes. What is not known, however, is whether the regiments were advancing with them or were trying to get away from them.[19]

Despite this ambiguity, it is clear that interest in bagpiping is increasing throughout the world. Piping schools are found on all the major continents and the established piping centers, including the College of Piping and The Piping Center in Glasgow, The Piobaireachd Society and the Army School of Piping in Edinburgh, and the Royal Scottish Pipe Band Association in Glasgow carry on the proud traditions of piping and piping instruction first begun many generations ago in Scotland.

THE PIPES AND HIGHLAND SOCIETY
(SCENES FROM THE PAST)

`Upoho Uka Nui `O Kekokia – 23

1. Cockney tourists have donned the kilt: they buy a set of bagpipes.
2. And bear them off in triumph.
3. Attempt to play: chanters and drones get rather mixed.
4. Directions: "Ye'll jist pit a guid blaw intil them, set them under one arm, an' gie them a wheeze."
5. Unearthly scream.
6. Sudden collapse.
7. It knocks him down.
8. Rescued from suffocation.
9. "No more of the bagpipes for me!"

Amateurs With The Highland Bagpipes
By Evelyn Hardy (1889)

The Highland Piper By J. Richardson (1865)

Highland Games At Aboyne, Aberdeenshire (1871)

The Prince Of Wales In The Highlands (1880)

`Upoho Uka Nui `O Kekokia – 27

The Court In The Highlands – the Queen and The Prince Of Wales Going To The Gillies Ball, Abergeldie Castle (1880)

*Sword Dance Of The Royal Caledonian Asylum
At Westbrook Park, Godalming* (1881)

`Upoho Uka Nui `O Kekokia – 29

The Queen Keeping Halloween At Balmoral (1885)

Highland Pipers Practicing In Hyde Park (1890)

`Upoho Uka Nui `O Kekokia – 𝄞 – 31

*The Coming Of Age Of Lord Warkworth:
The Garden Party At Alnwick Castle By John Charlton* (1892)

*Lord Campbell and His Pipers Marching Through The Pass
At Glencoe (1895)*

`Upoho Uka Nui `O Kekokia – 33

*The Queen's Long Reign:
A Celebration At Dublin Castle* (1897)

An Old Highland Custom: Celebrating A Marriage Outside The Bride's House By A .G. Small (1899)

The Gran Hieland Bagpipes, The Pride O' The Land (1917)

The Pipes and The Military
(Scenes From The Past)

`Upoho Uka Nui `O Kekokia – 39

MOUNTED PIPERS FOR THE HIGHLAND REGIMENTS—WHAT MIGHT HAPPEN AT THE FIRST PARADE

*Mounted Pipers For The Highland Regiments —
What Might Happen At The First Parade* (1889)

Amusements In The Camp Of The London Scottish,
Wimbleton (1871)

`Upoho Uka Nui `O Kekokia – 41

*A Highland Soldier's Wedding —
Chairing The Bridegroom* (1876)

*The Halloween Dinner Of The London Scottish Volunteers —
Bringing In The Haggis By Lockhart Bogle* (1891)

*The Queen At Aldershot: Military 'Tattoo'
and Torchlight Procession* (1894)

Queen Victoria Loved The Pipes — The Queen At The Birthday Party Of The 2nd Scots Guards At Windsor: The March Past By W. Small (1899)

England – Africa

The Zulu War: Embarkation Of The 91ˢᵗ Highlanders At Southampton (1879)

Africa

En Route To The Zulu War: The Mess Piper Of The 91st On Board The Pretoria (1879)

AFRICA

The Zulu War: The 91ˢᵗ Highlanders Leaving The Pretoria At Durban (1879)

Africa

The Zulu War: The 91st Regiment Leaving Camp At Durban For The Front (1879)

Africa

The Evacuation Of Zululand: The 21ˢᵗ Royal Fusiliers On The March Homewards (1879)

Africa

The Eve Of Departure (1881)

INDIA

The Rival Pipers From A Sketch Taken At The Wawul Pindi Durbar By An Officer Of The Seaforth Highlanders (1885)

Egypt

The King's Own Scottish Borderers Leaving The Citadel, Cairo, Egypt En Route For India (1890)

At Home

The Highland Brigade On The March (1897)

India

*The Storming of the Dargai Ridge by the Gordon Highlanders:
Piper Findlater Continuing to Play though Wounded in Both Legs*
(1898)

World War I

Highland Pipers Playing The Canadian Scottish Into Ypres: Heroic Canadians Honoured By Their British Comrades On Their Return From The Fight At Langemarck (1915)

56 – 𝄞 – Scotland's Great Highland Bagpipe

World War I

58. "Black Watch" Pipers Playing to the Captors of Longueval.

Highlanders Pipe Themselves Back from the Trenches.

138. The Black Watch Returning to Camp.

"Daily Mail"
Official Photograph
Crown Copyright reserved

'Upoho Uka Nui 'O Kekokia – 57

World War I

The Scotch Band

Joueur de Cornemuse.

ARMÉE ANGLAISE.

Chapter 2
First Encounters

When did Hawaiians first hear the majestic sounds of the bagpipe? While we will never know the answer to this question, it affords us the opportunity to review a fascinating history from what is known.

Hawaiians first heard the sound of western instruments during Captain James Cook's sojourn in Hawai`i. The American John Ledyard reported in January, 1779, at Kealakekua Bay that when Hawaiian chief Kalaniopu`u was transported from the *H.M.S. Resolution* to the *H.M.S. Discovery* one of the crew heralded the event by playing his French horn.[1] He goes on to describe what could be called the first concert in Hawai`i. It occurred the following day on shore:

> *One of the gentlemen of the* Discovery *brought his violin, and one from the* Resolution *a german-flute, and as the party seemed to want a variety, they played upon each in turn. The violin produced the most immoderate laughter among the natives, who seemed to relish it as many do the bagpipes.*[2]

Certainly an auspicious beginning for our instrument of preference! Ledyard may have been aware of the great interest in the bagpipe exhibited by the Tahitians during Cook's visit there in 1773 (See note below). However, he completes his account by simply stating *the flute they very much admired and examined very curiously. The drum and fife is the music they most delight in.*[3]

NOTE: First Bagpipes In The Pacific. Capt. James Cook on his second voyage to the Pacific aboard the *H.M.S. Resolution* along with the *H.M.S. Adventure* specifically requested that some of his Royal Marines be pipers.[4] One of his pipers has been identified as Archibald McVicar, Private, Portsmouth Division.[5] It was McVicar's playing skills which were noted by the voyage's naturalist George Forster in Tahiti on the islands of Tahiti-Nui and Huahine.[6] Forster's Swedish assistant Anders Sparrman[7] and the Captain himself[8] also noted the contributions of the ships' pipers.

Monday, August 23, 1772, on Tahiti-Nui at Tiarapu:

> Forster Entry: In the afternoon the captains went on shore with us again to the king, whom we found where we had left him in the morning. He took the opportunity of requesting the captains again to prolong their stay at least a few days; but he received the same answer as before, and was plainly told, that his refusing to provide us with livestock was the reason of their intended departure. Upon this he immediately sent for two hogs, and presented one to each of the captains, for which he received some iron-wares in return. A highlander, who was one of our marines, was ordered to play the bagpipe, and its uncouth music, though almost insufferable to our ears, delighted the king and his subjects to a degree which we could hardly have imagined possible. The distrust which we perceived in his looks at our first interview was now worn off; and if we had staid long enough, an unreserved confidence might have taken place, to which his youth and good-nature seemed to make him inclinable. The studied gravity which he had then affected, was likewise laid aside at present, and some of his actions rather partook of puerility, among which I cannot help mentioning his amusement of chopping little sticks and cutting down plantations of bananas with one of our hatchets. But, instead of cultivating any further acquaintance with him, we took our last leave towards the close of the evening, and returned to the sloops, which unmoored before night (p. 171-72).

> Sparrman Entry: The King sought, by the promise of hogs and fruit, to persuade Captain Cook to stay in the district of Tiarabu, but, on account of the former ban on the sale of pork, the Captain was distrustful of these blandishments, a distrust which he later, however, had cause to regret, for in reality the confidence appeared to have grown.

All distrust was finally banished from the young King's face when we asked, to the great distress of our own ears, a young Scots sailor to entertain the King with some airs on his bagpipes. The Scots Orpheus delighted the ears of the King's ladies no less than his subjects, from which it was easy to form an opinion of their musical tastes (p. 55-56).

Sunday, April 11, 1773, in Dusky Sound, New Zealand (southern tip of South Island):

> Cook Entry: About 10 o'clock the family of the Natives paid us a visit, seeing that they approached the Ship with great caution I met them in my Boat which I quited and went into their canoe, nevertheless I could not prevail upon them to put along side the Ship and was at last obliged to leave them to follow their own inclinations; at length they put ashore in a little creek hard by us and afterwards came and set down on the shore abreast of the Ship near enough to speak to us. I caused the Bagpipes and the fife to be played and the Drum to be beat, this last they admired most, nothing however would induce them to come a board....(p. 118).

Thursday, August 26, 1773, on Tahiti-Nui at Matavai:

> Forster Entry: While we were engaged in this conversation, our Highlander performed on the bagpipe to the infinite satisfaction of all the Taheitians, who listened to him with a mixture of admiration and delight. King O-too in particular was so well pleased with his musical abilities, which I have already observed were mean enough, that he ordered him a large piece of the coarser cloth as a reward for his trouble (p. 181).

Friday, August 28, 1773, on Tahiti-Nui:

> Cook Entry: When Otoo came aboard and one or two of his friends were siting in the Cabbin covered, the moment they saw the King enter they undress'd themselves in great haste, that is they put off their ahows or clothes because the Arree was present, and this was all the respect they paid him for they never rose from their seats or paid him any other obeisence. When the King thought proper to depart I carried him again to Oparre in my Boat and entertained him with the Bag-pipes of which musick he was very fond, and dancing by the Seamen; he in return ordered some of his people to dance also which dancing consisted chiefly in strange contortions of the Body, there were some of them that could however immitate the Seamen tollerable well both in Country dances and Horn pipes (p. 208).

Sunday, September 5, 1773, on Huahine:

> Forster Entry: Oree came on board early the next morning with his sons, the eldest of them a handsome little boy, about eleven years old, who received our presents with great indifference; but he, as well as all the people of the island, were highly delighted with the bagpipe, and required it to be constantly played (p. 207).

> Sparrman Entry: On the 5th, Ori and his young son came on board and were offered a performance on the bagpipes by way of entertainment. (p. 77)

October 2, 1773, on Middleburg Island (Eua island) in Tonga:

> Cook Entry:....delightful spot, the floor was laid with Matting on which we were seated, the Islanders who accompanied us seated themselves in a circle round the out sides. I ordered the Bag-pipes to be played and in return the Chief ordered three young women to sing a song which they did with a very good grace. When they had done I gave each of them a necklace, this set most of the Women in the Circle a singing, their songs were musical and harmonious, noways harsh or disagreeable... (p. 246).

> Sparrman Entry: Once ashore, we saw at closer range the splendour of the island's plantations and fruit groves...As we wandered...we observed general rejoicing...in short, generosity, signs of friendship, cries of delight, and song prevailed.

This song (which we believed we could play on our bagpipes afterwards) was song by three women, and although it was simple, I agree with Messrs. Forster and Cook that it produced

a pleasant effect and, with this melodious and gentle song, the beat was snapped with the thumb and first finger, which made a not unpleasing harmony......

...Our Scots virtuoso, who had been accustomed to arouse general delight in Otaheite with his wailing bagpipes, seemed here to be denied all approbation. Did this betoken a higher musical sense and taste here than in Otaheite? (p. 92)

A final footnote on Captain Cook; the Captain was killed at Kealakekua Bay on the island of Hawai`i on February 14, 1779, in an unfortunate confrontation with the local community. Almost one hundred years later the area in which Cook was killed was set aside as a monument to him. The land was donated to the British Government for the monument by Miriam Likelike, sister to King David Kalakaua and Queen Lili`uokalani, and her Scottish husband

Archibald Cleghorn. At the time Princess Likelike was serving as Governor of the Big Island of Hawai`i.[9] Today, the parcel of land is still owned by the British Government.

A. Hawaiians Traveling The World

The first Hawaiians to hear bagpipes were probably not in Hawai`i at all but in some far away ports, or, perhaps in England, itself. The first recorded Hawaiian to leave Hawai`i was a Hawaiian woman named Winee who left Hawai`i in 1787 as a 'personal servant' to the Captain's wife of the British ship *Imperial Eagle*.[10] At least eighteen other vessels, fourteen of which were of British registry, ported in Hawai`i during the ten year interval between the departure of Captain Cook's ships in 1779 and 1789.[11] It is probable that Hawaiians found their way to foreign ports and seas on some of these ships. Indeed, Winee, herself met up with the noted Hawaiian chief Kaiana and two other Hawaiians in China before beginning her return voyage to Hawai`i in 1788.[12]

Many Hawaiians found their way to North America's West Coast. This emigration particularly to western Canada and what now is the Pacific Northwest has been documented.[13] By 1825 more than 300 Hawaiians had left the islands in search of adventure, many finding employment with the Hudson's Bay Company or the Pacific Fur Company, or on sailing ships plying the high seas between China, Hawai`i, Alaska, and the Pacific Northwest.[14]

One such person was George Kaumuali`i, son of the last *Ali`i Nui* of Kaua`i. Sometimes known as *Humehume* or 'George Prince,' George left Hawai`i in 1806 at the age of seven in the care of an American sea captain. After a number of years in school on the East Coast of the United States, he enlisted in the Marines and later in the US Navy (the first known Hawaiian to serve in the American Armed Forces) and fought for the United States in the War of 1812. While there is a discrepancy on which ships he served, it is clear that he was wounded in battle and recovered.[15] After visits to Napoli and Gibraltar, he returned to the East Coast and eventually moved to Cornwall, Connecticut where he entered the Foreign Mission School with fellow Hawaiians; Henry Opukahaia, Thomas Hopu, William Kanui, and John Honoli`i. Then in 1820 with his countrymen, he returned home to Hawai`i with the missionaries on the brig *Thaddeus*. He is noteworthy in music history for introducing Hawaiians and Hawai`i to the bass viol, an instrument he played with great skill.[16]

Many of these early voyagers, including Kaumuali`i, could have heard the bagpipe in their travels. As the bagpipe was viewed on occasion as an instrument of war, Kaumuali`i could possibly have heard the pipes in battle during his engagements with the British Navy in the War of 1812.

Another Hawaiian whose life was dramatically affected by the War of 1812 was Naukane, who in 1811 was appointed by King Kamehameha I to accompany John Jacob Astor and oversee a number of Hawaiians whom Astor had hired on a three-year contract to work at his newly found community of Astoria in Oregon. On the voyage to the Pacific Northwest aboard the *Tonquin* Naukane's resemblance to one of the crew member named John Coxe was uncanny and soon he, too, bore the name; one that would stay with him throughout his life. Shortly after his arrival in Astoria, Naukane left his friends and journeyed with the North West Company as a scout across the Rockies to Fort William on Lake Superior(today's Thunder Bay, Ontario). War was soon declared between the United States and England and the North West Company sent a delegation to London to obtain a ship and eventually return and seize Astoria. Coxe journeyed with the group and became something of a celebrity in London. And, by 1813, when he returned with the group on the *H.M.S. Racoon*, he found that Astoria had already been taken by the North West Company. He returned to Hawai`i where, in 1823, he accompanied Liholiho and his Queen to England because of his prior knowledge of the country. After their deaths in London, Coxe was in the surviving party which brought their bodies home. It was a sad homecoming coupled with accusations of financial wrongdoings. By 1827, Coxe had returned to the Pacific Northwest and was living at Fort Vancouver (today's Vancouver, Canada) where he lived out the rest of his life as a farmer.[17] Somewhere along the way it is quite possible and, indeed, probable that Naukane, a.k.a. John Coxe, heard the sounds of the pipes.

The first Hawaiian known to have ventured to England was a lad from Moloka`i named Kualelo ('Towereroo'). His story is told by Clarice Taylor in her series "Tales of Hawaii" which appeared for almost ten years in the *Honolulu Star-Bulletin*.[18] Kualelo found his way to England via one of the Northwest American traders in July, 1789. He may have gotten into some trouble in London as Captain George Vancouver's orders issued in January 1791, specifically mention that he was to return Kualelo to his homeland on the voyage.[19] After deserting for a brief love affair in Tahiti, Kualelo was returned to Vancouver's ship by the island chief. Finally, in March, 1792, Vancouver left him in the care of Kaiana on the island of Hawai`i.[20]

Other Hawaiians besides Kualelo and Naukane also found themselves in England. Two others, 'Boose oh Hoo' and 'Tuano,' were 'billed' at the time as the first "Sandwich Islanders" to visit England. They arrived in London in November 1820, after more than three years of tragedy and adventure. They had been 'pressed' into service on an American vessel.[21] It is unfortunate that more is not known of these early Hawaiian adventurers and their observations to what must have been something of a strange yet exciting new world. They certainly could and probably did hear the sound of bagpipes on their overseas adventures in England.

In November 1823, Liholiho (Kamehameha II) and his wife Queen Kamamalu, as well as a contingent of Hawaiians including Boki and his wife Liliha, set sail from Hawai`i to visit King George IV in London.

> NOTE: Hawaiian Royalty In England. During the years of the Kingdom, seven royal visitations were made to England and three to Scotland:
>
> > May 1824: Kalani kua Liholiho (Kamehameha II) and Kamamalu, his favorite wife, visited London to visit with His majesty the King (George IV) to receive friendly counsel and advice for the Government of these far-distant isles, to increase their acquaintance with the world, enlarge their views of human society, and observe the laws, customs, institutions, religion, and character of the country beneath whose guardian friendship and protection they and their countrymen who remain have chosen with confidence to place themselves.[22]

Unfortunately, both contracted measles and died in London before meeting King George.

> January 1850: Dr. Gerritt Judd, serving as Hawai`i's Minister of Finance, took Lot Kapuaiwa (then 18 years old and eventually to become Kamehameha V) and Alexander Liholiho (then 15 years old and eventually to become Kamehameha IV) with him on his journey to the United States and Europe for the purposes of negotiating treaties. In London, Dr. Judd met with Lord Palmerston and other members of government and with members of the Royal family.[23]

> July 1865: Dowager Queen Emma, recovering from the deaths of her young son, Prince Albert Edward Kauikeaouli, and husband, Kamehameha IV, accepted the invitation of Lady Jane Franklin to be her guest on a visit to England. While in England, Emma met with Queen Victoria, the Archbishop of Canterbury and other members of government and the Royal family. Queen Victoria was godmother to Prince Albert.[24]

> August 1875: Princess Bernice Pauahi Bishop and her husband Charles Bishop visited Ireland, England and Scotland. Arriving in Queenstown, Ireland in July, the couple journeyed on to England and Scotland in August and departed for New York in September and returned to England and the Continent in November 1875. In May 1876, she was introduced to Queen Victoria. Shortly, thereafter the couple returned to Honolulu.[25]

> September 1881: King David Kalakaua, on his trip around the world, visited England and Scotland and met with Queen Victoria and other dignitaries of government and the Royal Family. He also visited Scotland.[26]

> June 1887: Queen Kapi`olani, wife of King David Kalakaua, and Princess Lydia Kamakaeha Lili`uokalani, sister of Kalakaua and heiress apparent, were sent to officially represent the Kingdom of Hawai`i at Queen Victoria's Jubilee Celebration in London. Queen Victoria met with the delegation.[27]

> 1891-97: Princess Victoria Kawekiu Ka`iulani Lunalilo Kalaninuiahilopalapa, heir-apparent and good friend of Robert Louis Stevenson, attended school in England. Also in England attending school for a portion of this time was her cousin, Prince David Kawananakoa. Princess Ka`iulani's father, Archibald Cleghorn, came from Edinburgh, Scotland, arrived in Hawai`i in 1851, and married the sister of Lili`uokalani, Miriam Kekauluohi Likelike in 1870. While in England, Ka`iulani visited Scotland on a number of occasions. On her first visit to Edinburgh with her father, both stayed at

Dreghorn Castle as guests of the MacFees – just as her uncle the King had been in 1881. While at Dreghorn, Ka`iulani planted two trees which may be still present. On another trip to Scotland, the Princess met and became close friends with Princess Titaua Marama (from the Pomare family), the Tahitian wife of a Scottish businessman named George Darsie. They were living in Anstruther. The only other member of the Royal family to visit Scotland was Ka`iulani's uncle, King David Kalakaua (See Appendix 1 for accounts of his trip). Ka`iulani returned to Hawai`i in 1897 and sadly, suddenly died in 1899 at the age of 23.[28]

In mid-May, 1824, the party arrived in London, but before the scheduled June 21st meeting with King George could occur, Queen Kamamalu and, shortly thereafter, Liholiho died from the measles. Boki met with the king and after a number of months sightseeing in London and its environs, the Hawaiian party left London in September, 1824, returning home on the *H.M.S. Blonde* under the command of Lord Byron (George Anson). On May 6, 1825, the *H.M.S. Blonde* arrived in Honolulu Harbor, returning the bodies of Liholiho and Kamamalu and more than eight Hawaiians who had been away for more than two years. It is almost certain that members of this group heard first-hand the music of the bagpipe during their sojourn in England.

On May 11, 1824, the funeral was held for the former king and his wife with members of the ship's company participating. It is noteworthy in that the ship's band played a funeral dirge from the wharf to Kawaiahao Church but there is no mention of bagpipes being part of the ship's band.[29]

Another of Hawai`i's kings, David Kalakaua, was familiar with the pipes for not only did he hear them at the Palace as a youngster at the Royal School in 1845, he was probably also present at the Palace in 1869 when pipes were again played in the presence of Hawai`i's royalty (See next section). In 1881, Kalakaua journeyed to Scotland and was received 'Highland Style' during his visits to Edinburgh and Glasgow. Shortly thereafter in 1882, he sent some of Hawai`i's brightest youth to

Scotland to study engineering as part of his 'Hawaiian Studies Abroad' program.

Decorated Gate Across King Street At Richards Welcoming King Kalakaua Home After His Trip Around The World, 1881
(Note "Scotland" Inscribed At The Top Of The Left Pillar – see Next NOTE)

Kalakaua was the first monarch of any country in the world to circumnavigate the globe. He left Honolulu on January 20, 1881, and returned home almost ten months later. The last European country he visited was Scotland from September 7-12, 1881.[30] While in Scotland, the King was entertained by pipers from the 'Royal Highlanders' or better known as the 'Black Watch.' *The Glasgow Herald* and the *Edinburgh Courant* as well as Honolulu's *Pacific Commercial Advertiser* detailed the King's visit to Scotland (See Appendix 1 for the newspaper accounts of the King's Scotland visit).

NOTE: King Kalakaua Returns Home. The decorations prepared for the King's return to Honolulu were extensive. A number of decorative arches were constructed along the route the King took from the wharf to the palace. The account in the *Pacific Commercial Advertiser* notes: ...Some little way beyond Richards Street (on King Street before the entrance to the Palace) stood the handsome arch which the members of the Civil Service, whose duties gathered them daily at Aliiolani Hale, had erected as a greeting to His Majesty. From Alakea Street to this arch five pairs of standards with their strings of flags were to be seen. The arch itself was lofty and of greater width than any of the others. The piers were finished by small turrets and above the arch was a battlement, and in the center, surmounting all, a huge crown in crimson and gold. The arch bore on its Ewa side the inscription, "E ka Lani, e Ola" – (Live O King); and on the other side "Welcome Home." Beneath the arch was drapery in red and white to represent a curtain drawn up and hanging in folds. On the piers on either side were emblematic pictures – one a screw steamship, the other an express locomotive. The other sides of the piers bore shields with the names of the countries which the King had visited during his tour, thus: –

Japan	India	Scotland	Spain
China	Egypt	Germany	Portugal
Siam	Italy	France	United States
Singapore	England		

The arch was also tastefully decorated with flags and with wreaths of ferns.........[31] See photograph previous page.

Realizing the value of education, Kalakaua, in conjunction with legislator Robert Ho`apili Baker, introduced a bill into the 1880 legislature to provide funds to educate "Hawaiian Youths Abroad." This was the beginning of a program which lasted for more than ten years and saw 18 young Hawaiians (17 men and 1 woman) dispersed to the major cities of the world to learn and ultimately return to Hawai`i bringing with them knowledge to serve the Kingdom well. Most did return to the Kingdom and did make great contributions in future years. Of particular interest was the fact that six young Hawaiians were sent to England and Scotland, and it is with certainty that their ears heard the strains of bagpipes during their educational journey abroad.

NOTE: Kalakaua's Students Abroad. 17 men and 1 woman journeyed to the world's cities to educate themselves in accordance with the needs of the Kingdom:[32]

Name	Local School	City/Country (Dates)	Studies

Italy:
James Kaneholo Booth*	Punahou	Prussia/Naples (1880-84)	Sciences
Robert Napuuako Boyd	Punahou	Prussia/Leghorn (1880-87)	Sciences
Robert W. Wilcox	Maui	Prussia/Turin (1880-87)	Sciences
August Hering		Turin (1887-88)	Sculpture
Maile Nowlein		Turin (1887-89 ?)	Art/Music

England:
Joseph A. Kamauoha**	Punahou	London (1882-86)	Sciences
Mathew Makalua***	Iolani	Denstone/London (1882-)	Medicine
Abraham Piianaia	Royal School	Denstone/London (1882-87)	Law

Scotland:
Henry Kapena		Glasgow (1882-86)	Engineering
Hugo Kawelo	Punahou	Glasgow (1882-85)	Engineering
John Lovell	Punahou	Glasgow (1882-86)	Engineering

China:
James Kapaa		Canton (1882-85)	Culture/Lang.

Japan:
James Hakuole		Tokyo (1882-88)	Culture/Lang.
Issac Harbottle	Kamehameha	Tokyo (1882-88)	Culture/Lang.

United States:
Thomas Pualii Cummins	Punahou	San Mateo, CA (1885-87)	Liberal Arts
David Kawananakoa	Punahou	San Mateo, CA (1885-87)	Liberal Arts
Henry Grube Marchant		Boston, MA (1887-90 ?)	Engraving
Thomas Spencer		San Mateo, CA (1882-87)	Liberal Arts

* Died in Naples, Italy of cholera in 1884
** Died in Torquay, England in 1886
*** Stayed in England, married, practiced medicine, and died in 1929

The three Hawaiians who found themselves in Scotland were apprenticed to the Scotland Street Iron Works, an affiliate of the large firm of Mirrlees, Watson & Company in Glasgow. This firm produced large machinery for sugar plantations found throughout the Kingdom. Despite the unhealthy environment in 19th century Glasgow, Henry Kapena, Hugo Kawelo, and John Lovell survived their first few years and found time to participate in local football(soccer) and bicycle clubs; but in 1885 Kawelo returned home because of ill health ("pluerisy and kidney infection"), and eleven months later both Lovell and Kapena returned to Hawai`i having been away for almost four years.[33]

The unhealthy air of 19th century Glasgow was due primarily to coal burning activities related to the Industrial Revolution. Not only did it affect the three lads in Scotland, but also those who went to Italy and England. Two did not survive their training primarily because of these poor environmental conditions which prevailed in Europe.[34]

No records have been found documenting how these youth sent to Europe felt about the pipes, but it is with great certainty that those who were sent to Scotland and England were exposed to the unique sounds of the great highland bagpipe during their lengthy stays.

Other Hawaiians probably were introduced to the pipes through military service. Solomon L. Peleioholani whose great grandfather was high chief Ke`eaumoku has a fascinating story of bravery and adventure. His constant childhood companion was young Prince Albert of Hawai`i, the child of Kamehameha IV and Queen Emma. Both Albert and Solomon were slated to be sent to England for schooling prior to the young Prince's death in 1862. In 1869, the Duke of Edinburgh visited Hawai`i stopping first in Hilo (See next section). While in Hilo, the Duke met young Solomon. Both were to remember the meeting a year or two later. Peleioholani left Honolulu on the steamer S.S. *Nevada* shortly after the Duke's Hilo visit bound for Australia where he joined the British Army and found himself and his unit being transported to Africa to fight in South Africa. He gave an account of his African services in the *Pacific Commercial Advertiser* in 1902:

> *I was sent north with a large force and upon one of our expeditions we were attacked by a body of blacks under command of a man of rank from Morocco, part Russian and part Moroccan, who was called a prince. Our troops were sent across a river to engage his force. We had to fight while wading across and at last met them on the opposite bank. The Prince was on a horse and the squad with which I was connected engaged the prince directly. I was struck by a bullet as I rushed forward toward the Prince, who was on a horse. I caught his bridle and was struck on the head. At the same instant Captain Bickerton made for the Prince, who struck at Captain Bickerton with his sword. I threw my arm around his neck and received the point in my left forearm. Before the Prince had time to recover I thrust him with my sword, the blade entering his right side and coming out near the neck. I obtained possession of the sword and a medal which he wore upon his breast and carried them with me into camp, where I turned them over to the corps commander...When we went to England to be mustered out, we were marched in review before Queen Victoria, who distributed medals to the men. The sword and the medal of the Prince were presented to the Queen and I was questioned as to my nationality. I told her my grandfather had accompanied Kamehameha II to England. I told her Kamehameha V was my King. The Duke of Edinburgh recognized me as being the native who had assisted him to land in Hilo from the Galatea and procure the hula girls to give a dance before his Highness.*[35]

Despite Peleioholani winning this battle and his brave exploits, the British Army eventually was forced to withdraw from Africa but the sounds of bagpipes continued strong in the British Army.

Almost twenty years later, another Hawaiian serving in another war with the British Army again received royal recognition. Heali`i Kahea Beckley, a descendant of Captain George Beckley, a military advisor to Kamehameha I, served along with about 200 others from Hawai`i in British or

Canadian units in World War I. Beckley enlisted as a rifleman in the Liverpool Rifles and was awarded the Military Medal by King George V for his actions in 1918. The *London Gazette* of October 7, 1918, reported that Beckley left Hawai`i and crossed the Atlantic on a mule boat as one of the "livestock chambermaids." Arriving in France, he left the ship and joined the British Army and was wounded shortly thereafter at the Front. Following his convalescence, he returned to the Front and was wounded again; afterwhich he was sent to the Balkans where he received additional wounds attempting to retrieve the body of his captain. Certainly Rifleman Beckley became acquainted with the sound of bagpipes during his tour of duty. The newspaper account noted that Beckley remarked after receiving his medal, "I hope I have done my bit for the Beckley family. That is the reason I joined the British army." He went on to note in a letter home that he was sorry "that the First and Second Hawaiian Infantry regiments of Hawai`i did not get across to Europe to show what Hawaiians can really do...."[36]

It is clear from the numbers of Hawaiians moving about the world in the late 18th, 19th, and early 20th centuries that the first Hawaiians to hear bagpipes were, in fact, not in Hawai`i but in such countries as England, Scotland, China, Canada, or what is now the Pacific Northwest of the United States, or, perhaps, even somewhere on the high seas. Wherever the instance when the instrument became familiar in Hawai`i, it quickly became known for what it was, an instrument whose sound produced 'chickenskin' for those who understood and honored its significance in peace and war.

B. Bagpipes Arrive In Hawai`i

The first recorded instance of bagpipes being played in Hawai`i was in 1845. There may have been other instances but these have been lost in time. Between 1779 and 1845, more than 290 ships recorded visitations to the port of Honolulu. Of this number, 51 were of British registry and 25 were vessels of the Royal Navy.[37] Additionally, by 1845, more than fourteen immigrants from Scotland were living in Hawai`i and had become Hawai`i residents.[38] It is possible that bagpipers were on board some of the visiting British Naval vessels and, perhaps, some knowledge of the instrument's playing was held among some of Hawai`i's early Scottish residents, however, written documentation of this knowledge or musical talent has yet to be found.

The first known instance of bagpipes being played in Hawai`i was by piper Nichol MacIntyre from the *H.M.S. America*, arriving in the port of Honolulu on October 20, 1845. His musical talents were documented by *The Polynesian* during an evening spent at the Palace with Kamehameha III and his guests on Wednesday, October 29, 1845 (See APPENDIX 2 for the complete article):

> **Musical Soiree At The Palace.** — *The Honorable Capt. Gordon, of H.B.M.'s ship* America, *had the kindness to send on shore, on Wednesday evening, for the entertainment of the king, his fine band, composed of about twenty well trained musicians of an excellence in their art far beyond anything that had ever before been heard in Honolulu. MacIntyre, his Scotch Piper, struck up the wild and exciting strains of old Scotch martial airs, at half past 6 o'clock, and the band commenced soon afterwards, beginning with the national anthem, alternating with the piper, till about 10 o'clock, when the national anthem was repeated, and the musicians retired...*
>
> *After the missionary families had retired, dancing commenced with the reel of Tulloch-gorum, played by the piper; quadrilles, &c., followed to the music of the band.*
>
> *MacIntyre, the Scotch Piper, in the romantic garb of Caledonia, was an object of great and universal interest. He played round the drawing rooms repeatedly during the evening, measuring his steps to the time of the air that he was playing. The bagpipes and every article of his attire down to his dark kilt, garter, dirk, hose and buckles, excited the curiosity of the company. The good humored Highlander had often to stop to allow some part of his dress and equipment to be examined.*

The piper belongs to Argyleshire, but he wore on the occasion the Gordon tartan, with silver buckles and shoulder ornaments richly chased. The Scotch cap and eagle's feather formed his head dress.

The kind courtesy to the King and Chiefs of the honorable Capt. Gordon, upon this occasion, has reanimated the never forgotten impressions left by the earlier British navigators; and we know it was much appreciated by their Majesties, the King and Queen….[39]

**NOTE: First Bagpiper In Hawai`i.** A search of the log book for the *H.M.S. America* found entry for one Able-Bodied Seaman Nichol MacIntyre from Argyleshire. From the entry information this voyage to Hawai`i was McIntyre's first voyage in the service of the Queen (Victoria). McIntyre was 25 years old at the time of his Palace performance, stood 5 feet 9 inches in height, was of fair complexion, and had black eyes and black hair. He was single and had learned the trade of a 'cornfactor' – another way of describing a corn dealer or merchant.[40]

The evening event with its Scottish Captain and bagpiper was also highlighted in one of the earliest Hawaiian language newspapers, *Ka Elele*. It carried the following account in its October 21, 1845, edition:

Manuwa Beritania

I ka la 20 o Okatoba nei, ku mai ma monolulu (Honolulu) nei, kekahi manuwa Beritania, o Amerika kona inoa. A. Gordon ka inoa o ke Lii; he kaikaina oia no ka haku Abedeen, ke kakauolelo kaulana no ko na aina e ma Beritania. No Sokotia ko lakou hanauna i kinohi.

British Man-O-War

On October 20 last to Honolulu came the British warship *America*. A Gordon is the name of the Captain. He is the younger brother of Lord Aberdeen, the noted secretary of internal Affairs. His family is Scottish.

I kela po aku nei, ua hoomakaukauia ka hale o ka Moi, a hele nui malaila na haole a me na kanaka Hawaii kekahi o Honolulu nei, e lohei ka poe kani o ua manuwa nei. Maikai loa ke kani ana; lealea ku pepeiao i ka lohe. Paapu hoi koloko, a me ko waho o ka hale, i na kane a me na wahine haole, a me na kanaka maolikahi.

Last evening there was prepared at the King's home in Honolulu a party to which many haole and Hawaiians came. There the people heard the musicians from the aforementioned Man-O-War. The beautiful sound was a pleasure to the ears. The place was crowed inside and out with haole and Hawaiian men and women.

Eia nae ka mea kupanaha a makou i ike ai malaila; he kanaka Sokotia, he koa; ano e loa kona kahiko ana, e like me na kanaka no kuahiwi ma Sokotia. Aneane me keia kii kona helehelena.

Also there was the wonderful sight of a Scottish man, a soldier. He was awesome and dressed in the custom of the Highlands in Scotland.

He mea kani ano e ko keia kanaka; he eke makani malalo o kona lima, a he mau ohe manamana e moe ana maluna o kona lima hema, a holo kona mau manamana lima maluna o kekahi ohe. Ano e loa ka leo o keia mea kani; kaapuni keia koa i ka hale o ke alii me ka hookani a nui hoi ke hapaha a me ka mahalo iaia no kona ano e loa. He okoa ke ano e na kanaka Sokotia e noho ana ma kahakai a he okoa ke ano o ka poe noho ma kuahiwi. Pau loa no nae ko kela aina i ka naauao; aole kanaka Sokotia i ike ole i ka palapala. He aina naauao loa ia nui na kula; nui na hale pule; nui na Baibala, ua malama loa ia ka la Sabati, a ua maluhia ka noho ana.

An incredible thing was that he had a windbag under his hand – a flute-like instrument in his left hand – his fingers running up and down on this instrument. Awesome is the sound of this instrument. So the soldier went around the house of the King sounding this instrument and all admired him because of his talent. Those Scottish people living by the coast are different from those living in the Highlands, but many of the people in this land are proficient in this instrument; they are civilized and educated – no Scottish people don't know how to write. There are many schools, many churches, many Bibles, and the people observe the Sabbath, a truly peaceful place.[41]

Many of Honolulu's social elite were at the Palace that evening and also noted the event in their journals. One such person was the eccentric trader and planter, Capt. Stephen Reynolds who recorded a few lines about the evening in his journal entry for Wednesday, October 29, 1845:

Fresh breezes & rain – Ships unable to get in – Gerty requiring repairs. Dull, did not sell an inch of piece goods ...Evening the band from the America – & Best band ever I heard on the island – a Scotchman with his bagpipes dressed in Scotch costume – were at the King's – General notice to the residents &c to call – I went for the sole purpose of seeing the Bagpipes – with which I was much pleased....[42]

Other entries have been found in the journal and correspondence of Honolulu entrepreneur Gorham Gilman and missionary educator Amos Starr Cooke. Gilman noted about the evening:

In the year 1846(sic-1845), the English Frigate America Capt Gordon – paid a visit to the island – which will long be remembered for the pleasant nature of the intercourse with her gallant and gentlemanly commander and officers. Capt. Gordon was one of the members of the Gordon clan of Scotia (and brother to the Earl of Aberdeen) – and fellow countryman of Mr. Wyllie – who upon learning that there was a piper on board the ship – requested that Captain Gordon would allow him to bring his piper onshore and perform before the King – to which he readily consented. Mr.

78 – 𝄞 – Scotland's Great Highland Bagpipe

Kamehameha III and Queen Kalama Who Entertained Piper Macintyre In 1845

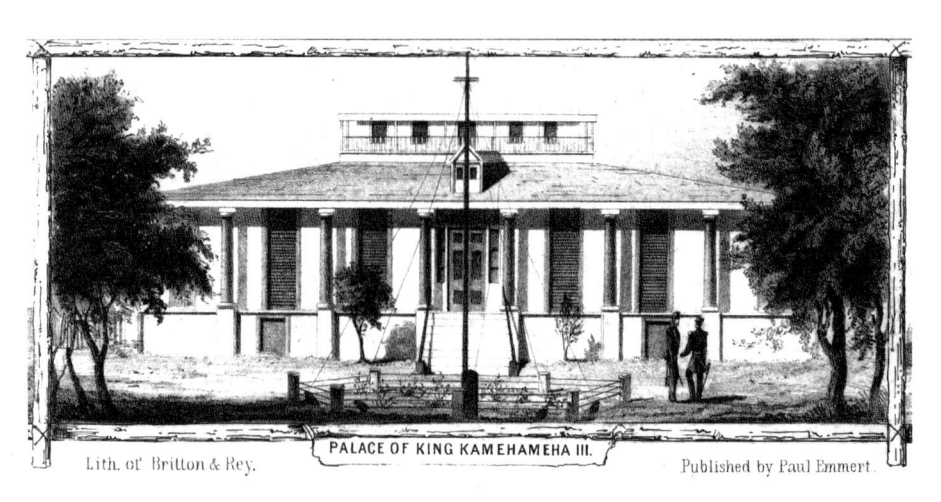

Kamehameha III's Palace In 1845

> *Wyllie issued notice that His Majesty would hold a levee in the evening and it was known that the piper would be present – and at the hour (8:00 pm) there was a large assembly of the beauty and rank of Honorables present. The band of the America were also in attendance and had the award of being the best practiced band that had visited the islands. The piper made his appearance clad in the kilts and tartan with his cap and eagle plume in real Highland style, and being the first that had ever visited the islands, afforded much pleasure and diversion as he passing in and out before His Majesty who seemed highly delighted while some of the members of the Court were terrified at the strange sounds and appearance of the piper. A Scotch reel was got up by Mr. Wyllie and was the first dance ever executed in the Palace and by its singular figures and movements caused much amusement. The French Consul and sister also performed a very graceful waltz in the beautiful manner before the King. The evening passed rapidly and agreeably and is not yet forgotten. These evenings at the Palace serve a good purpose to bring together the people and keep up the respect and regard for His majesty.*[43]

In a letter home, Gilman further wrote that the children from the Chiefs' Children's School were also present for the piper's performance:

> *A most pleasing entertainment was offered by the King in a general invitation to attend a luau at the palace to hear a Scotch bagpiper with his pipes, in tartan clothes, kilts, and stocking legs, – altogether a novelty in Honolulu. The children of the school were, of course, present as members of the court circle and they entered into the spirit of the evening with a zest that showed their enjoyment of the release for awhile from the study hours to innocent recreation. Not that they were deprived of this at the school home, where all was done consistent with the Christian principles of the servants of the Board of Missions. Mr. and Mrs. Cooke were ever alive to what would help in forming character in those under their charge who were destined to exert such important influence in the future of the Island Kingdom.*[44]

Cooke himself reported in his journal entry for Friday, October 31, 1845, about the evening:

> Tuesday we had a visit from brother and sister Hitchcock. In the evening a call from Mr. Wyllie and Dr. Judd. The former invited us to the Palace to hear a Highlander play his Bagpipe, the next evening....Wednesday I did not accomplish much. In the evening I went to meeting conducted by brother Andrews and from thence home and to the Palace (the children went before) with Miss. Wyllie. The band of the America was there and played all the evening, also the player on the Bagpipe....[45]

Thus, Hawai`i's future monarchs and their brothers, sisters, and cousins were exposed to the sounds of the bagpipe (See listing in #43). As the *H.M.S. America* sailed out of Honolulu Harbor a number of days later, the sounds of this new instrument were left in the mind's eyes and ears of Honolulu's citizenry.

Nothing further has been found in the written record about bagpipes in Hawai`i until 1869 when H.R.H. Prince Alfred, the Duke of Edinburgh, on the *H.M.S. Galatea* arrived in Honolulu's port on July 21, 1869, after a brief sojourn in Hilo. The young Prince, second son of Queen Victoria, was on a trip around the world and was accompanied on the voyage by his piper and physician, the renown piper J.F. Farquharson. Queen Victoria had been the Godmother to Hawai`i's Prince Albert Edward Kauikeaouli, the young son of Kamehameha IV and Queen Emma. Thus, the Hawai`i visit was special to the British Prince and to Queen Emma. Throughout the rest of July Prince Alfred and his piper were recognized and entertained by Hawai`i's monarchy.

Upon arrival, the Duke and his company were whisked off by King Kamehameha V to his father's home in Waikiki. Here they stayed, meeting Emma and then being entertained at a royal state dinner on the evening of July 27th followed by a grand ball at Iolany Palace on the 28th. During this time, the Duke's personal piper, Farquharson, became somewhat of a celebrity. The *Pacific Commercial Advertiser* noted:

> ...The Highland piper, in his original Scotch costume, is an object of marked attention wherever he goes, and is most certainly one of the most accomplished musical artists we have ever been permitted to hear.[46]

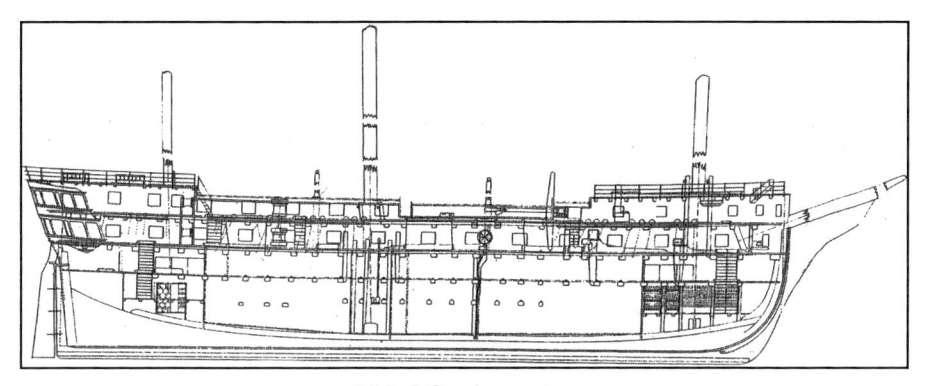

H.M.S. America

Piper Nichol MacIntyre, the first known bagpiper to play in Hawai`i, served on this ship which arrived in Hawai`i in 1845. It was classified as a frigate.

H.M.S. Galatea

Piper J.F. Farquharson and Prince Alfred arrived in Hawai`i on this ship in 1869. It was classified as a wooden screw frigate.

A striking account of the State Ball given by Kamehameha V for the Prince mentions the piper on a number of occasions. This may have been the first time that the traditional music of the pipes – Piobaireachd – was played and heard in Hawai`i. It is referenced in the *Hawaiian Gazette*'s account of the Ball. After an evening of ceremony and dancing, it was time for dinner:

> *At 12, precisely, after the close of an animated quadrille, a Piper, in attendance on His Royal Highness, the Duke, arrayed in Highland costume, stepped on to the ballroom floor, – the observed of all observers, – and with stirring notes and martial tread, promenaded the room, while the company parted right and left for him as he advanced; and as they gazed with curiosity and admiration, many felt,*
>
> *"How, in the noon of night, that pibroch thrille, Savage and shrill."*
>
> *The Piper was, for the moment, the hero of the scene. Soon, His Majesty, taking on his arm Mrs. Wodehouse – the Duke taking Queen Emma – led the way to the supper-room, marching always to the sound of the bagpipes....*[47]

The account goes on to mention a night of toasts, continued dancing and piping, and general good cheer. Archibald Cleghorn, a Scotchman from Edinburgh who married Princess Miriam Likelike, sister of future King David Kalakaua and Queen Lili`uokalani, noted in his journal for that day....

> *Gust trade winds*
> *The natives took presents to H.R.H from 10 till 2 (pm).*
> *Ball given at the Palace in honor of H.R.H.*
> *Got home from the ball at 3 (am)....*[48]

Even the small local newspaper *Punch Bowl* reported on the occasion:

> *...Last Wednesday, the King gave a State ball at Iolani, to which several hundreds of guests were asked. The Galatea's fine band and the Duke's Highland piper constituted the orchestra, and the programme of eighteen dances was consequently very well carried out. The quadrille d'honneur,*

a quadrille introducing several well-known sailors' songs, a waltz composed from a Tahitian melody, and a Scotch foursome reel were the most interesting dances, the last name being played by the piper and performed by Mrs. Sterling and Mrs. Poor, the Duke of Edinburgh and Mr. Sterling. The brogan and the whisky punch, we doubt not, would move some of our Caledonian friends to a most sentimental pitch; and certainly, this old fashioned dance excited great admiration

The ball, which by all who attended was noted a great success, is now over; requiescat in pace![49]

NOTE: The Prince's Piper. The piper, J.F. (James/John Forbes) Farquharson, is noteworthy for a number of reasons. He was a rare right-shouldered piper. Born in 1845 on the Donside estate of Sir Charles Forbes of Edinglassie, he was taught by such famous pipers as Donald Cameron and John Ban MacKenzie while studying medicine at Aberdeen Medical College. In 1865 by command of Queen Victoria he was appointed medical advisor and piper to H.R.H. Prince Alfred Duke of Edinburgh, the second son of Queen Victoria. His piping career continued throughout his life. He "retained his knowledge and interest...to the end of his life and was still playing the chanter until a week before his death. He died at his home in London in 1935 in his 92nd year."[50] In his diary still retained by his family, he recounted his travels with the Duke and noted about his early life:

> I was born 1845, December 23rd at Strathdon, Aberdeenshire. I was educated at the Parish school, Strathdon then at Braemar and at St. Andrews College, Aberdeen. My father was a farmer and wished to make me a doctor. But I took to bagpipe playing and a roaving, roaving life. I went with the best teachers in pipe music in 1857-58. I was with Duncan Campbell, then with the Mackenzies and Ross Her Majestys piper afterwards with Cameron and MacAllister and MacDougal in Edinburgh. I was very successful at Inverness and gained the champion dirk-broaches, sporrans and other prizes. My godfather Sir John Forbes of Inverness paid my teaching and I was friend to him in 1860-64. I then went to Edinburgh to finish my music lessons. I then returned home.[51]

Also in his diary he included a composition on which he noted: *A few good old notes which J.B. (John Ban) McKenzie and D. (David) Cameron always made use of in the year 1867 – Very good notes for Tulloch Gorm or Prince Alfred's March 1888.* SEE Appendix 4.

Donald Mackay (Left), Piper To The Prince Of Wales and J. F. Farquharson (Right), Piper To The Duke Of Edinburgh (1876)

In his diary for that day, J. F. Faquharson simply noted:

> *Very hot day. There was a Ball at the Palace given by the King. I played several times. I got home at 2 am – and very tired.*[52]

Indeed, over the course of the visit's eleven days in Honolulu there was hardly a day when the piper did not play. It was a sad farewell when on August 2, 1869, the Prince and his Piper departed Hawai`i for Yokohama, Japan on their continued world cruise.

A year later, the sounds of bagpipes again graced the ears of Honolulu's citizenry. Or did they? An article appearing in the October 5th, 1870, edition of the *Hawaiian Gazette* notes:

> *Scotch Bagpipes.– Last Wednesday evening Honolulu was treated to a rarity in the shape of serenade. It was a species of music seldom heard here – the veritable Scotch Bagpipe. One of our residents from the land "O" Cakes was honored with a "play," perhaps because he had lately taken to himself a better half. Captain Alexander Adams, our oldest foreign resident, who had not heard the pipes for many a long year, felt young again and could have danced the Highland Fling with any one of his numerous descendants, and doubtless much better than any of them.*[53]

A few days earlier a small unobtrusive notice had appeared in the *Hawaiian Times* and the *Pacific Commercial Advertiser*:

> *"Married" Cleghorn-Kapaakea. On Thursday evening, September 22, at Washington Place, the residence of Mrs. Mary Dominis, by the Rev. C.G. Williamson of St. Andrews Church, Mr. Archibald Scott Cleghorn to Miss Miriam Likelike Kapaakea, daughter of the late Hon. C. Kapaakea, and sister of the Hon. Mrs. Dominis and the Hon. David Kalakaua. No cards.*[54]

Local Scottish businessman Archibald Cleghorn had married Miriam Likelike, the younger sister of future King David Kalakaua and the Queen Lili`uokalani.

When these two notices are taken together, a story emerges. On the evening of Wednesday, September 28, 1870, someone seemingly played the pipes for a newly married Archibald Cleghorn; but who?

In 1870, newly arrived businessman Alfred H. Havell opened a new music business out of his home on Nu`uanu Avenue in downtown Honolulu. He defined himself as a "piano forte Maker, Organ builder and Manufacturer of Harmoniums." But during the summer of 1870, he declared his intention to leave Hawai`i which he did in November. Prior to leaving, however, he desired to make a contribution of his talents to the Masonic Building Fund in Honolulu.[55] And so, on Thursday, August 11, Mr. Havell gave his concert. The *Pacific Commercial Advertiser* reported:

Masonic Building fund. – On Thursday evening, August 11th, Mr. A.H. Havell gave an entertainment at the Kaumakapili Church for the benefit of the Masonic Building Fund of the city. The concert was well attended by the brethren and others, and the receipts were, we learn, very satisfactory. Mr. Havell's lecture was really a fine literary production, interspersed with songs and piano forte playing. For one unassisted person to please and entertain a Honolulu audience – rather a critical audience, by the way – is no easy task, but Mr. Harvell succeeded admirably. Among the songs which were received with marked applause, without further mention were – "Jenny Lind's Good Night," "the Maniac," "Little Fat Man," and "Rocked in the Cradle of the Deep." But the instrumental triumph of the evening was "imitations of the Bagpipe."[56]

"Imitations of the Bagpipe"…This is the only mention of bagpipes or anything resembling bagpipes in the Honolulu's papers at that time. Could Havell have given a repeat performance for Cleghorn a month later in honor of his marriage? If so, then the bagpipe noted in the initial *Hawaiian Gazette* article was in fact a piano, or, perhaps, an organ, and our piper a 'manufacturer of harmoniums."

While this is but one scenario, there are some other possibilities. On Tuesday, September 27, 1870, one day before the identified concert for Cleghorn occurred, the *H.B.M.S.S. Ringdove* arrived in Honolulu after a 21 day voyage from Mazatlan.[57] It is possible that one of its crew members was a bagpiper who could have been approached to play for Cleghorn during the 'play' dedicated to him on the following day.

A third but unlikely possibility; the famed 'Flying Squadron' of six British Navy vessels under the command of Admiral Hornby "going around the world, visiting the various naval stations, and relieving such ships whose time has expired…" had put into Honolulu's port six weeks prior to the 'play'.[58] The squadron had two excellent bands which the newspaper account in the *Pacific Commercial Advertiser* described:

> *Two of the bands belonging to the squadron were on shore during the day, which happened to be the anniversary of the succession of Queen Victoria, and delighted our residents by their beautiful music.*[59]

The bands played at the residence of the British Commissioner and Consul General and in Emma Square. Though none are mentioned, perhaps a piper or two were in the band or in one of the ships' company. Perhaps one of them was waylaid a bit in Honolulu and participated in Cleghorn's 'play.'

For both of these scenarios, however, it seems unlikely that given the uniqueness of the bagpipe some notice of a piper's presence in Honolulu would not have been reported in one of the local newspapers of the day.

At any rate, in 1940, the *Honolulu Advertiser* recalled the 'bagpiping' instance as noted in the *Hawaiian Gazette* in its "History From Our Files" column, but it still remains a mystery as to who was playing what and for what purpose.[60]

In more recent years visiting pipers from British, Australian, Canadian, or New Zealand military units have continued to grace Hawai`i's shores.

One of the more notable visits occurred in August, 1928, during commemoration ceremonies of the 150th year of Captain James Cook's arrival. Bagpipes again were heard in Hawai`i.

On Kaua'i where Cook first landed in Hawai`i, an international ceremony was held in Waimea town on Thursday, August 16, 1928. Official representatives arrived on the battleship *U.S.S. Pennsylvania*, carrying Secretary of War Dwight F. Davis, three cruisers including the British Royal Navy's *H.M.S. Cornwall*, the New Zealand Navy's *H.M.N.Z.S. Dunedin*, and Australia's *H.M.A.S. Brisbane*, three US submarines and two destroyers, and six American seaplanes. The *Honolulu Star-Bulletin* captured the spirit of the day:

> *A gorgeous sunrise beyond Waimea Canyon revealed the flotilla anchored near the spot where Cook's* Resolution *and* Discovery *lay on January 7, 1778. The bay was filled with bedizened sampans and Waimea pier and the black sand beach was thronged with spectators. Ship's boats were escorted shorewards by sampans driven by laughing Japanese and Hawaiians.*

> *On the pier were 300 Japanese children of the Waimea Japanese language school waving flags of the United States, Great Britain, New Zealand and Australia. The pier was a colorful sight as the naval and civilian parties arrived.*

> *A detachment of 100 sailors from the Pennsylvania came ashore first, followed by 150 British marines and the bagpipe corps from the Cornwall.*[61]

The *Honolulu Advertiser* recounted:

> *The two great maritime powers of the Pacific had united in embellishing the program of the Kauai committee in charge with more than one new landmark in their history. In addition to providing them with their first sight of British Marines in a century and a half. The day also gave them their chance to hear the bagpipes.*

> *A kilted piper shrilled and droned for them as the marines from the British cruiser Dunedin marched up from the wharf to take their positions in Waimea Park where the monument stands. He was the first ever seen or heard under orders on Kauai.*[62]

`Upoho Uka Nui `O Kekokia – 89

Cook's Commemoration Service At Waimea, Kaua`i

British Detachment Arrives On The Wharf (Top); Ceremony In Waimea Town Dedicating Monument; British On The Left, US Navy On The Right (Bottom), August 16, 1928

The *Garden Island* also noted that the piper was a great hit with Waimea's children:

> One of the interesting features of the affair from the standpoint of children was the bagpiper from one of the British ships. It was probably the first piper that most of them had seen and he was quite the center of attraction.[63]

On O`ahu in Waikiki, local playwright James A. Wilder, produced a play "Hawaii 150 Years Ago" for Captain Cook's commemoration. His play included a "Mr. Cherry, as Cook's drummer, and another haole who played the bagpipe."[64] The *Honolulu Advertiser*'s account of the play notes:

> ...All is excitement. You hear the roar of cannon from the ships, which the natives take for rainless thunder. Then there are the bagpipes of this ship "singing in the nose" and presently Captain Cook, Vancouver, Lieutenant Wilkinson, marines and sailors enter upon the scene. The grouping of the sailors in uniform with the Hawaiians clean limbed, the girls in soft tapa skirts, the elderly men and women in more dignified costumes makes a picture to be remembered....[65]

Unfortunately, the bagpiper is never identified in these accounts. However, in 1928, there was only one known resident bagpiper in Honolulu, Donald Mackay. In all likelihood, it was he who so ably played with 'Mr. Cherry.'

As bagpipes were heard more and more on Hawai`i's shores, greater interest developed among local residents to learn and play the instrument. This interest was magnified as local celebrations of Scottish and Irish culture continued to emerge in Hawai`i society.

Finally, there are a few historical events which occurred in Hawai`i which deserve mention; not because there is mention of bagpipes but rather because there is no mention of them.

In 1889 and for six months thereafter, the pride of Scottish writers, Robert Louis Stevenson, and his family visited Hawai`i.

They spent most of their time in Waikiki, in Kailua-Kona, and on Moloka`i and became close friends with King Kalakaua and Archibald Cleghorn and his family. In 1893, he returned to Hawai`i for a five weeks visit just prior to his passing in Samoa in 1894. Stevenson was an accomplished player of the flageolet but no where in his writings about Hawai`i is there any mention of bagpipes or pipers.[66] Had he found any along the way in Hawai`i, it is with certainty that he would have mentioned this in his writings.

The world famous song and dance man of his time, Sir Harry Lauder, found Honolulu a truly beautiful place and visited the islands no less than six times between 1914 and 1937. His most publicized visit occured at the end of World War I. He had just established his "Lauder Fund" for disabled British soldiers and traveled the world raising money for the fund. In April 1918, Lauder arrived in Honolulu making a plea for his newly established fund. He returned on April 14, 1919, on the *S.S. Ventura* and spent the day raising money for the fund first at a reception at the Alexander Young Hotel and later in the afternoon giving a performance at the Bijou Theatre. That evening he sailed on to Australia and his efforts had raised slightly over $6,000 for his fund. This, coupled with over $5,000 raised in the previous year, gave Hawai`i a total of over $11,000 raised for the Lauder Fund.[67] Lauder returned to Honolulu in October 1919 and, again, in 1929 and 1937 on his farewell swing around the world. In all his visits and performances, there is no mention of bagpipes which may be reflective of the fact that Honolulu at that time simply had no available resident piper.

A year later in 1920, H.R.H. Crown Prince Edward, Prince of Wales, visited Honolulu twice in the course of the year; in April for one day and in August for three days. Unlike his great uncle who had visited Hawai`i some fifty years earlier, Prince Edward had no personal piper.[68] In newspaper accounts of the day, brief biographies of the main officers aboard Edward's flagship, the battle cruiser *H.M.S. Renown*, included that of the ship's accomplished bandmaster –

> *Lieutenant Percival S. G. O'Donnell, Mus. Bac. L.R.A.M., director of music (temp.), joined the South Wales Borderers in 1897, taking part in the Boer War. In 1905 he joined the Black Watch as band master, and in 1915 he was appointed band master of the Royal Artillery. He became band master of the Plymouth Royal Marine Light Infantry Band four years ago, his band being engaged for the royal tour.*[69]

With such credentials and with such a royal visitor onboard, it is surprising that no bagpiper was included in the band or attached to the Prince's party for the duration of the voyage. What is identified by the newspapers was Edward's deep enthusiasm for and enjoyment of paddling and surfing with the Kahanamoku brothers.[70] During the Prince's second visit in August, Duke Kahanamoku was away in Europe with Pua Kealoha winning Gold Medals at the Olympics in Antwerp, Belgium. His brothers, however, kept the Prince occupied and enthralled during his two-day visit to Waikiki.

The final event occured in 1920 and was, in fact, attended by the visiting Edward in April during his one day visit to Honolulu. This was an extravaganza held on the slopes of Punahou School's Rocky Hill (*Pu`u o Manoa*). The show attempted to capture Hawai`i's history in a half-day's performance of nine distinct picture "recreations" of history. The cast included hundreds of Honolulu residents. The *Pacific Commercial Advertiser* noted:

> *Living pictures of a hundred years of Hawaii's progress passed in dramatic review before 10,000 fascinated spectators...At the conclusion of the first of the nine pictures, the Prince of Wales... accompanied by his staff took his seat in a box especially arranged for his benefit. He was greeted by Prince David Kawananakoa... The Hawaiian Band (Royal Hawaiian Band) played 'God Save the King,'....*[71]

What is noteworthy about this show is that in the seventh picture which portrayed 'Hawaiian Industries' including the importation of labor from Asia and Europe, there was a 'piper.' The piper's name was Rosamona Morgan. She also 'piped' in the final scene of the show. Was this reference to the great highland bagpipe? In reviewing all the newspaper accounts and in searching through photographs of the event in the Punahou School Archives, no where is there any mention or photographic record of any bagpipe. Yet the reference still leads one to ponder.[72]

Chapter 3
Social Acceptance Achieved

So far our story has focused on individual incidents of bagpiping either possibly heard by Hawaiians abroad or individual performances by visiting pipers to Hawai`i. What about the development of resident pipers in Hawai`i?

A. Celebrations and Parades

Bagpipes are intimately connected with commemorations and celebrations. The development of local pipers in Hawai`i is intimately connected with such events and with celebrations specific to Scotland and Ireland by those of Scottish, Irish, Welsh, or English descent or related cultures in Hawai`i.

Three of the more notable Celtic celebrations; Burns Night in remembrance of the Scottish poet and songwriter Robert Burns, St. Patrick's Day, and the Highland Games, or Festival, have been largely responsible for developing a demand for resident pipers and pipe bands in Hawai`i.

These celebrations were, and continue to be, intimately tied to social activity in Hawai`i. The tracing of pipers' and pipe band appearances at these events provides a synopsis of piping and pipers in Hawai`i and the shift which piping has undergone from that of being a music only played by visiting musicians to that of becoming a truly local music played by resident pipers.

Hawai`i in the mid-19th century had many European and American residents, a number of whom belonged to their own 'clubs' or associations which, according to a 1901 edition of the *Pacific Commercial Advertiser*, served the purpose of home and hostelry, and *distinguished guests from abroad were constantly being entertained....*[1] Archibald S. Cleghorn, a Scotchman and father of Princess Ka`iulani, wrote in 1902 about Honolulu's club life:

> *Club life in the earlier days was somewhat different to what it is now. The club house was used as a home – not many of the members had other homes – where they spent their evenings in a social manner and receiving their friends.*

> *This club (The British Club) has had the honor of entertaining several distinguished and prominent visitors during its existence, among whom may be mentioned the Duke of Edinburgh who visited Hawaii in 1869, the officers of the "Flying Squadron" who were here in 1870, the officers of the famous "Merrimac," and many other naval, military, diplomatic and civil officials who have visited Honolulu. Kings Kamehameha the fourth and fifth were frequent visitors to the club, while Kalakaua and his brother Leleiohoku, were on its role of membership, as were also members of the diplomatic corps.*[2]

The British Club was one of the older clubs in Honolulu having been organized in 1852. Its legacy continues today in Hawai`i as The Pacific Club.

Additionally, Cleghorn as 'Honorable Chief' along with 'Honorable Chieftains' J. S. Walker, H. R. Macfarlane, H. E. McIntyre, and Alexander Young formed the Scottish Thistle Club of Honolulu in April 27, 1891.

> *The objects of this club shall be to provide opportunities for more intimate social intercourse among 'Brother Scots' in the Hawaiian Islands; to maintain a Club Reading Room, furnished with Scottish newspapers, periodical literature, and a library of standard Scottish works; to hold weekly or fortnightly meetings; to foster Scottish music, songs and games; and, when expedient, to give public social entertainments.*[3]

(1) Burns Night

In 1892, the Scottish Thistle Club sponsored the first public celebration of Burns Night in Hawai`i, a tradition the club maintained for almost twenty years.[4] It was not until ten years later in 1902 that references to bagpipes at Burns Night first appeared in Honolulu newspapers:

1902:

Highland Fling (In costume)....Piper **R. McDonald Murray**

Bagpipes Selection....Piper **R. McDonald Murray**
"The braw bagpipes is gran, my frien's,
The braw bagpipes is fine
We'll tuk't another pibroch yet,
For the days o' auld syne."

Sword Dance....Ghillie Callum by Piper **R. McDonald Murray**[5]

Piper **R. Macdonald Murray**, *the champion piper of the Pacific, was a general favorite, and the shrill tones put the audience in the best of spirits. They beat time with their feet and clapped with their hands. The piper responded to an encore and the enthusiasm was greater than before. Murray wore the costume of the Highlands and made a picturesque figure in his tartan skirt and green military coat. His bare knees seemed proof to the assaults of the clannish mosquitoes.*[6]

Mighty enthusiasm was created by the performance on the bagpipes of **R. Macdonald Murray**, *dressed in Highland costume of his own clan's tartan, as well as by his dancing of the Highland fling and "Gillie Callum" (the Sword Dance) at intervals....*[7]

...and Piper **R. Macdonald Murray** *danced some Scottish dances.*[8]

Pipers appeared at two additional Burns Nights sponsored by the Scottish Thistle Club of Honolulu in 1907 and, again, in 1908:

1907:

Piper **Fraser** *followed with a bagpipe selection rendered in his own inimitable style...*

Piper **Fraser** *next set feet a-stamping to popular Scotch tunes played on his weird instrument. He can give a realistic imitation of a pig being killed by torture which must be heard to be believed.*[9]

> Chief J.C. McGill opened the program...He was followed by Piper **Frazer**, who brought out the wild thrill of the bagpipes and aroused all the Scotch blood in the hall...
>
> ...afterwith the music of the bagpipes as played by Piper **Frazer** made the windows rattle....[10]

1908:

> The Burns concert will start promptly at 8 p.m. One of the chief drawing cards is the piping of Piper **Stewart** who is said to be the finest performer on the pibrochs that has ever visited Honolulu.
>
> The bagpipe is a wonderful instrument and although as old as the highlands themselves some new and strange charm about them is constantly being discovered.
>
> Quite recently in a backwoods settlement in Canada, Donald McLean, Late of Scotland, was deer hunting and had two fine bucks hanging from a tree near by his little shanty. One evening he heard the howls of a big pack of timber wolves. He didn't want to lose his deer and he knew that his rifle would be useless in the dark. So he seized his trusty bagpipes.
>
> "The Campbells are Coming-tra-la, Tra-la" he piped. The wolves stopped a short way from camp. The strains of "Loch Lomond" next shivered the wintry air. The howling ceased for a moment. McLean sent one of his own compositions over the waste, and the wolves turned and loped for the woods. There hasn't been a wolf near the camp since.[11]
>
> Piper **Stewart** played the overture on the bagpipes and made things ring – or the Scotchmen did![12]

As to who these early pipers were, nothing is known. It is probable they all were visitors to the islands who were pressed into service for the occasion.

Shortly after the 1908 Burns Night celebration, the Scottish Thistle Club disbanded and many of its members joined its successor, the Pacific Club. Burns Night celebrations, however, continued in Honolulu as an annual affair under the auspices of another social club, the British Club. Except for 1919's event when it was canceled due to influenza outbreaks, the British Club maintained the event for more than twelve years. No pipers appeared at these later years until 1917, when the celebration was held at Phoenix Hall:

1917:

One of the special features of the evening was Scottish dancing by Miss. Commin-Smith in Highland costume, to music by Piper **Burns**....[13]

Pipers continued occasionally to appear at Burns Night celebrations over the next two decades (1921, 1928, 1929, 1930, and 1934) but after 1935, the celebration took a 10 year hiatus. Shortly after 1921, the British Club disbanded, leaving Burns Night without a permanent sponsor. The British War Veterans Club assumed sponsorship for a few years (1928 and 1929), followed by the Hawaiian Board of Missions (1930), and the Pacific Club (1934 and 1935). As most of the participants at Burns Night were affiliated with one or a number of these groups, the changing sponsorship was of little consequence.

1921:

The program was opened with a bagpipe selection by **William McDougall**, *followed by brief introductory remarks by John Watt, the president of the British Club...*

There was generous appreciation, too, for the dancing of Miss. Janet Ross and Mrs. Sibyl Campbell Davis. Miss. Ross danced a sword dance and the Highland fling. Mrs. Davis danced "Shean Trews," a Scottish folk-dance. Mr. **McDougall** *accompanied the dancers with his bagpipe....*[14]

In 1928 a new piper, Donald MacKay, appears in the Burns Night newspaper accounts. Born in Scotland on October 17, 1885, MacKay developed his performing skills early in life. He performed with Harry Lauder on stage and later served as a piper with the Black Watch. He left Scotland via Canada and found his way to Los Angeles where he joined a pipe band with future Honolulu resident and long-time family friend, Aggie Wallace. Arriving in Honolulu in 1926, or thereabouts, MacKay continued to play the pipes and quickly became involved in local golfing society.

100 – 𝄞 – Scotland's Great Highland Bagpipe

*Donald MacKay at the Mid-Pacific Club House – 1931
(left to right: Bob McQuigan, Mary MacKay (wife),
Donald MacKay, Rea Commeford (foreground))*

The appearance of Donald MacKay in 1928 and years thereafter marks a new chapter for piping in Hawai`i. He was the first known Honolulu resident piper to perform at Burns Night in Hawai`i.

1928:

*British Veterans will Celebrate Burns' Birthday – "Bagpipe selection: Piper **Donald R. Mackay**."*[15]

Donald R. Mackay *bagpiped until he had all the Scots in the house rocking in their seats....*[16]

1929:

'Scotchmen and Otherwise Do Honor to Bobbie Burns On His 170th Birthday'

Mission Memorial hall was full of Scotchmen and Aloha Tower siren had not quit blowing curfew when the drone of bagpipes of Piper **Donald Mackay** *announced the nationality of the evening...*

The opening skirl of the bagpipes was followed by a series of Scotch airs played by the Kyles of Bute Orchestra...

The sword dance and Highland fling danced by Miss Estelle Crawford to **Mackay**'s *pipes were as Scotch as could be....*[17]

1930:

'Scots Celebrate Poet's Birthday This Evening'

Songs written by the famous bard to the folk-tunes of his native Scotland will be sung by a number of Honoluluans of Scotch descent and the program will be varied with bagpipe numbers by Piper **Donald Mackay** *and the sword dance and Highland fling by Miss. Estelle Crawford....*[18]

1934:

Celebration dinner was held at the Pacific Club — 'Scots Will Honor Burns at Dinner'

*...***Donald McKay**, *professional at the Lanikai Golf Club, and his son* **Donald, Jr.**, *will be present with pipes, kilts, and all*

> *the trimmings down to the skean dhu. McKay and his son are two of the foremost pipers in the United States and their public appearances are rare....*[19]

> *'Local Scots Honor Famed Poet at Annual Bobby Burns Dinner'*

> *...During the dinner Donald McKay, professional at the Lanikai Golf Club, and one of the foremost pipers in the United States, skirled the pipes in centuries-old Scottish tunes which set feet a-stamping....*[20]

Donald MacKay's great love of golf was exemplified by his becoming the first golf professional at the Lanikai Golf Club (now Mid Pacific Country Club) in 1928. He later designed the Moanalua Golf Course. An older resident of Lanikai, Jiro Tanabe, remembered MacKay:

> *Donald MacKay, the manager and pro up there, was a good guy but a real Scotsman. When he got in the mood-good fun guy. He had a bagpipe, and all by himself he walked back and forth playing that thing. I guess he had to march when he played that thing.*[21]

Donald passed on his love of the pipes to his son, Donald Rea MacKay, who also played in his early years and went on to become active in Honolulu business circles.[22]

Donald MacKay played with his friend Aggie Wallace when she arrived in Honolulu in 1938. She formed Honolulu's first pipe band and MacKay continued to play with her until his passing in 1965. It was fitting that Aggie Wallace played at his funeral November, 1965.

After Honolulu's Burns Night celebration in 1934, there seems to have been a ten year hiatus in celebrating the bard's birthday.

From 1944 when Burns Night once again resumed at the Pacific Club till 1950, the celebration was held on occasion but remained 'piperless.' 1950 was a landmark year for Burns Night... Piper Agnes Wallace first appeared on the program.

Her appearance further solidified the shift in piping in Hawai`i from one of dependency upon visiting pipers to one of having resident pipers perform. Ms. Wallace had arrived in Hawai`i in 1938 as a piper for E.K. Fernandez's shows.

'Aggie,' as she was fondly referred to, was born in Kilsyth, Scotland on December 28, 1902. Her father, Alexander Wallace, was an accomplished piper who played at King Edward VIII's funeral and served as Pipe Major for the Thistle Pipe Band of Kilsyth, the Roman Catholic Pipe Band (Croy), and the Glasgow Police Pipe Band (1900).[23] Young Agnes started playing pipes at the age of five "on a 300-year-old, quarter-size bagpipe originally made for a Stuart prince."[24] In 1911, her father moved the family to Canada when he was appointed Pipe Major of the 50th Gordon Highlanders Regiment of Canada. Aggie continued to play her bagpipe as well and within three years she was known as "The Champion Piper of Canada and the United States." She played with John Philip Souza's band when it came to Calgary for the Stampede and spent the years from 1921 until 1930 moving around vaudeville. Later, she moved to Hollywood where in 1938 E. K. Fernandez heard her play and contracted her to play in his shows in Hawai`i.

On April 16, 1938, she arrived in Hawai`i and began a fifty year career of playing and teaching the bagpipe to island residents. It was due to her influence and teaching that the first pipe band was formed in Hawai`i.

> **NOTE: Pipe Major Agnes Wallace.** Aggie Wallace was married three times; first to William Ross in New Jersey in October 1925, second to a fellow named Hendrix in 1947, and a third brief encounter with a physician. Her only child, Ian Ross, was born in March 1928, and became a drummer in his mother's band. He married and had five children. He died in June 1981, at the age of 53. Aggie died less than a month later on July 11, 1981. Her grandchildren continue to live in Hawai`i today.

Young Piper Agnes Wallace

'Upoho Uka Nui 'O Kekokia – 105

Piper Aggie Wallace Leading The Labor Day Parade, 1938

Another piper friend of hers from Los Angeles, Glen 'Brick' Johnson also had moved to Hawai`i a year earlier in 1937 to teach at Punahou School. He stayed only a year but on occasion played his pipes while successfully coaching football at the school.[25]

Punahou's annual *Oahuan* for 1938 noted:

No record of the year's activities would be complete without a mention of a friend who the athletes of '37-'38 will never forget. In September as an exchange director of boys' physical education and coach came a genial, quiet, red-haired man who soon became not only a teacher but friend to the boys. Now after just one short year with us he is returning to his home in Piedmont, California. We like to think that he may become a member of the "Come-back Club." He may be sure that whether or not he does return he has won a place among those who learned to know him that will not be filled. It is with a heavy heart that we let 'Brick' Johnson go. Says one of his boys, "We have yet to know a coach more efficient or more popular." If Aloha means not goodbye but 'Auf Wiedersehen,' then the whole school joins in saying, "Aloha, 'Brick!' Aloha!"

Returning to the Burns Night story, another Anglophile organization, the Daughters of the British Empire, was in its second year of existence in 1950. The continuation of Burns' Night became its challenge; one which it ably undertook until 1967 when The Caledonian Society of Hawai`i assumed responsibility for Burns Night. It continues today under The Caledonian Society's auspices with its location having moved from the `Ilikai Hotel to the Japanese Cultural Center in 2001.

1950:

The birthday of the great Scottish poet Robert Burns was observed last night at Tenney Hall, St. Andrew's Cathedral, under the sponsorship of Daughters of the British Empire.

Many of Burns' famed poems were recited in an atmosphere kindred to the Scotland of his day and age.

'Upoho Uka Nui 'O Kekokia – 107

*Pipe Major Aggie Wallace and Piper Sandy Gair With 'Moki'
At The Burns Dinner,* 1965

Participating in the program were Mrs. **Agnes W. Hendrix**, William H. Atwell, Jack Coale and Mr. and Mrs. Alec Gordon of Los Angeles.

Mrs. Ann Grace Chapple presided.[26]

1951:

'Bagpipes, Dancers Honor Bobby Burns'

The Skirl of bagpipes and the swirl of kilts made this program, observing the 192nd birthday of Bobbie Burns, a colorful bit of Scotland transplanted to Hawai`i. After greetings by Mrs. Ann Grace Chappie, DBE Territorial President, a band of pipers, including Mrs. **Agnes Wallace Hendrix, Alexander G.S. Blake, James McClelland, Alexander Gordon** *and* **Ian Ross** *opened the tribute to Scotland's poet laureate.*[27]

1965:

It (haggis) was flown in yesterday by BOAC from Scotland and warmed in the Halekulani oven by a man who doesn't claim Scottish ancestry – Chef Moses (Moki) Kawaha. In strict tradition, two bagpipers – **Sandy Gair** *and* **Agnes Wallace Hendrix** *– piped in the haggis, borne proudly by the smiling Kawaha.*[28]

1967:

'Pipin' in the Haggis'

The Caledonian Society of Hawai`i is sponsoring a party celebrating the 208th anniversary of Scottish poet Robert Burns Friday. Ready to 'pipe in the haggis' or pudding before it is served at the traditional celebration are...Alexander MacGregor, Al Douglas, Mrs. **Agnes Wallace**, *Ernest Lewis and William Morrison, in their tartans and kilts. The party begins at 6 p.m. in the Pacific Ballroom of the Ilikai Hotel.*[29]

Over the years under auspices of The Caledonian Society, Burns Night in Honolulu has developed into an annual local tradition. Accomplished individual pipers continue to play during the evening. In recent years, Pipe Major David Furumoto

Celtic Pipes and Drums Of Hawai`i At The Burns Bicentennial Dinner Held At The Ilikai, 1996

(Honolulu Pipes and Drums), Pipe Major A.P. Frappia (Honolulu Pipes and Drums), Pipe Major Lawrence Coleman (Celtic Pipes and Drums of Hawai`i), Pipe Major Jacob Kaio (Hawaiian Thistle Pipe Band), Pipe Major Dan Quinn (Celtic Pipes and Drums of Hawai`i), and Scotland's Gold Medal winner Andrew Wright have all performed at Burns Night festivities and continue a tradition established one hundred years earlier by Piper R. Macdonald Murray.

On occasion Burns Night celebrations have been and continue to be held on the neighbor islands. Hawai`i's Hamakua Coast has traditionally been known as the 'Scottish Coast' because many of the sugar plantations there were managed by Scots or had Scots in management positions in the 19th and 20th centuries. When Honolulu businessman Francis Morgan asked why, his respondent simply said, "Any Scotsman with any brains left Scotland."[30] The first Burns Night Celebrations on the island of Hawai`i occurred in Hilo at the end of the 19th century. Bagpipes appeared on the program shortly thereafter in 1905 when the Big Island's pioneer piper Robert Forbes began to entertain at these early functions.[31]

1905:

The Hilo Burns Club are renowned for their excellence of their entertainments, and Saturday night's affair added another success to their reputation ... as a prelude **R. Forbes** *in costume played a bagpipe refrain, which was roundly applauded.*[32]

1906:

A large audience was present at the entertainment given at Spreckels Hall Saturday evening ... the first number, selection, on bagpipes, by Mr. **R. Forbes** *in full costume, was well performed....*[33]

1907:

... 300 attendees at Spreckels Hall under the auspices of the Hilo Burns Club – Bagpipes....Mr. **Robert Forbes**[34]

Piper Robert Forbes continued to play at these events for a number of years. Both he and his brother William were the only known pipers on Hawai`i for many years.

On Maui, Burns' Night was first instituted in 1932.

> Highlanders of Maui, together, with other friendly lads and lassies to the grand total of 53 met at the Maui Country Club... for a Scotch feast in honor of the memory of Bobbie Burns....
>
> It was the first Burns dinner to be staged on the island...There was Scotch broth and oat cakes to begin with, then came chicken with oatmeal stuffing and "Chappit Neeps and Tatties," tea, scones, marmalade, short cake and apple dumplings completed the menu.
>
> John Moodie served as toastmaster...The entire Bobbie Burns dinner was staged under the chairmanship of John Moodie, assisted by Robert Bruce of Wailuku.[35]

However, this first celebration was 'piperless.' For the past ten years there has been a casual Burns Night celebration in Kihei. In 2004 a new formal Burns Night was celebrated at Mulligan's Irish Pub in Wailea sponsored by Maui Celtic, a local business. The evening included piping in the haggis and all the correct adresses and toasts.

Most recently, Kaua`i also has begun to celebrate Burns birthday. A number of Scotchmen emigrated to Kaua`i in the 19th century to work in the sugar industry. Scotchman and Kaua`i County fireman David Walker spearheaded efforts for Kaua`i's first Burns' Night celebration held on February 4, 2001, at the Waimea Plantation Cottages. In the finest tradition of Robert Burns, Walker organized a remarkable evening with his cousin, also David Walker, from Edinburgh presiding over the haggis. Pipe Major Emeritus Lawrence Coleman and Piper Hardy Spoehr from the Celtic Pipes and Drums of Hawai`i were in attendance providing tunes for the evening... a great beginning for the island. In its second year, Kaua`i's Burns Night under David Walker's direction, hosted the Pipes and Drums of the Atlantic Watch under Pipe Major Ernie Lackey, a pipe band from Red Bank, New Jersey; Ian Howarth, a Black Watch retiree;

Kaua`i's First Burns Night Celebration – (Top): Serving The Haggis, (Bottom) David Walker and Family, Waimea, Kaua`i, 2001

and a three-person contingent from the Celtic Pipes and Drums of Hawai`i…another great evening with more than 150 Kaua`i residents in attendance. In February 2003, the Atlantic Watch returned for a repeat performance at Kaua`i's Burns Night, and today this celebration has become an island tradition.

(2) St. Patrick's Day

The Irish, also, have been active Hawai`i advocates for piping over the years. When Captain George Vancouver arrived in Hawai`i in 1792, he found an Irishman present and residing on O`ahu.[36] Since then, numerous Irishmen have found their way to Hawai`i's shores. Names like James Campbell, John A. Hughes, Robert Lewers, George Lucas, Francis Mills Swanzy, the McInerny twins – Jim and Will, and former Governors Charles McCarthy, William Quinn, and Jack Burns have all left their mark on Hawai`i's history.

By 1869, Hawai`i's Irish citizenry were celebrating St. Patrick's Day in Honolulu in what some would say was in typical Irish fashion. The *Pacific Commercial Advertiser* reported:

> *Concerning St. Patrick's Day. — The Irishmen are squabbling over the preliminary arrangements for properly observing their approaching anniversary. High-toned citizens have arranged for a fifteen-dollar dinner at the Occidental, much to the disgust of the poorer Celts, who are obliged to do the honor to the occasion by partaking of a cheaper meal at the Brooklyn. Still a third dinner is talked of. Besides generous provision for the inner man, a procession will take place, and whisky 'galore' will be furnished.*[37]

In accounts for the following year, 1870, the day's observance had become more organized and well in tune with Honolulu's society:

> *St. Patrick's Day.— In this city on Thursday last, on the "17th of Ireland," some of the sons of the Green Isle, never forgetful of the dear old sod, made a demonstration in commemoration of their country by providing a bountiful spread of all the luxuries in eatables and drinkables that the markets of the country could*

afford. Several toasts were proposed and received – the King – the day we celebrate – Queen Victoria – President of the United States – the Emperor of France – all of which were appropriately responded to. The company separated at quite an early hour for Irishmen on the birthday of their patron saint, giving three hearty cheers for their entertainers.[38]

Another account appeared in the Honolulu newspaper *Bennett's Own*:

St Patrick's Day

…The anniversary of the patron of the Emerald isle, the 17th inst, passed off without any fenian demonstration in this city. Although the shamrock was a conspicuous patriotic badge on the breast of several of our inhabitants of the Hibernian persuasion, we do not think that the attention of the police was called particularly to this 'Wearing of the Green.' No thrilling lines of patriotic songs – no recitals of Shamus O'Brien – were heard in our streets; nor was "Arrah na Pogne" enacted in the Royal Theatre – nevertheless, the day was duly remembered and celebrated.

The proprietors of the Royal Hotel gave an entertainment in the evening to their friends, in excellent style. The table was spread in the large and airy Billiard Room, and certainly did great credit to the hospitable hosts of the Hotel. It was spread with all the substantials and luxuries which our market can afford, and there was everything that could revive the spirits and exhilarate the inner man, from genuine mountain dew, down to bottles and syphons of the effervescing soda. It was a festive and happy company – purely democratic. There was present high social feeling, and a total absence of shillelahs. Any person who had seen the radiant and happy countenances of the Celtic brothers present would never believe that they belonged to a race that would 'shoot landlords for snipe' in the ould country, and St Patrick himself could have smiled upon them benignantly.[39]

On the neighbor islands, St. Patrick's Day as a special day for the Irish seems to have first been celebrated on Maui in 1903. The Irish and Irish-at-heart gathered for a St. Patrick's Day ball at the

Dr. John 'Doc' Sheedy – St. Patrick's Day, 2000

St Patrick's Day Parade, 1980s – Drum Major Bill Morrison

Aloha Lodge, Knight of Pythias, at Wailuku at a function "given by the patriotic sons of the ould sod." The *Maui News* reported:

> At eight o'clock, the grand march was formed with Dr. and Mrs. John Weddick as leaders, and over fifty couples in line, the music being furnished by Mr. George B. Schrader at the piano. An elaborate program of dances followed, with Mr. J.J. Walsh of Kahului as floor manager and a most delightful and successful evening of dancing followed, during which refreshments were served. At 12:30 the train whistles announced that the time for departure had arrived and brought to a close one of the most delightful dances ever given at Aloha Lodge Hall.[40]

There is no mention of pipers being present on Maui until recent times. Most recently, in 2004, the Maui Celtic Pipes and Drums along with visiting Canadian Champion piper Jack Lee with his sons Andrew, Colin, and John perfomed throughout the day.

Traditionally, the St. Patrick's Day parade has been one of the events which has brought people of the Irish persuasion together and has attracted pipers and pipe bands.[41]

The current annual St. Patrick's Day parade in Honolulu dates back to 1969. The first parade slipped by with little or no preliminary announcements. The holding of the 'second' annual parade, however, gained some notoriety in the *Honolulu Advertiser* in 1970:

> St. Patrick's Day Parade In Waikiki — The second annual St. Patrick's Day Parade will begin at 1:30 pm today from the Kapiolani Bandstand and wind through Waikiki.
>
> Termination point for the parade is Ft. DeRussy, but participants will go to the Hilton Hawaiian Village for refreshments.
>
> A Marine color guard will lead the parade. Among those scheduled to participate are Mayor Frank F. Fasi, who is being made an 'honorary Irishman' for the day, and an Irish colleen, Roberta Rutledge of Dublin.
>
> The King and Queen of Aloha Week and their kahili bearers will be there, as well as a bagpipe band, Marine band, Air

The Royal Scots At The First Games In Waimea In 1973

> Force band, Kalani High School band, and a Damien High School float.
>
> Representatives of all the military services will be in the parade.[42]

Except for its direction, the parade has changed little since its inception. Today's parade begins at Ft. DeRussy and ends at Kapiolani Park and over the years has been led by such honorary 'Irish' as the Mayor of the City and County of Honolulu, Frank F. Fasi (Italian American) and noted entertainer, Al Harrington (Samoan American).

Two Irish organizations in recent times have continued to keep the Irish heritage alive in Hawai`i; Clan Na Gael (Family of Ireland) founded in 1983 to be a 'family-oriented' organization and the local chapter of the Friendly Sons of St. Patrick founded in 1955 and the organizer of Honolulu's annual St. Patrick's Day parade.[43]

(3) Highland Games / Festival

The Highland Games, or Festival, as it it now known, is the third contributing factor to the demand for and growth of pipers and pipe bands in Hawai`i. The first Highland Games was held in Waimea on the Big Island of Hawai`i between October 6-7, 1973. It was the 'brainchild' of Angus Coombs, a native Scot who emigrated to Waimea and who managed the former Waimea Village Inn which is now part of Hawai`i Preparatory Academy.

> The hills of Waimea were alive with the sounds of Scotland yesterday as the 1st annual Scottish-Hawaiian Highland Games got underway at the the Hawaii Preparatory Academy Field...
>
> Several bagpipe bands from Canada, the Mainland and Hawaii performed. George Naope's Hawaiian troupe and the Kaneohe Marine Drum and Bugle Corp were also featured....[44]

Besides the famous Vancouver Police Pipe Band, Aggie Wallace's Royal Scots Pipe Band was present representing Hawai`i at these first Games. One of her piping students, David Furumoto, won the piping competition adjudicated by renown piper, piping instructor, and Pipe Major James McMillan who had been brought to Waimea by Coombs from Canada to judge the piping contests.

In following years, the Games have continued on O'ahu in Honolulu. Venues have been diverse ranging from Iolani and Punahou Schools, the Navy's Richardson Field, the Holy Nativity Church, the Bishop Museum, and, most recently, Kapiolani Park. Generally, the games have been held in March or April and have attracted not only local pipers and pipe bands but have been enriched by visiting pipers and pipe bands from the continental United States, Canada, Australia, and New Zealand.

NOTE: Honolulu's Highland Festival. Between 1982-1985, the Highland Festival reached its peak in terms of performing pipe bands. During all four years, P/M James McMillan attended the festivals as chief judge. The festivals were held:

> March 28, 1982: Iolani School
> March 27, 1983: Punahou School
> March 25, 1984: Richardson Field
> March 26, 1985: Richardson Field

In 1984, Seven pipe bands participated in the competition – the most ever recorded. The pipe bands included:

> Anchorage Pipe Band, Anchorage, Alaska
> Auckland Police Pipe Band, Auckland, New Zealand
> Honolulu Pipes and Drums, Honolulu, Hawai`i
> House of Scotland Pipe Band, La Jolla, California
> Los Angeles Police Pipe Band, Los Angeles, California
> Penticton Pipe Band, Penticton, British Columbia, Canada
> Prince George Pipe Band, Prince George, British Columbia, Canada

Since 1984 the mainstay to the Games has been Honolulu's local pipes bands. Most recently, these have been the Celtic Pipes and Drums of Hawai`i and the Hawaiian Thistle Pipe Band. The R.P. Blanford & Sons Pipe Band from California has also participated in recent years.

For these celebrations and festivals, the occasional individual piper has made a public impression, but what has largely been responsible for the growing popularity of the pipes has been the formation and performances of pipe bands in Hawai`i.

B. Pipe Bands and Pipers

(1) Pipe Bands

Pipe bands developed in the 19th and early 20th centuries in the British military and soon became part of the civilian community as well, representing universities, towns and cities, or public service agencies. Today pipe bands are found in all corners of the world and many participate in local, national, and international competitions. There are four established levels of pipe band proficiency with Grade 1 being at the top or world class descending to Grade 4 at the community level or the beginning level for competition. In recent years, the top Grade 1 pipe bands in the world have included Canada's Simon Fraser University Pipe Band, Northern Ireland's Field Marshal Montgomery Pipe Band, Australia's Victoria Police Pipe Band, United States' City of Washington Pipe Band, and Scotland's Shotts & Dykehead Caledonia Pipe Band, Strathclyde Police Pipe Band and 78th Fraser Highlanders.

Most of the top bands in the United States are considered Grade 2 bands and include the Nassau County Police Emerald Society Pipes and Drums, Alameda County Sheriff's Pipe Band, and R.P. Blanford & Son Pipe Band.[45]

The essential ingredients of a pipe band include a Drum Major and a Pipe Major and a compliment of pipers and drummers; the latter including a bass drummer and one or more snare and tenor drummers. The Drum Major generally serves as coordinator of the band and leads the band when it is in formation on street marches or in field performances. The Pipe Major is the understood leader and director of the band. One published authority notes:

> *In the pipe band, it is the 'heart' of the pipe major that is most vital to the musical development of the group. Only his 'style,'*

122 – 𝄞 – Scotland's Great Highland Bagpipe

British Army Pipe Bands:
(Top) Seaforth Highlanders; (Middle) Argyll and Sutherland Highlanders;
(Bottom) Queen's Own Cameron Highlanders

`Upoho Uka Nui `O Kekokia – 123

British Army Pipe Bands:
*(Top) Gordon Highlanders; (Middle) Royal Scots;
(Bottom) Black Watch*

his ability to teach it, and his band's ability to learn it, can bring forth from the group a concerted musical effort. Naturally the pipe major should seek input and support from the group in musical matters, but attempts to run the musical approach of a band by committee or through other 'democratic' processes generally end in disaster.[46]

NOTE: Pipe Majors and Drum Majors — In Appendix 3 there is a listing of past and present Pipe Majors and Drum Majors of Hawai`i's pipe bands.

Pipe Major Emeritus Lawrence Coleman of the Celtic Pipes and Drums of Hawai`i described the operations of pipe bands in a 1995 interview:

The traditional way a pipe band is organized is that the Pipe Major is the musical director of the band. The Drum Major has the most visibility because he is the person out front on parade or in the middle of the circle when playing in circle with his mace or staff. He is usually tall and impressive looking. He is called the Drum Major because traditionally he comes up through the ranks from the drum section and knows percussion very well as well as military drill. So when the band is in the field...the Drum Major, traditionally, is the leader of the whole unit because it is marching, changing direction, and going through intricate movements. The Drum Major is the person who controls all that with his mace. The Pipe Major will determine in advance what tunes will be played and how they are going to be played, but the Drum Major through specific movements of his mace will bring all the ranks — percussion and pipes — in and out of these tunes. Thus, the Drum Major is a very formidable position in most pipe bands.

The Pipe Major is usually positioned at the right front of the ranks because that is the easiest place for him to be identified by the other members in the ranks. He gets his say with the Drum Major.

> *In civilian bands...there is also usually a set of band officers elected by the membership. Each has the usual duties associated with nonprofit organizations.*
>
> *Finally, there are also military or regimental pipe bands which are organized on the military side. Within their ranks they have military schools of piping which keep the tradition of piping alive and well within the British military structure....*[47]

The uniforms of pipe bands are also extremely important. Military pipe bands, particularly those associated with regiments in the British Army, have unique uniforms associated with their regimental histories and traditions. Civilian pipe bands generally have less ornate uniforms but still maintain the 'spit and polish' uniform appearance so important in any performing band.

One of the standard uniform items associated with pipe band recognition is the kilt and its associated tartan. Hawai`i's pipe bands have worn kilts with a number of distinguishing tartans. These have included the Royal Stewart tartan, the Irish Saffron tartan, the Black Watch tartan, the Scott tartan, the U.S. Marine Corps tartan, and the Hawai`i tartan.

> NOTE: Hawai`i Tartan. The Hawai`i Tartan was designed by Douglas Herring in 1997 and has been adopted by the Caledonian Society as Hawai`i's official tartan. In 2001, the Senate Committee on Hawaiian Affairs of the Hawai`i State Legislature passed a resolution adopting the Hawai`i tartan as Hawai`i's official tartan (S.C.R. No. 63, S.D. 1). The tartan reflects the colors of Hawai`i; blue for its oceans and skies, green for its forests and landscapes, brown for the `aina, the life-giving soil, and red and yellow for its royal legacy and fiery origins (Thread Count: B/8(blue), R4(red), Y4(yellow), B48(blue), T16(brown/tan), G40(green), Y4(yellow), R6(red)), and it has been registered with The Scottish Tartans Society.

Hawai`i's pipe bands have generally been at the Grade 4 level and have all been community oriented and composed of volunteers. Their history begins with the arrival of Aggie Wallace to Hawai`i's shores in 1938. Shortly after her arrival, she began attracting local

Hawai`i Tartan

pipers and drummers. Pipers Donald MacLeod, ship's carpenter on the S.S. Lurline, Donald McKay, pro golfer at Lanikai, Alexander 'Sandy' Blake, and Huntley McLean joined Joe Dickson, Danny Redmond and others on the drums to perform under Aggie's direction in 1939 and 1940.[48] They eventually called themselves "The Royal Scots" with Aggie Wallace serving as Pipe Major. This was the first pipe band established in Hawai`i.

One of the band's first performances occurred at `A`ala Park in support of the China Relief Program just prior to December 7, 1941. Aggie related the story in an interview:

> *Well, Mr. Ching Alai did not know what the bagpipes looked like, and had never heard them before and he was a little skeptical about having us on the program because he didn't know whether it would be an asset or not. And so, anyway, we went down... and he says, "Just play one number." So we started off and played "The Black Watch," the one number. After we started to play, it would have done your heart good to see those poor old Chinamen, Chinese men with big, long beards, coming right up to the platform there and throwing $20 bills at our feet. In no time at all, it took about six or eight men to pick up the money before it would all blow away. And they were so excited and Ching Alai was one of the men picking the money up. And he came over to my shoulder and said, "Please can you play one more, one more?" And he kept doing that several times because as long as we played, the money was flowing onto the stage. And it was so terrific, I'm telling you, we couldn't believe our eyes ourselves.*[49]

With this performance, the history of pipe bands begins in Hawai`i. This section identifies some of the highlights of pipe band history in the islands through the present time (2004).

When the war broke out, Aggie was asked to participate in the USO, and so her civilian pipe band took a hiatus. The Army took advantage of her organizing talents and asked her to form a military pipe band, the first in Hawai`i. It quickly took shape under her direction:

> *I taught one chap who was stationed out at Schofield Barracks... One day he was practicing outside by the ambulance in the*

*Hawai`i's First Pipe Band about 1940.
(Aggie Wallace is far left and Donald MacKay is far right.
Young piper on MacKay's right is Rae Commeford-Donald
MacKay's nephew)*

field and he heard a great commotion over the wall and the next thing he knows that a colonel is standing on top of the wall and he says, "Young lad," he says... "Where did you learn to play the bagpipes?" "Sir, I'm just learning," he says...So when he found out there was a teacher here, he said, "I want your lady teacher to come up here and pay me a visit." So I went up, and when I got up there, it was Col. Moore, and he told me he wanted a pipe band taught for the 25th Division Artillery. So that was arranged...So that was their duty, to come down every day for a lesson. And in three months' time we were playing at the hospitals....[50]

After the war, Aggie reformed the Royal Scots which continued intermittently with bagpipers, drummers, and dancers. By the 1950s, it had become a band in demand among Honolulu's social circles. Aggie's pipers Bill Davidson, Sandy Lauchlin, Bill Savage, George Parker, and E. Petrongilli, all with the Army's 25th Division Artillery at Schofield Barracks and dancers Sandy Ross and May Louise Mulvehill, formed the nucleus of the band. In the 1960s the band continued to grow in popularity. Its mainstays included Aggie, her son, drummer Ian Ross, and a few of her piper friends including Alexander 'Sandy' Blake, Sandy Gair, a few military personnel and a number of young local students including David Furumoto and Roberta Jones. Unlike the 1950s, the 1960s began to see more local residents becoming interested in learning how to play the pipes and eventually joining the band.

> **NOTE: Clan MacLeod Chieftain Visits Hawai`i.** One event which was greatly heralded in Hawai`i was the arrival of the Chieftain of the Clan MacLeod, Dame Flora MacLeod, in 1955. From her home at Dunvegan Castle in Scotland, Dame MacLeod traveled to Hawai`i for a ten day visit. Welcomes began when Dame Flora and her traveling companion, Miss Hopeton Kneeland (of New York City) arrived at the Honolulu International Airport and were met by a familiar sound. The highland favorite, "Over the Seas of Skye," was piped for her pleasure by Mrs. Agnes Wallace Hendrix, dressed in Royal Stewart kilts. Lei were piled to the wide brim of Dame Flora's black hat by the time all MacLeods on hand had said 'Aloha".[51]

130 – 𝄞 – Scotland's Great Highland Bagpipe

(Top) Aggie Wallace Playing At USO Camp Show,
Schofield Barracks, 1942
(Bottom) fellow Piper Sgt. Bill Gillespie (Us Marine Corps) Playing At USO Show
On Ford Island, 1945

After more than thirty years in Hawai`i, anything or anyone involved with piping knew and treasured Aggie Wallace. Her former student, David Furumoto recalled:

> *At times we would have visits from her contacts as she had many with the piping community in Canada…Generally, whenever anyone who had any connections with piping was coming through (Hawai`i) they invariably would be there visiting with Aggie in her little apartment….*[52]

By the early 1970s, Aggie began to find it more and more difficult to continue as pipe major because of failing health. In 1973, she asked her student David Furumoto to take over the band. Aggie continued to train and teach piping to individuals who made the commitment and felt the passion to learn the pipes.

In 1974, an advertisement appeared in a local Honolulu newspaper asking local pipers to please identify themselves. The ad had been placed in the newspaper by Radioman First Class Charles R. Anderson, a Coast Guard serviceman who had been playing the pipes for 15 years on the continental United States and who desired to form his own band in Hawai`i. Soon five pipers and two drummers answered the call and in discussions with the remaining members of the Royal Scots and with Aggie's blessings, a new pipe band – the Honolulu Pipes and Drums – was born. Within a year and a half the band had grown and included such members as Charles Anderson as Pipe Major, John Patella and Bill Morrison as Drum Majors, and A. J. Frappia, David Furumoto, George Maclellan, Dick Markoff, Rick Shuman, Larry Samuels, Bob Cent, Robert Green, Michael Mendenhall, David Siegel, and John Johnson.

Starting a pipe band is a very expensive undertaking. Uniform costs including kilts and other implements of Scottish and/or Irish dress often exceed $1,000 per band member. A good set of bagpipes costs well over $1,000 and drum costs are about the same. Even with pipers and drummers purchasing their own instruments, new band outlays often exceed $25,000.

Pipe Major Anderson had to find financial support for his new Honolulu Pipes and Drums, and he found major support from the local distributor of Johnny Walker whisky. Initial sponsorship

(Top) Piper Aggie Wallace Greets The Clan MacLeod Chieftain, Dame Flora MacLeod, At Honolulu Airport In 1955.
(Below) piper Aggie Wallace and Her Royal Scots Dancers In The 1950s.

brought the funds to outfit the band as well as a mascot, a dog named "Johnny." The band adopted the Royal Stewart tartan for its kilt.

The popularity of the band grew quickly. Besides playing Burns Night, demand grew to a point where the band had to limit its performances. In 1976, one band member, A. J. Frappia, who was eventually to become the band's Pipe Major, noted:

> Now the band has to decline some requests. Frappia, a claims adjuster for the Fireman's Fund Insurance Company and the band's business manager, said they try to accept no more than two or three dates per month since members are all working men or students.[53]

The band became a regular not only at Burns Night, St. Patrick's Day, and Highland Games gatherings, but also at many of the Honolulu parades. The band cut a striking image in a local setting:

> Striding down sunny Kapiolani Boulevard, wearing sparkling white military blouses and kilts in the traditional piper's Royal Stewart tartan, they might have been lifted whole from the heathered slopes of Ben Lomond.[54]

In 1978, Pipe Major Anderson was transferred and the band selected A. J. Frappia as its new Pipe Major.[55] The Honolulu Pipes and Drums continued to function as Hawai`i's sole pipe band for almost ten years.

On July 11, 1981, Aggie Wallace died at the age of 78. She had devoted her life to the bagpipe and in Hawai`i was responsible for training more than two generations of pipers.[56] Her legacy was her students who were to lead piping efforts in Hawai`i for the next twenty years and into the new millennium. These included three pipers who rose to the rank of Pipe Major in Hawai`i's pipe bands – David Furumoto, A. J. Frappia, and Lawrence Coleman – and Dr. John Sheedy who was a founding member of the Shamrock Pipe Band and the Celtic Pipes and Drums of Hawai`i.

Pipe bands, generally, do not handle dissent among members well. The necessary autocratic nature of leadership within the band structure can magnify dissenting opinions. When pipe major decisions are met with dissent, that dissent often leads to individuals leaving bands and, either joining other bands or forming new ones.

In April 1985, when dissent within the Honolulu Pipes and Drums among some members grew to a point of no return, a few members left and, having no other band to join, formed their own; the Shamrock Pipe Band under the auspices of the local Irish organization Clan Na Gael. The band under the direction of Pipe Major Lawrence Coleman included pipers John 'Doc' Sheedy, Capt. Barry Cronin, Glenn Wheaton, Jean Smith, Norm McCormick, Melany Henderson, David Curry, Cora Dargan, Charles Ireland, student piper Sean O`Reilly, Drum Major Jamie McCormick and drummers Jon Quigg, Paul Lynch, Shannon O'Hannigan, Robin Corbin, Scotty Dawson, and Pete Donahue. Jack Sullivan, later to be known as Honolulu's St. Patrick's Day leprechaun, served as the band's tenor. The band focused on an Irish repertoire and outfitted itself in an 'Irish sort of way':

> *(The women) wear green kilts, and the men wear the uniform of the Royal Irish Guards, the orange-brown kilt. All wear kelly green knee-length socks held up with garters trimmed with saffron ribbon….*[57]

Soon the band found its Irish focus too limiting. In 1987, the band "disestablished" itself from Clan Na Gael and became its own entity. Former Pipe Major A.J. Frappia of the Honolulu Pipes and Drums joined the band as Pipe Major Emeritus, and in January 1988, the band changed its name to the Celtic Pipes and Drums of Hawai`i in and effort to broaden its scope to a true "United Kingdom" (Scottish, Irish, Welsh, and British) character.

The Honolulu Pipes and Drums continued to perform under the direction of a number of competent Pipe Majors. David Furumoto took charge of the band and brought it to a high level of playing ability. In 1986, however, Furumoto resigned his position to focus on his own personal development as a piper. Under the tutorage of such instructors as James MacMillan and Lt. Col. John McEwing, he was the first person of local descent to achieve national recognition for his piping ability in piping competitions held in Canada and the

United States in such places as Vancouver, Canada; Bellingham, WA; Portland, OR; Anchorage, AK; and Monterey, CA.[58]

> NOTE: First Hawai`i Pipe Band Travels Overseas. Under the direction of Pipe Major David Furumoto, the Honolulu Pipes and Drums' trip to the Highland Games in Anchorage, Alaska in 1986 marked the first time a pipe band from Hawai`i performed overseas. This has only happened once since then... the Celtic Pipes and Drums of Hawai`i traveled to Taiwan, China representing the City and County of Honolulu and played in a music festival there in January, 2000.

Accomplished piper Barbara Macaulay took over as Pipe Major of the Honolulu Pipes and Drums in 1986. She had started piping at the age of 12 in Vancouver, Canada and was a member of the famed Vancouver Ladies Pipe Band from 1959 to 1967. As a band member, she had performed at the Edinburgh Tattoo and took first place at the European Championships at Shotts, Scotland. In 1970, she was the sole piper for the British Columbia Pavilion at Expo '70 in Osaka, Japan. In 1985, she joined the Honolulu Pipes and Drums along with her husband, Douglas Macaulay, who served as Band Manager. It was at this time that he was able to secure financial support for the band from Anheuser Busch, and it was through this support and sponsorship that enabled the band to travel to the Highland Games in Anchorage, Alaska in 1986.

Known to some as Honolulu's 'Johnnie Walker' or 'Budweiser' Band, the Honolulu Pipes and Drums continued to grow and improve with such such pipers as former Pipe Major David Furumoto, David Siegel, Larry Jones, Kanoe Miller, Dr. Rob Knudson, and Tom Campbell and drummers John Quigg, Jim Crisafulli, and Stuart Cowan.

Native Hawaiian piper Kanoe Miller also introduced Hawaiian hula into the band repertoire dancing to such tunes as *Hawaiian Lullaby*, *Aloha `Oe*, and *Hawai`i Aloha*. This is the first known instance of the hula being done in a pipe band.

In 1988, Barbara Macaulay stepped down as Pipe Major due to work commitments, but she remained with the band until 1989 when she moved to the continental United States. Through her hard work and that of her fellow band members, the band was playing at a 'solid' Grade 3 competition level at the time of her departure. She was followed by fellow piper Tom Campbell who continued as Pipe Major until 1991 when he was followed by piper Glenn Stewart. Pipe Major Stewart was followed by Alexander Causey a little over a year later in 1992.

> NOTE: First Native Hawaiian Pipers and Pipe Major. In the mid 1980s, under Pipe Major Barbara Macaulay's tutorage and mentorship, Hawai`i's first Native Hawaiian bagpiper, Kanoe Miller, began piping and developed her playing skills to a high level of proficiency. A former "Miss Hawai`i," she continued to play in the Honolulu Pipes and Drums for a number of years. Today, Miller is one of Hawai`i's foremost hula dancers and continues to dance professionally. The sound of the pipes continue to sound in her soul.
>
> Maui's first Native Hawaiian piper, Trinette U`ilani Furtado, began her piping career in 2003 and is presently a member of the Maui Celtic Pipes and Drums.
>
> Beginning his piping career under Pipe Major Lawrence Coleman, Jacob Kaio, Jr. has had a passion for the bagpipes and its music. He quickly rose in the ranks of the Celtic Pipes and Drums of Hawai`i and when Pipe Major Coleman retired in 1999, Kaio was appointed by the band as its new Pipe Major, thereby becoming the world's first Pipe Major of Native Hawaiian ancestry. Later, in 2000, he left the Celtic Pipes and Drums and formed the Hawaiian Thistle Pipe Band where he served as its Pipe Major until 2003 when he left the band to focus on his own personal piping skills. Today, Kaio is one of Hawai`i's most accomplished pipers.

Under Pipe Major Causey the Honolulu Pipes and Drums continued to participate in many different functions on O`ahu including Burns Night celebrations, St. Patrick's Days, Aloha Week Parades, and Highlands Festivals.

With Causey's departure in 1993, Air Force Col. Richard Adams took over as Pipe Major. A proficient piper, Col. Adams continued to raise the level of piping in the band. Noted Canadian piper Rene Cusson journeyed to Hawai`i during this time and provided the piping community with additional instruction. Gradually, however, the band grew smaller as many of its members moved from Hawai`i. The Colonel, himself, was transferred in 1996.

Unfortunately, during the last few years, the Honolulu Pipes and Drums has moved into obscurity and has ceased piping, losing its last Pipe Major, Craig Macdonald, to mainland employment in 1999. Prior to his departure, however, the band was instrumental in hosting renown piper and North American Piobaireachd Society's instructor Alan Walters for a 1998 piping concert and workshop in Honolulu. Noted Australian piper Michelle Mussett also provided band members with ongoing instruction during short visits to Hawai`i between 1998 and 2001.

During the last decade, the Celtic Pipes and Drums of Hawai`i also has grown and developed. In 1989, Honolulu Police Chief Douglas Gibb, realizing that many large cities on the continental United States had pipe bands, approached then Pipe Major Lawrence Coleman with the idea of having the Celtic Pipes and Drums represent the Honolulu Police Department(H.P.D.) at official police functions. Not only was his idea accepted but he and other members of H.P.D. such as bass drummer Bill Burgess joined the band.

Sister Roberta Derby, H.P.D. Chaplain, also became the band's chaplain. She always took great delight with the band and so enjoyed it when the band struck up the tune Garyowen. Upon her death in April 1996, musician and piper Alan Miyamura composed the first of his many tunes *God In the Midst of You* in her memory. In 2001, Father Richard Ruby was inducted into the band as its second official chaplain, a position he continues to hold today.

NOTE: Honolulu Police Department Pipe Band. The HPD Pipe Band was formed through the Celtic Pipes and Drums of Hawai`i and the relationship with Pipe Major Lawrence Coleman and then Chief of Police Douglas Gibb. Chief Gibb was able to get private funding to outfit the new band. He also had a set of bagpipes made for him out of the native Hawaiian wood of koa (Acacia koa). This is the only known set of bagpipes to be made of this traditional wood.

Honolulu Pipes and Drums Piper Kanoe Miller,
1st piper of Native Hawaiian ancestry- 1987

The Celtic Pipes and Drums of Hawai`i's affiliation with the Honolulu Police Department(HPD) has continued under Chiefs Gibb, Michael Nakamura, and Lee Donohue. This affiliation is one of the reasons why the band wears with pride the tartan of the Black Watch.

Another reason is that the band has developed an ongoing relationship with the Black Watch Regiment of the British Army. Former Honolulu Police Chief Gibb initiated dialogue with the Black Watch in the early 1990s when he contributed memorabilia from a family member who had served in the Black Watch to the Black Watch Regimental Museum at Balhousie Castle in Perth, Scotland.

Over the past ten years members of the regiment occasionally have passed through Honolulu and have played with the pipe band. One memorable event occurred in 1996 when pipers of the Black Watch joined the band in the traditional July 4th Kailua Parade on O`ahu. After asking what the occasion of the parade was and being told that it was a commemoration of gaining independence from England, one young Scottish piper replied 'jolly good show.' More recently in 2001, Black Watch retiree and Secretary to the Black Watch Retirees Association, Mr. Ian Howarth, a frequent visitor to Hawai`i, was inducted into the band and recognized for his volunteer service to the band.

Besides those band members previously noted, stalwarts during the early years of the band included pipers Glenn Wheaton, Bruce Middleton, Joe Miller, Dave Reid, Marcus Reed, Mark Reed, Chris Brown, Hunter McEuen, Montie Derby, Dave Graham, Christina Mackay, Gary Kanaya, Craig Ross, Scott Morgan, Rob Duncan; Drum Sergeant and snare drummer Shannon O'Hannigan, snare drummer Chuck Fells, Drum Major and bass drummer Joe O'Hannigan and then alternate bass drummer and sometime piper Hardy Spoehr and Drum Major Bill Hart. Others in the band organization included Bob Graham who served as the band's Operations Officer and HPD Sgt. John Shaw who directed the band's color guard unit. Life member James Brown was also inducted into the band at this time.

Between 1993 and 1996, the band also had a relationship with St. Andrews Cathedral and on occasion would perform as the St. Andrews Pipe Band. The establishment of the Anglican Cathedral represents one of many close ties the Hawaiian monarchy had with England. Land was given by Kamehameha IV for the Cathedral in 1866, and it was finally completed more than 90 years later. Queen Emma while in England in 1865 personally paid for blocks of sandstone cut from English quarries for the Cathedral's construction. She also commissioned English architects to design the Gothic structure. Today, the Cathedral continues its Scottish tradition by holding the annual 'Kirkin of the Tartan' service for its congregation and the resident Scottish clans in Hawai`i.

> NOTE: The Anglican Church In Hawai`i. The Anglican Church's influence in Hawai`i dates back to Captain Cook's arrival when he held a Christian service at Kealakekua Bay. Further, the first resident missionary living in Hawai`i was the Anglican minister John Howel who lived at Kealakekua from 1794-95. This was more than twenty years before the missionaries from the Boston Missionary Society arrived in 1821.
>
> St. Andrew's Cathedral continues the Anglican religious tradition in Hawai`i. The Cathedral's major stained glass window depicts the monarchy's close relationship with the church with the inclusion of miniature depictions of Kamehameha IV and his wife, Queen Emma, in its design.

In 1997, the Celtic Pipes and Drums of Hawai`i's H.P.D. affiliation was expanded to include the Honolulu Fire Department (H.F.D.). With support from then Fire Chief Anthony Lopez, Jr. and, more recently, under Chief Attilio Leonardi, the band continues to represent H.F.D. throughout the year during the annual 4th of July Parade in Kailua, O`ahu and the City Lights Parade at Christmas time. In March 2004, the band dedicated Alan Miyamura's composition *Honolulu Fire Brigade* to the Honolulu Fire Department at its annual Retirees' dinner.

In the intervening years, the band increased with additional pipers including Jacob Kaio, Jr., Dr. Rob Knudson, Tina Berger, Dan Quinn, Pat Roberts, Susan Yamamoto, Frank Talamantes, Tom "Buck" Buchanan, Pat McGuigan, Brent MacNab, Andrew Sullivan, Macha Buchner-Hawkins, Les Enderton, David Mackay, Erin Brown,

`Upoho Uka Nui `O Kekokia – 141

Noted Piper Kathy Kinderman and Pipe Major Jacob Kaio, Jr.
(2000)

*Noted Piper Andrew Wright With
Drum Major Kevin Richard and His Wife Alison*
(2000)

and Elizabeth Kent; Drum Sergeant and piper Alan Miyamura; tenor and snare drummers Marilyn Giese, Brian Naughton, Frank Lude, Matt Enderton, Laurie Yagi, Gene Marcus and his wife Sandy, Tomiko Salz, and Brian Overby; bass drummers Bonnie and Ron Graff and Jamie Buchanan; and Drum Major Kevin Richards.

Over the years, the band also has had a number of dancers including Irish dancer Katherine Kane; Scottish dancers Carol Brown and Karen Toy; and hula dancer Debbie Nakanelua-Richards. Most recently, Irish dancer and instructor Annette Johansson and her school of Irish dancing, "Jig This," has affiliated with the band. Ms. Johansson also is a tenor drummer in the band.

> NOTE: First Hula Dancer In A Pipe Band. Native Hawaiian piper Kanoe Miller of the Honolulu Pipes and Drums was the first person to perform the hula as part of a pipe band's repertoire in the late 1980s. Ms. Debbie Nakanelua-Richards continues the tradition today having joined the Celtic Pipes and Drums of Hawai`i in 1998. She dances to such tunes as *Aloha `Oe, Hawai`i Aloha,* and *Amazing Grace.*

Since 1988, the Celtic Pipes and Drums has continued to distinguish itself as a community band making more than 50 appearances a year. Besides the usual Burns Night, St. Patrick's Day, and Highland Festival activities, the band's memorable appearances have included playing before Prime Minister Margaret Thatcher at Washington Place; participating in commemorative ceremonies for the end of World War II in the Pacific with President Bill Clinton; participating in numerous July Fourth and Christmas parades including having two pipers from the famed British Army's Black Watch Regiment march with the band in the 1996 Fourth of July Parade; beginning every St. Patrick's Day with breakfast at the Sheraton Waikiki with friends such as former New York State Trooper Dennis Higgins and his wife; commemorating the World War II actions of Hawai`i's famed U.S. Army's 100th Battalion and the 442nd Regimental Combat Team; participating in the U.S. Army's annual Tattoo at Fort DeRussy including having Pipe Major CWO Alexander Sandy Dewar and piper MWO Ian Ferguson from the

Canadian Armed Forces Pipes and Drums of the 48th Highlanders join with the band in the March 2000 Tattoo; leading numerous March of Dimes and 'Silver Streak' Walks for charity; participating with Hawai`i's famed Royal Hawaiian Band in a number of public concerts including playing with Gold Medal piper Andrew Wright, chief instructor at Coeur d'Alene's School of Piping and Drumming and president of Scotland's The Piobaireachd Society, from Dunblane, Scotland, and piper Kathy Kinderman from Washington State in the January 2000 concert 'Aloha Kekokia'; and in January 2003 and 2004, playing with the Pipes and Drums of the Atlantic Watch on the deck of the battleship U.S.S. Missouri at Pearl Harbor and playing together at Honolulu's annual Burns Night dinner in 2004.

In 1999, founding Pipe Major Lawrence Coleman retired as Pipe Major and was appointed Pipe Major Emeritus of the band. During his pipe major career, Coleman kept the band together for more than ten years and, taking up where Aggie Wallace had left off, was singularly responsible for teaching a whole new generation of pipers in Hawai`i. Almost all of the pipers of the Celtic Pipes and Drums of Hawai`i at that time had been trained by Coleman.

In 1999, piper Jacob Kaio, Jr. was appointed Pipe Major of the band, the first Native Hawaiian to achieve such a distinction. A year later Pipe Major Kaio and a number of pipers and drummers left the band and former Pipe Sergeant and piping instructor Dan Quinn was elected Pipe Major. He continued in his role as Chief Instructor for the band as well. During these years additional pipers and drummers joined the band including returning piper Craig Ross and pipers Andrew Grandinetti, Alicia Delos Reyes and her son Daniel Eisen, Howard Lavy, Rick Cuthbertson, Joyce Finley, Dan Sinclair, Rodney Takeuchi, Ian Styan, Ashley Fergeson, Mike Hudgins, and Toni Stevens; side and tenor drummers Mickey Keahi and Justin Sinclair; and bass drummers Sita Seery, veteran Honolulu Pipes and Drums drummer Stuart Cowan, and Scott Wallace.[59]

The Hawaiian Thistle Pipe Band came into existence in March 2000. Under the direction of Pipe Major Jacob Kaio, Jr., the band formed to focus on competition venues for its pipers. Accomplished piper Jim Kennedy and others including James Dasinger, Luke Hunter,

Playing On The U.S.S Missouri – Pipes and Drums Of The Atlantic Watch and The Celtic Pipes and Drums Of Hawai`i
(2003)

Alex Moxey, Marcus 'Pappy' Reed, Mark Reed, Michael Riedel, Alison Sherwood, Ian Styan, Charles Whitehill, Brent MacNab, Pat McGuigan, and Susan Yamamoto along with lead drummer Craig Dolack, bass drummer Bonnie Graff and side drummers Joe Beebe and Brian Overby formed the nucleus of this new band. Another notable member included band manager Ron Graff.

Initially, the band performed throughout Honolulu with monthly performances in Waikiki at the Kapiolani Park Bandstand, participation in the annual St. Patrick's Day Parade, the Highlands Festival, the annual 'Kirkin of the Tartan' at St. Andrew's Cathedral and at other community functions. Pipe Major Kaio resigned as Pipe Major in 2003 to concentrate on his personal piping. He continues to be recognized as one of Hawai`i's most talented pipers, receiving national and international acclaim for his piping ability.[60] Piper Mark Reed assumed the Pipe Major role for the band in 2003.

Since early 2000, a former member of both the Celtic Pipes and Drums of Hawai`i and the Hawaiian Thistle Pipe Band, Lt. Justin Stodghill, has worked hard to form the 'Marines Own Highlanders.' While bagpipes have never officially been part of the Marine Corps, there have been at least two unofficial groups of Marine bagpipers; a pipe band composed of members from the 1st Provisional Battlegroup stationed in Londonderry, Ireland in 1943 and a small group led by Captain Joe Cason who began playing 'Cock of the North' when they 'hit the beach' at Iwo Jima in 1945. Presently, Stodghill continues to teach Marines to become pipers and drummers in the ranks of this new unofficial band which Stodghill hopes will gain official recognition in the near future.[61]

All the pipe bands mentioned previously have been formed on the Hawaiian island of O`ahu. There is only one known pipe band which has been formed on a neighbor island, the island of Maui. The Maui Celtic Pipes and Drums had its early beginnings in December 1999, when five individual pipers on Maui began to practice as a group in Kula. The five consisted of Hamish (Jim) Douglas-Burgess, a former member of the Cornish Caledonian Pipes and Drums (United Kingdom), who was tutored in Hawai`i by Craig MacDonald, then Pipe Major of the Honolulu Pipes and Drums; Michael Riedel; John Grant, a piper since 1959 who formerly played with the U.S. Army 36th Regiment Pipes and Drums. He served as Pipe Major of the Central Coast Highland Society Pipe Band(California) and was originally trained by Donald Henry Maich, a Scotsman who moved to Toronto and was in the Canadian Highland Light Infantry; John Impey, a New Zealander; and local resident Will McBarnet. Within a year, this group was joined by two Maui County firefighters, James Brent and Mike MacDougall, who were being tutored by then Pipe Major Lawrence Coleman of the Celtic Pipes and Drums of Hawai`i.

In the summer of 2000, Maui pipers in the persons of both Hamish (Jim) Douglas-Burgess and Michael Riedel journeyed to Scotland where they represented Maui and the Hawaiian islands in 'The Millennium Pipe March.' The march brought together over 10,000 pipers and drummers in Edinburgh to march for the Marie Curie Cancer Research charity.[62]

The first 'official' function of the Maui Celtic Pipes and Drums occurred in the September 11th Memorial in 2002. Today, the band consists of eight pipers and two drummers. The pipers are under the direction of Pipe Major John Grant. Pipers include Hamish (Jim) Douglas-Burgess, John Impey, James Brent, Mike MacDougall, Roger McKinlay Pleasanton, Jason Wolford, and Trinette U`ilani Furtado. The drum section is under the direction of Peter Della Croce and includes drummer Matt Gilman and bass drummer Colin Hanlon. Former band members include piper Michael Riedel now playing with the Clan MacLeay Pipe Band in Portland, Oregon; piper Will McBarnet who is at Princeton University; piper and instructor Richard King, now playing with the L.A. Scots, drummer Michael Buono, and drummer Bradley Salter. The band wears kilts of mixed tartans. The pipe band continues to play for many of Maui's community events including the Maui County Fair, the yearly Burns Night dinner in Kihei, the St. Patrick's Day Party in Wailea, the 4th of July Makawao Parade, and at official County functions. Of particular note is that over Thanksgiving weekend 2002, and again in March 2004, band members organized a Maui visit for World Champion bagpiper Jack Lee from Simon Fraser University. He put on a piping school for Maui bagpipers and played recitals which "were nothing short of brilliant."

`Upoho Uka Nui `O Kekokia – 147

Robert Anderson, Perhaps Honolulu's First Resident Piper, 1898

A final note: since the mid 1980s, many Hawai`i pipers and drummers have attended the North American Piobaireachd Society's Summer School of Piping and Drumming in Coeur d'Alene, Idaho. Founded in 1968 by Lt. Col. John McEwing, USAF(ret), pipers David Furumoto, Lawrence Coleman, and A. J. Frappia initiated a relationship with the school's chief instructor, Pipe Major Evan MacRae. More recently, under chief instructor Andrew Wright, pipers Jacob Kaio, Jr., Dave Reid, Montie Derby, Hardy Spoehr, Les Enderton, Marcus Reed and his son Mark Reed, Tina Berger, and Jim Kennedy, as well as drummers Ron and Bonnie Graff, Marilyn Giese, Matt Enderton, and Tomiko Salz have maintained this Coeur d'Alene connection. A number of the School's piping instructors have come to Hawai`i and provided instruction as has already been noted. The School's Chief Instructor Andrew Wright and instructor Kathy Kinderman came to Hawai`i in 2000 as did renown Canadian pipers Alan Walters and Rene Cusson in years previous. More recently, renown Canadian piper and piping instructor Jack Lee has performed twice on Maui and has provided instruction there to Maui's pipers. These relationships have provided inspiration to all pipers in Hawai`i.

Thus, the future of piping in Hawai`i is bright. More people are playing bagpipes now than ever before and at higher competency levels. The instrument is no longer seen as a 'foreign' one. Many local folks – Hawaiian, Japanese, haole, and others – have embraced this instrument first played in Hawai`i at Kamehameha III's Palace ballroom more than one hundred and fifty years ago and first heard by Native Hawaiians residing in far away lands more than two hundred years ago.

(2) Noted Local Pipers

The growing popularity of piping in Hawai`i is due in part to the legacy of a number of talented local residents who have either contributed and continue to contribute their piping talents to the community and to their fellow pipers.

On O`ahu, the exploits of such resident pipers as Donald MacKay, Aggie Wallace, David Furumoto, Lawrence Coleman,

Jacob Kaio, Jr., and Dan Quinn have already been discussed; but what of O`ahu's earlier resident pipers?

One of O`ahu's first resident pipers was Robert Anderson, born in Selkirk, Scotland. He arrived in Honolulu in 1898 as an accountant for the engineering and manufacturing firm of Catton-Neil. Eventually he became manager of this firm's successor, Honolulu Iron Works. In a photograph of Mr. Anderson appearing on the cover of *The Story of Scots in Hawai`i* (Honolulu, 2000), he is in full regalia carrying a set of bagpipes.

Another early local resident who had some knowledge of the pipes was Honolulu businessman Malcolm MacIntyre (1879-1934). He arrived in Honolulu in 1900 and in an interview with his wife, she noted:

> *I remember my husband on one trip back to Scotland outfitted himself with a highland outfit...kilts and even bagpipes....Yes, he brought back bagpipes and kilt. And I remember once there was a parade. I don't know what they called it or what was the occasion, but he marched in the parade, and as I remember, I think he carried his bagpipes with him...He never learned really to play them as a player. He could demonstrate to his children.*[63]

Other early pipers noted in newspaper accounts as perfoming in Honolulu including R. MacDonald Murray and pipers named only as 'Fraser,' 'Stewart,' and 'Burns' may or may not have been local residents. They remain for future researchers to reintroduce them to us for their piping accomplishments.

On the neighbor islands, occasional resident pipers were also present and brought the sound of the pipes to their respective communities. Many initially were involved with the sugar industry, but, more recently, others are reflective of the teaching efforts of Aggie Wallace, Lawrence Coleman, and Jacob Kaio, Jr. who on occasion journeyed to the neighbor islands to assist those with a desire to learn the pipes.

On Kaua`i, a number of Scots in the 19th century found themselves in Koloa and Waimea working for sugar plantations. Undoubtedly, some must have had some knowledge of the pipes.

150 – 𝄞 – Scotland's Great Highland Bagpipe

(Top) William Forbes, (Bottom) Robert Forbes –
Ribbons Say "See Hawaii First." (See Note #66).
Both Photos Taken In The Early 1900s

Similarly, many Scots resided on Maui and on the 'Big Island' of Hawai`i, most having come directly from Scotland to work for the sugar plantations. As previously noted, Hawai`i's Hamakua Coast was known as the 'Scotch Coast' between 1880-1930 because of the number of Scotchmen working on plantations along that coast as managers, engineers, or accountants.[64] This, too, became a rich cultural area for things Scottish including bagpipe music. In a 1980s oral history project focusing on Hawai`i's Scottish heritage, some interviewees reminisced about bagpipes and bagpipers in their respective communities.

Hilo resident Mrs. Margaret Cushnie Burso remembered the Forbes brothers:

> My uncles were both bagpipe players...Bill Forbes and Bob Forbes. They were very good, and very attractive in their kilts because they were big sturdy men. They looked so nice in their Forbes Tartans….[65]

William and Robert Forbes were two brothers in a family of twelve children who emigrated to Hawai`i's 'Scotch Coast' from Aberdeenshire, Scotland; William in the late 1890s and Robert in 1904. William, who never, married, was born in 1864 and worked for Onomea Sugar Company as a blacksmith. He died in 1938. Robert was born on June 2, 1879, and worked as a blacksmith at Hilo Sugar Company until his retirement in 1943. He died on July 8, 1954. A family member noted that both learned their piping skills early in life within the family setting playing for dances which were the prevalent form of entertainment at the time and having a father who was an accomplished violinist.[66]

On Maui, Mr. Robert P. Bruce, born in 1907 in Inverness, Scotland and first president of the St. Andrews Society on Maui, recalled a renown Maui piper:

> …Jack Hendershot…he got very interested in things Scottish and he made a trip to Scotland, and…he learned to play the bagpipes. This old Aggie Wallace came up too…we got her to come up to all our affairs, and she came up and gave bagpipe lessons to

Hendershot and he learned the bagpipes. He got the full dress and everything, and he got me interested in the thing. I bought my kilt in 1955….[67]

Another early resident piper on the island was Jim O'Donnnell who moved to Maui in the late 1950s and taught a few local residents how to play the pipes including Stewart D. Mackay. Mackay was born in Largs, Scotland in 1945, met his wife Shawn Lyons from Maui in Europe whereafter shortly they were married. In 1968, they moved to upcountry Maui (Olinda) where he began taking lessons from Jim O'Donnell in the early 1970s. In 1978, O'Donnell passed away and in 1996, Mackay passed away. Maui resident and noted artist James Peter Cost played at his funeral. Cost learned his piping from Seumas MacNeill through the College of Piping courses in California in the 1970s. He joined the Salinas Valley Highlanders (now known as the 'Monterery Pipe Band') and in 1992 moved to Maui from Pebble Beach where he played for many weddings and for community events. In 2001, he returned to Carmel.[68] Maui now has a number of accomplished pipers who have formed the Maui Celtic Pipes and Drums.

Thus, as the new century begins, the skirl of bagpipes can be heard throughout Hawai`i. Its music has changed from being something deemed 'foreign' to something today which is commonly accepted and expected at island celebrations and ceremonies relevant not only to Scottish and Irish traditions but to all gatherings recognizing the spirit to which the pipes are dedicated – honor, pride, and devotion to duty and service. This has come about because of the influence of dedicated pipers who integrated their talent into the communities in which they lived or continue to live.

Some of those pipers who have left or are leaving their legacy on piping in Hawai`i include:

> Agnes Wallace:

LIFE: b. 12/1/1902 – Kylsyth, Stirlingshire, Scotland; d. 7/11/1981 – Honolulu, HI

TEACHERS: Alexander Wallace (father)

ACCOMPLISHMENTS: started piping at age 5 in Scotland; named 'Amateur Champion of the Pacific Coast' (1914 Caledonian Games in Vancouver, Canada); member of Jessie Blair Sterling's 'Glasgow Maids'(Canada); 'Kincade Kilties'(Canada); Jack Wyatt's 'Scots Lads and Lassies'(Canada); vaudeville circuit; 'Highland Society Pipe Band'(Los Angeles); Ringling Brothers Circus; Pipe Major – Glendale Ladies Pipe Band(Glendale, CA); and Pipe Major – the Royal Scots(Honolulu, HI)/Piping instructor in Hawai`i (1938 - 1981)

> Dr. John Austin 'Doc' Sheedy:

LIFE: b. 6/17/1920 – Wilmington, Delaware d. 2/22/2003 – Honolulu, Hawai`i

TEACHERS: Pipe Major Aggie Wallace

ACCOMPLISHMENTS: Member, Honolulu Pipes and Drums, Shamrock Pipe Band; Pipe Sergeant – Celtic Pipes and Drums of Hawai`i

> A.(Armel) J.(Jennings) 'Frap' Frappia

LIFE: b. 3/25/1927 – Minnesota   d. 1/3/1999 – Honolulu, Hawai`i

TEACHERS: Pipe Major Aggie Wallace

ACCOMPLISHMENTS: Pipe Major – Honolulu Pipes and Drums; Pipe Major Emeritus   Celtic Pipes and Drums of Hawai`i

> Lawrence Coleman:

LIFE: b. 9/5/1930 – Hubbard, Ohio

TEACHERS: Pipe Major Seamus McInnis; Pipe Major Aggie Wallace; Pipe Major Even MacRae

ACCOMPLISHMENTS: Pipe Major – Shamrock Pipe Band; Pipe Major – Celtic Pipes and Drums of Hawai`i; Pipe Major Emeritus – Celtic Pipes and Drums of Hawai`i/Piping instructor in Hawai`i 1980s – ongoing; Scott of the Year (1994) – Caledonian Society of Hawai`i.

> Alan Miyamura:

LIFE: b. 2/19/1951 – Honolulu, Hawai`i

TEACHERS: Pipe Major Lawrence Coleman

ACCOMPLISHMENTS: Drum Sergeant – Celtic Pipes and Drums of Hawai`i; Piper and composer of pipe and drum tunes including *God in the Midst of You*, *Pipe Major Lawrence Coleman*, *The Caledonian Society in Hawai`i* and *Honolulu Fire Brigade*; tin whistle player in Hapa's recording Namahana.

> Dan Quinn:

LIFE: b. 4/28/1953 – Inglewood, California

TEACHERS: Pipe Major Lawrence Coleman

ACCOMPLISHMENTS: Pipe Sergeant – Celtic Pipes and Drums of Hawai`i; Piping instructor 1998-present/Pipe Major – Celtic Pipes and Drums of Hawai`i 2000-present

> Jacob Kaio, Jr.:

LIFE: b. 7/2/53 – Honolulu, Hawai`i

TEACHERS: Pipe Major Lawrence Coleman, Pipe Major Alexander 'Sandy' Dewar; Andrew Wright; Roddy MacLeod (Scottish National Piping Center)

ACCOMPLISHMENTS: Piping instructor 1998-present/Pipe Major – Celtic Pipes and Drums of Hawai`i 1999-2000; Pipe Major – Hawaiian Thistle Pipe Band 2000-2003; competition piper in Canada, Scotland, and the United States; 2003 – invited observer at the Glenfiddich Piping Championship, Blair Castle, Scotland.

> David Furumoto:

LIFE: b. 8/7/54 – Honolulu, Hawai`i

TEACHERS: Pipe Major Aggie Wallace; Pipe Major James MacMillan; Lt. Col. John McEwing; Pipe Major Evan MacRae

ACCOMPLISHMENTS: Pipe Major – Honolulu Pipes and Drums; competition piper in Canada and the United States; Piper of the Day, Alaska Highland Games (1986); 1st place – Highland Games, Waimea (1973).

These are but a few of the many pipers who have been responsible for the growth and development of pipe bands and pipe music in Hawai`i.

Hawai`i's piping tradition continues to flourish. Its ongoing legacy continues to stir the heart and soul reminiscent of the words in the popular song *When the Pipers Play*:

I hear the voice, I hear the war
I hear the sound on a distant shore
I feel the spirit of yesterday
I touch the past when the pipers play.

The pipes kept playing for you and me
They kept on saying we'll soon be free
And your soul will never fade away
You'll live forever when the pipers play.

The people fear its deadly cry
And some will live and some will die
And though they rest so far away
I feel their presence when the pipers play.

It speaks of love that I have lost
It speaks of my eternal past
It speaks the price of peace to pay
A price remembered when the pipers play.

We do remember when the pipers play.

* This tune is similar to "O' Waly, Waly" which is published as The Water is Wide in the Spaulding Collection (page 131)

BAND PHOTOGRAPHS

The Royal Scots
Honolulu Pipes and Drums
Shamrock Pipe Band
Celtic Pipes and Drums Of Hawai`i
Hawaiian Thistle Pipe Band
The Marine's Own Highlanders
Maui Celtic Pipes and Drums

Royal Scots

Pipe Major Aggie Wallace and The Royal Scots (1954)

Pipe Major Aggie Wallace and The Royal Scots (1957)

Honolulu Pipes and Drums

Johnnie Walker Pipes and Drums
Budweiser Pipe Band

Honolulu Pipes and Drums (1970s)

Honolulu Pipes and Drums (1970s)

Honolulu Pipes and Drums (1970s)

*Honolulu Pipes and Drums
aka Johnnie Walker Pipes and Drums* (1970s)

*Drum Major Bill Morrison (Left) &
Pipe Major A. J. Frappia (Right) (1970s)*

Honolulu Pipes and Drums, Pipe Major A. J. Frappia (1970s)

Honolulu Pipes and Drums, Drum Corps (1980s)

Honolulu Pipes and Drums, Bass Drummer Stuart Cowan (1980s)

'Upoho Uka Nui 'O Kekokia – 173

Honolulu Pipes and Drums, Pipe Major David Furumoto
(1980s)

Honolulu Pipes and Drums, Pipe Major David Furumoto
(1980s)

Shamrock Pipe Band

`Upoho Uka Nui `O Kekokia – 177

Shamrock Pipe Band, Pipe Major Lawrence Coleman (1980s)

Shamrock Pipe Band, Pipe Major Lawrence Coleman (1980s)

CELTIC PIPES AND DRUMS OF HAWAI`I

Honolulu Police Pipe Band
St. Andrews Pipe Band
Honolulu Fire Pipes and Drums

`Upoho Uka Nui `O Kekokia – 181

*Celtic Pipes and Drums Of Hawai`i, Aloha Week Parade,
Pipe Major Lawrence Coleman (1993)*

Celtic Pipes and Drums Of Hawai`i,
Pipe Major Lawrence Coleman
(1990s)

Celtic Pipes and Drums Of Hawai`i, Pipe Major Jacob Kaio, Jr.
(1998)

Celtic Pipes and Drums Of Hawaii, Pipe Major Dan Quinn, St. Patrick's Day Parade, March 19, 2002

`Upoho Uka Nui `O Kekokia – 185

*Celtic Pipes and Drums Of Hawai`i
aka Honolulu Police Pipe Band, Pipe Major Lawrence Coleman
(1990s)*

186 – 𝄞 – Scotland's Great Highland Bagpipe

*Celtic Pipes and Drums Of Hawai`i
aka Honolulu Police Pipe Band
Founding Members, Pipe Major Emeritus A .J. Frappia and
Honolulu Police Chief Douglas Gibb* (1990s)

`Upoho Uka Nui `O Kekokia – 187

Celtic Pipes and Drums Of Hawai`i
aka Honolulu Police Pipe Band, Lawrence Coleman
Note Hula Dancer Debbie Nakanelua-Richards In White Mu`umu`u – first Hula
Dancer To Dance To The Pipes, Central Union Church Concert (1998)

Celtic Pipes and Drums Of Hawai`i
aka St. Andrews Pipe Band, Pipe Major Lawrence Coleman
(1993)

Celtic Pipes and Drums Of Hawai`i
aka Honolulu Fire Department Pipes and Drums,
Pipe Major Lawrence Coleman, 4th Of July Parade (1998)

Celtic Pipes and Drums Of Hawai`i
aka Honolulu Fire Department Pipes and Drums,
Pipe Major Dan Quinn, 4th Of July Parade (2000)

`Upoho Uka Nui `O Kekokia

*Celtic Pipes and Drums of Hawai`i
Aka Honolulu Fire Pipes and Drums
Pipe Major Dan Quinn, March 5, 2004
"Inaugural Performance of Honolulu Fire Brigade"*

Hawaiian Thistle Pipe Band

Hawaiian Thistle Pipe Band, Pipe Major Jacob Kaio, Jr. (2001)

Hawaiian Thistle Pipe Band, Pipe Major Jacob Kaio, Jr. (2002)

Marines Own Highlanders

Marine 1st Lt. Justin Stodghill, Founder and Pipe Major, Marines Own Highlanders (2002)

Maui Celtic Pipes and Drums

`Upoho Uka Nui `O Kekokia – 203

*Pipe Major John Grant and The Maui Celtic Pipes and Drums
4th Of July Parade, Makawao, Maui (2003)*

Bibliographical Notes

Introduction

[1] Berger, Henry. "Music in Honolulu," *Honolulu Almanac*, 1885, pp. 72-74.

See also:

McClellan, Edwin. "How Haole Music Came to Hawaii," *Paradise of the Pacific*, February, 1938, pp. 23-25.

McClellan, Edwin. "New and Old Oral Music of Hawaii," *Paradise of the Pacific*, 1939, pp. 71-73.

Chapter 1. The Bagpipe — An Instrument Of Calling

[1] Baines, Anthony. *Bagpipes*, Occasional Papers on Technology, 9, Pitt River Museum, Oxford, 1995, p. 54.

See also:

Cannon, Roderick. *The Highland Bagpipe and Its Music*, Edinburgh, 1997, p. 4.

Gioielli, Mauro. Julius Caesar's Bagpipes, *Piping Times*, Vol. 46, No. 3, December 1994, pp. 25-27.

[2] Baines, Anthony. *Woodwind Instruments and Their History*, New York, 1991 – See section on "Bagpipes".

See also:

Cannon, Roderick. *Op, Cit.*, 1997, pp. 10-18.

Cheape, Hugh. *The Book of the Bagpipe*, Contemporary Books, Chicago, 2000.

Baines, Anthony. *Op. Cit.*,1995

Video Presentation
The Pipes, the Pipes Are Calling, SeaBright Video Productions, Canada, 1996, (90 minutes)

For additional information about some of the physical attributes of the bagpipes and pipers
see:

Black, W.W. "The Highland Bagpipe and the Comma" (Scale), *Piping Times*, Vol. 49, No. 2, November 1996, pp. 14-16, 18.

MacNeill, Dugald. "Piping A Health Hazard? No Cause for Alarm," *Piping Times*, Vol. 53, No. 5., February 2001, pp. 9, 11.

"The Great Highland Bagpipe Scale," *Piping Times*, Vol. 50, No. 1, October 1997, pp. 41-44.

Wallace, Robert. "Silver Standards Change under European Law," *Piping Times*, Vol. 52, No. 7, April 2000, pp. 13, 15, 17.

Wallace, Robert. "More on Silver Pipes: Hallmarks of the Glasgow Makers," *Piping Times*, Vol. 52, No. 8, May 2000, pp. 11, 51.

Walsh, Dr. E. Geoffrey. "Scientific Tests Prove Pipers

Surpass All others in Fingering," *Piping Times*, Vol. 55, No. 4, January 2003, pp. 21, 23, 25, 27, 29.

[3] Cannon, Roderick. *The Highland Bagpipe and Its Music*, Edinburgh, 1997 – pp. 10-18. (2nd Edition, 2002)

For additional information on piobaireachd and canntaireachd see:

Buisman, F. "From Chant to Script. Some Evidences of Chronology in Colin Campbell's Adaptation of Canntaireachd," *Piping Times*, Vol. 39, No. 7, April 1987.

Buisman, F. "Canntaireachd and Colin Campbell's Verbal Notation – An Outline, Part 1," *Piping Times*, Vol. 50, No. 3, December 1997, pp. 24-27, 29-30.

Buisman, F. "Canntaireachd and Colin Campbell's Verbal Notation – An Outline, Part 2," *Piping Times*, Vol. 50, No. 4, January 1998, pp. 28-33.

Cannon, Roderick(editor). *Complete Theory of the Scots Highland Bagpipe, c 1760*, as written by Joseph MacDonald, The Piobaireachd Society, Glasgow, 1994.

Cannon. Roderick. "The Campbell Canntaireachd Notation" in *General Preface to the Piobaireachd Society Collection*, The Piobaireachd Society, April 1997.

Kenneth, A. G. "The Campbell Canntaireachd," *Piping Times*, 17, No. 8, 1965.

MacNeil, Seumas and Frank Richardson. *Piobaireachd and Its Interpretation*, Edinburgh, 1996.

Excellent review of the bagpipe's classical music style.

McKay, Ian. *The Art of Piobaireachd*, Comunn Na Piobaireachd, New Zealand, 1997.

Smith, M.F. "Has Piobaireachd Changed? Clues from the Wider World, Part 1," *Piping Times*, Vol. 51, No. 5, February 1999, pp. 17-23, 25.

Smith, M.F. "Has Piobaireachd Changed? Clues from the Wider World, Part 2," *Piping Times*, Vol. 51, No. 6, March 1999, pp. 29, 31-35.

[4] MacNeil, Seumas and Frank Richardson. *Op. Cit.*, p. 25.

[5] Campbell, Jeannie. Is Perthshire the Real Home of the MacCrimmons?, Piping Times, Vol. 53, No. 7, April 2001, pp. 5-7.

For additional information on the MacCrimmons see:

"A MacCrimmon Relic," *Piping Times*, Vol. 46, No. 11, August 1994, pp. 36-41, 43.

Campbell, Jeannie. "More on the Early MacCrimmons," *Piping Times*, Vol. 54, No. 1, October 2001, pp. 35, 57.

Campbell, Jeannie. "MacCrimmon, Son for the Fox," *Piping Times*, Vol. 54, no. 4, January 2002, pp. 13.

Cheape, Hugh. "The Origins of the MacCrimmons," *Proceedings of the Piobaireachd Society Conference*, Vol. XXVI, 1999.

[6] Wallace, Robert. "A Fine Tradition of Royal Support for the Noble Instrument," *Piping Times*, Vol. 53, No. 7, April, 2001, pp. 5, 7, and 9.

For additional information on the Sovereign's Piper see:

McKay, Neville T. "Playing Waist Deep in a River – All Part of Royal Duty for Pipers," *Piping Times*, Vol. 53, No. 8, May 2001, pp. 24-25, 27.

McKay, Neville T. "Bonfires, State Banquets, A Flying Ham and a Thirsty Cameron," *Piping Times*, Vol. 53, No. 9, June 2001, pp. 25-28.

Wallace, Robert. "A Fine Tradition of Royal Support for the Noble Instrument," *Piping Times*, Vol. 53, No. 6, March 2001, pp. 5, 7.

Wallace, Robert. "Sovereign's Piper on the Army Payroll and a tune called 'Mallorca'," *Piping Times*, Vol. 53, No. 10, July 2001, pp. 29-31.

[7] *IBID*, p. 49.

[8] Keeling, Brian and John MacLellan. "Notes on the Pipes, Drums and Military Bands to 1973," Scottish Military Historical Society, 1973, p. 1.

[9] MacNeil, Seumas and Frank Richardson. *Op. Cit.*, p. 49.

[10] MacNeil, Seumas and Frank Richardson. *Op. Cit.*, p. 50.

For additional information about early piping in America see:

Donnelly, Sean. "Bagpipes in Revolutionary America," *Piping Times*, Vol. 50, No. 4, January 1998, pp. 46-47, 49.

For additional information on pipes in the military see:

General Reference:

Baynes, John. *Soldiers of Scotland*, New York, 1988, pp. 96-106.

Black Watch Regimental Trustees. *The Black Watch: The Black Watch Photographic Archive*, Gloucestershire, 2000.

Brander, Michael. *The Scottish Highlanders and Their Regiments*, New York, 1971, pp. 84-94.

Gray, Pipe Major Michael. "Army Piping and Drumming in the 21st Century," *Piping Times*, Vol. 53, No. 11, August 2001, pp. 27-29.

Henderson, Diana M. *The Scottish Regiments* (Second Edition), Glasgow, 1996.

Malcolm, C. A. *The Piper in Peace and War*, London, 1993.

Manson, W. L. *Tunes of Glory*, Glasgow, 1992.

Murray, Lt. Col. D. J. S. "Piping in the Army," *Proceedings of the Piobaireachd Society*, March, 1975, pp. 1-28.

Murray, David. *Music of the Scottish Regiments*, Edinburgh, 2001.

[11] Liner Notes (VIDEO): "When the Pipers Play" by Isla St. Clair, produced by Patrick King and Ian Lynn, Westminster King Productions Ltd., London. 1998.

Bagpipes at the Alamo is also referenced in:

Petite, Mary Deborah. *1836 Facts About the Alamo and the Texas War for Independence.* Da Capo Press, 1999; p. 159:

One of Cockett's favorite ways to cheer the men during the siege was to stage a musical duel between himself and John McGregor. The 'Colonel' had found an old fiddle and challenged Mcgregor to get out his bagpipes and see who could make the most noise. McGregor always won.

[12] Lord, Walter. *A Time to Stand, The Epic of the Alamo,* University of Nebraska Press, Lincoln, 1961, p. 117.

and

Personal communication with Dr. B. Winters, Alamo Historian, Daughters of the Republic of Texas, San Antonio, Texas, November 13, 2001.

[13] Keeling, Brian and John MacLellan. *Op. Cit.,* p. 3.

[14] Henderson, Diana M. *The Scottish Regiments* (Second Edition), Glasgow, 1996 – excellent charts showing history of the Regiments and the conflicts in which they fought.

[15] Murray, David. *Music of the Scottish Regiments,* Edinburgh, 2001, p. 118.

See also:

"Queen Victoria's Legacy to Piping and Pipe Bands," *Piping Times,* Vol. 53, No. 7, April 2001, pp. 11-17.

[16] Crew lists in: Beaglehole, J. C.(Editor). The Journals of Captain James Cook; Vol. 1, p. 598; Vol. 2, p. 883 & 892; Vol. 3, p. 1470 and 1477; The Hakluyt Society, the Boydell Press, London (reprint 1999).

[17] For Information on the role of Army Pipers, See:

World War I:

1916, "Willie Ross and Pipers at the Somme," *Piping Times*, Vol. 45, No. 7, April 1993, pp. 35, 37-38.

Bryson, Willie. "Leading From the Front – A Veteran Piper of the Highland Light Infantry," *Piping Times*, Vol. 54, No. 2, November 2001, pp. 29-32.

Murrray, David. "'A Second Flodden' – Gallipoli from April to December 1915," *Piping Times*, Vol. 55, No. 8, May 2003, pp. 27, 29-31.

Video Presentations:
Instrument of War: Westminster King Productions, Ltd., HJN Communications, 1997.
> Part 1 – *Ladies From Hell* (52 minutes)
> Part 2 – *Call to the Blood* (52 minutes)

When the Pipers Play, Westminster King Productions, Ltd., REL Records, Inc., 1999 (57 minutes)

World War II:

"Aldershot 1939 and a Famous Regimental Pipe Band Prepares for War," *Piping Times*, Vol. 54, No. 9, June 2002, pp. 30-31, 33.

Murray, David. "Piobaireachd in the Jungle and a Real Piping Hero Passes On" (Jock Laidlaw), *Piping Times*, Vol. 54, No. 5, February 2002, pp. 23-25, 27, 58.

Murray, David. "How Archie MacDonald, South Uist, Had the Last Laugh," *Piping Times*, Vol. 54, No. 12, September 2002, pp. 11, 13, 15.

Murray, David. "The 51st Division at Alamein – Doing their bit for Tartan Tam," *Piping Times*, Vol. 55, No. 3, December 2002, pp. 33, 35, 37, 39, 41.

Murray, David. "The Battle of Loos: Giving their All for King and Country," *Piping Times*, Vol. 55, No. 12, September 2003, pp. 27, 29-31, 33.

Murray, David. "The Noble Instrument," *Scottish Life*, Autumn, 2003, pp. 12-13, 69 (story of action in Asia).

[18] Murray, David. "Pipes and Drums to the Fore From D-Day Until the End of WW2," *Piping Times*, Vol. 56, No. 9, June 2004, pp. 11, 13-15, 17.

See also:

Piper Bill Millin described his WW2 Normandy landing in his book: *Invasion*, The Book Guild, Ltd., UK, 1991.

[19] Quote attributed to Winston Churchill by Aggie Wallace in an interview appearing in the *Honolulu Advertiser*, "A Pipe Dream Come True," August 5, 1976, p. B-1.

For additional information in the bagpipe's general history see:

Campbell, Jeannie. *Highland Bagpipe Makers*, Magnus Orr Publishing, 2001.

Donaldson, William. *The Highland Pipe and Scottish Society, 1750-1950*, Scotland, 2000.

Donnelly, Sean. "Bagpipes in Masques at the English Royal Court 1551-1557," *Piping Times*, Vol. 49, No. 11, August 1997, pp. 26-28, 30.

Fox, Edward. "The Skirl of My Dreams," *Sky*, January, 1997, pp. 106, 108-109.

Livingston, Craig. "Instrument of Inspiration," *The Police Piper*, Nov/Dec. 1993, pp. 10-12.

Mackenzie, Bridget. *Piping Traditions of the North of Scotland*, Edinburgh, 1988.

Stephens, David. "History at the Margins – Bagpipes in Medieval Manuscripts," *History Today*, August, 1989, pp. 42-28.

Video Presentation:

Scotland The Brave, Adler Media, Inc., 1995 (50 minutes)

Chapter 2. First Encounters

[1] Ledyard, John. *A Journal of Captain Cook's Last Voyage*, Hartford, 1783 (reprint: Chicago, 1963), p. 114.

[2] *IBID*, p. 114.

[3] *IBID*, p. 114.

[4] Cook requested at least three pipers be assigned to his party on two occasions:

> Admiralty Secretary to Colonel Bell, Plymouth. "To order a recruit who plays bagpipes to hold himself in readiness to embark on one of the ships fitting out for making discoveries" (Adm 2/1166), January 25, 1772.

> Admiralty Secretary to Cook. "To apply to Captain Collier, Nore, for and embark two marines with bagpipes on board *Resolution* and *Adventure* and to discharge to headquarters at Chatham two marines to make room for them" (Adm 2/1166; CLB), May 9, 1772.

These dispatches are archived in the National Maritime Museum (Greenwich, London) and noted in:

Beaglehole, J.C. (ed). The Journals of Captain James Cook on His Voyages of Discovery, Vol. II – the Voyage of the *Resolution* and the *Adventure*, 1772-1775, Hakluyt Society, Extra Series No. XXXV, Cambridge University Press, 1961 (Appendix VIII, p. 912 and p. 928).

The names of Archibald McVicar and Thomas McDonald are noted in these Admiralty dispatches as being Marine pipers sent to join Cook's party. It appears that only McVicar made it for his name appears in Cook's ships' muster books (on the Resolution) leaving the whereabouts of McDonald a bit of a mystery.

The following is the account of Cook's drummers in the liner notes for a CD entitled "Sound the Alert – A Day in the Life of a Royal Marines Bugler," *Blue Band Magazine*, United Kingdom, 1992:

One of the most interesting and well documented historical stories is that of the Drummers who accompanied Captain Cook. Drummers were included on all three voyages made by Captain Cook to Australia and New Zealand. Cook first sailed in the HMS *Endeavour*, in 1768. In the ship's papers it is noted that on the 2nd of December 1769:

Rossiter, Thomas, Drummer. Punished for stealing rum.

In the ship's papers for 1769 we also find a mention of the Drummers nickname "Sticks." This nickname is still in use today. In the days of the Royal Marine Light Infantry and Royal Marine Artillery the Drummers were known as "Sticky Blue" and "Sticky Red." In the ship's papers for 1771 we find Drummer Rossiter in trouble again:

21 January 1771. Rossiter, Thomas, Drummer; flogged for drunkenness and assault.

Rossiter, the only Drummer in the ship's company of 85 Royal Navy Officers and men, with a detachment of 13 Marines, has the distinction of being the first British musician to set foot on New Zealand.

When planning his second voyage, Cook had much discussion with the Admiralty regarding the type and number of musicians that should accompany him. The Admiralty wanted Cook to take a Drummer who could play a violin plus two Marine bagpipers. Cook disagreed. Eventually a compromise was reached and two Drummers and one bagpiper joined Cook's two ships, *Resolution* and *Adventure*. The Drummers were Philip Brotherson and John Lane, and the piper was Archibald McVicar. Apparently when the ships reached New Zealand the Maoris were impressed with the playing of the side-drum but showed little interest in

either the bagpipes or the fifes.
For his third voyage Cook took French Horns, fifes and drums. Once again only the side-drum was held in esteem by the Maoris. At Petropavlosk, Marine Drummer Hooloway fell in love with a Kamchapal woman and tried to desert. This was Cook's last voyage because he was killed in Hawaii and buried at sea. When the ship returned to port, Drummer Michael Portsmouth had accumulated in wages, or bounty, the sum of 30 pounds/3/0. This compared with Corporal John Jackson who had 24 pounds/3/7 and Private John Perkins who had 16 pounds/14/5. The highlights of one of the problems that they faced upon the return home was a long trip. With these amounts of money on their person they were ideal targets for thieves.

For an additional discussion of Cook's music makers on his second voyage see:

Agnew, Vanessa. "A Scots Orpheus in the South Seas," *Journal of Maritime Research*, National Maritime Museum, Greenwich, London, May 2001.

[5] Beaglehole identifies one piper as Archibald McVicar (See reference noted above, Appendix VII, p. 884).

[6] Forster, George. *A Voyage Around the World*, volume 1, University of Hawai`i Press, Honolulu, 2000.

[7] Sparrman, Anders. *A Voyage Round the World with Captain James Cook in the H.M.S. Resolution*, Robert Hale, Ltd., London, 1953.

[8] Cook's entries in regards to bagpipes are noted in his journal:

Cook, Captain James. *A Voyage Towards the South Pole and Round the World Performed in His Majesty's Ships the Resolution and Adventure,* 1772-1775, London, 1777, (pp. 118, 208, and 246).

[9] The deed for the property on which the Captain Cook monument is located is dated January 6, 1877. 'A.S. Cleghorn and wife' (Miriam Likelike) conveyed the property to Major James Hay Wodehouse, British Commissioner, representing the Captain Cook Memorial Trust. The transaction is noted in Record 50, page 26 in the Bureau of Conveyances, State Department of Land and Natural Resources. For more information see:

Marshall, James S. and Carrie Marshall. *Adventure in Two Hemispheres, including Captain Vancouver's Voyage,* Talex Printing Service, Vancouver, Canada, 1955, page 201 (Appendices).

[10] Duncan, James K. "Kanaka World Travelers and Fur Company Employees 1785-1860," *Hawaiian Journal of History,* 7, 1973 - p.93.

[11] Judd, Bernice. *Voyages to Hawaii Before 1860,* Hawaiian Mission Childrens' Society, Honolulu, 1974 - pp. 1-9.

[12] Duncan, James. *Op. Cit.,* pp. 93-94.

[13] For additional information on Hawaiians Abroad see:

Dillon, Richard H. "Kanaka Colonies in California," *Pacific Historical Review,* vol. 24, 1955, pp. 17-23.

Duncan, Janice K. *Minority Without a Champion: Kanakas on the Pacific Coast, 1788-1850,* Oregon Historical Society, Portland, 1972.

Duncan, Janice K. "Minority Without a Champion: The Kanaka Contribution to the Western United States, 1750-1900," Master's thesis, Portland State University, 1972.

Illerbrum, William. "Kanaka Pete," *Hawaiian Journal of History*, 6, 1972, pp. 156-166.

Kittelson, David. "Hawaiians and Fur Traders," *Hawaiian Historical Review*, 1, January, 1963, pp. 16-20.

Kittelson, David. "John Coxe: Hawaii's First Soldier of Fortune," *Hawaiian Historical Review*, 1, January, 1965, pp. 194-198.

Koppel, Tom. *Kanaka – The Untold Story of Hawaiian Pioneers in British Columbia and the Pacific Northwest*, Vancouver/Toronto, 1995.

Lane, M. Melia. "Migration of Hawaiians to Coastal B.C.,1810-1869," Master's thesis, University of Hawai`i, Honolulu, 1985.

The Friend, February 20, 1863, "Hawaiians in California."

The Friend, August 25, 1868, "Hawaiian Settlements in California."

[14] Duncan, James. *Op. Cit.*, p. 98.

[15] George's service in the U.S. Navy is discussed by all the following authors. His account of serving on the *U.S.S Enterprise* and *U.S.S. Guerriere* during the times he had indicated has been called into question. It is clear that he was on both ships but perhaps at different times. He may have also served on the *U.S.S. Wasp*. For more information see:

Damon, Ethel (editor). "George Prince Kaumualii," *Hawaiian Historical Society, 55th Annual Report for the Year 1946*, Honolulu, February, 1948, pp. 7-12.

Spoehr, Anne H. "George Prince Tamoree: Heir Apparent of Kauai and Niihau, *Hawaiian Journal of History*, Honolulu, 1981, pp. 31-49.

Warne, Douglas. "George Prince Kaumuali`i, the Forgotten Prince," *Hawaiian Journal of History*, vol. 36, Honolulu, 2002, pp. 59-72.

[16] Kanahele, George (editor). *Hawaiian Music and Musicians*, Honolulu, 1979, pp. 27-28.

[17] Koppel, Tom., *Op. Cit.*, pp. 15-16 and 26-28.

[18] Taylor, Clarice B. "Tales of Hawaii – Kualelo of Molokai Sees England in 1789," *Honolulu Star-Bulletin*, March 23-April 4, 1953, pp. 26-29.

[19] Towse, Ed. "Some Hawaiians Abroad," *Hawaiian Historical Society, Paper 11*, Honolulu, 1904, pp. 12-13.

[20] IBID

[21] "Native Hawaiians in London, 1820," *Hawaiian Historical Society, 55th Annual Report for 1946*, Honolulu, February, 1948, pp. 13-17.

[22] Kuykendall, R.S. *The Hawaiian Kingdom 1778-1854*, vol. 1, Honolulu, 1980, p. 77: cited from letter to Directors, London Missionary Society from Ellis dated Nov. 22, 1833 and cited in London newspaper, 1824.

[23] Judd, Laura Fish. *Honolulu, Sketches of the Life (Social, Political, and Religious) in the Hawaiian Islands from 1828 to 1861*, Honolulu, 1928, pp. 150-162. Text provides letters from Judd describing her meetings with British government officials and royalty.

[24] See: Kanahele, George S. *Emma – Hawai`i's Remarkable Queen*, The Queen Emma Foundation, Honolulu, 1999.

[25] See: Krout, Mary. *The Memoirs of Hon. Bernice Pauahi Bishop*, Honolulu, 1908 (reprinted 1958), pp. 139-197. Text provides copies of the Princess' letters while on her extended trip.

[26] See: Appendix 1 for newspaper accounts of Kalakaua's visit to Scotland. His adventures in England can be found in *Pacific Commercial Advertiser*,

[27] The trip of Queen Kapiolani, Princess Lili`uokalani, and others to Queen Victoria's Jubilee is documented in *Pacific Commercial Advertiser*

[28] Many of the letters which Princess Ka`iulani wrote while she was in England to her auntie, Queen Lili`uokalani, are in the Lili`uokalani Collection and Cleghorn Collection at the Hawai`i State Archives.

See also:

Linnea, Sharon. *Princess Ka`iulani – Hope of a Nation, Heart of a People*, Cambridge, 1999.

Stassen-McLaughlin, Marilyn. "Unlucky Star – Princess Ka`iulani," *The Hawaiian Journal of History*, vol. 33, 1999, pp. 21-64.

Zambucka, Kristin. *Princess Kaiulani: The Last Hope of Hawai`i's Monarchy*, Honolulu, 1982.

[29] Bloxam, Andrew. *Diary*, Bishop Museum Special Publication 10, Honolulu, 1925, pp. 36-37.

Dampier, Robert. *To the Sandwich Islands on H.M.S. Blonde*, edited by Pauline King Joerger, Honolulu, 1971, pp. 38-42.

For additional information on Liholiho and Kamamalu's trip to England see:

Pleadwell, Frank. "The Voyage to England of King Liholiho and Queen Kamamalu," an essay read at a meeting of the Social Science Association, 71st Session, Honolulu, June 2, 1952.

Davis, Theo. H. "The Last Hours of Liholiho and Kamamalu," a letter sent to H.R.H. Princess Lili`uokalani and presented to the Hawaiian Historical Society, *Hawaiian Historical Society 4th Annual Report*, Honolulu, 1896, p. 30-32.

[30] "Kalakaua's Tour 'Round the World – A Sketch of incidents of Travel," Pacific Commercial Advertiser, October 1881, pp. 75-76.

See also:

Dye, Bob, "Kalakaua Also Paid a Visit to Scotland," *Honolulu Star-Bulletin-Advertiser*, December 8, 1991, p. G-1.

[31] *Pacific Commercial Advertiser*, November 5, 1881, p. 2.

[32] The story of Kalakaua's "Hawaiians Abroad" is detailed by Agnes Quigg in "Kalakaua's Hawaiian Studies Abroad Program," *The Hawaiian Journal of History*, Volume 22, 1988, pp. 170-208.

For the three young Hawaiians sent to Scotland, their story begins with the following memorandum sent to the Minister of Foreign Affairs W.E. Green by the King:

> *King to the Minister of Foreign Affairs W.E. Green*
>
> *Your Excellency.*
>
> *I have three young men 2 from Punahou and one from Mr. Mackintoshes School that I would like to send to Scotland by the steamer after next. It would require therefore a certain amount of the appropriation devoted for sending young men to be educated abroad to be drawn out of the treasury before the close of the biennial period. I would like to see your Excellency upon this matter this afternoon at 1 pm or when I return from Waikiki*
>
> *Kalakaua*

This memorandum is found in the Hawai`i State Archives, Honolulu, Hawai`i in the "Foreign Office File – Hawaiians Abroad."

[33] Correspondence and Materials relating to the "Hawaiians Abroad" are in the Hawai`i State Archives in Foreign Officials Abroad (FOA) File and Hawaiian Youths Abroad (HYA) File found in "Records of the Foreign Office and Executive," Hawai`i State Archives, Government Records Inventory, vol. 10. The materials relating to the Hawaiians in Scotland are in the folders labeled "FO and EX - 63, 64, and 65 (referencing Great Britain)."

[34] The files noted above contain reports from the guardian of the three Hawaiians, inventories of expenditures, and few personal notes. There is a letter from John Lovell (1886 File) and a physician's report on Hugo Kawelo (1885 File). Both Lovell and Kawelo suffered respiratory ailments because of the horribly polluted air of 19th century Glasgow.

[35] *Pacific Commercial Advertiser*, "Companion of a Prince, A Hawaiian Chief Who Fought in Africa." January 22, 1902, p. 1.

[36] *Pacific Commercial Advertiser*, "King Decorates Son of Hawaii." April 16, 1919, p. 4.

[37] Judd, Bernice. *Op. Cit.*

[38] List of Scottish Immigrants to Hawai`i compiled by The Caledonian Society, Honolulu.

See also:

Honolulu Star-Bulletin, "Famous Scotsmen in Hawaii," January 25, 1958, p. 6.

[39] *The Polynesian*, November 1, 1845, p.103.

[40] Log Book of *H.M.S. America* on file in the Public Records Office, Kew, Richmond, Surrey, England (ADM 53/1946).

[41] *Ka Elele Hawaii*, October 21, 1845, p. 126.

[42] Reynolds, Capt. Stephen. *Journal – July 1845 - August 1849* (entry for Wednesday, October 29, 1845), typed manuscript in the Hawaiian Historical Society Library, Honolulu.

[43] Gillman, Gorham. *Honolulu as it is – Notes for Amplification*, located in the Hawaiian Historical Society Library manuscript edited by Richard A Greer and Jean S. Sharpless, June 18, 1970, pp. 39-40 (200-201); and published in *The Hawaiian Journal of History*, Volume 4, 1970 – the Palace function for the Duke appears on page 120.

[44] Krout, Mary. *The Memoirs of Hon. Bernice Pauahi Bishop*, Honolulu, 1908, p. 88. (Reprinted Honolulu, 1958).

[45] Cooke, Amos Starr. *Journal*, No. 7, located in the Hawaiian Mission Children's Society Library, pp. 347-348.

The children of the school are noted in:

Richards, Mary Atherton. *The Chiefs' Children's School*, Honolulu, 1937, p. 241 also see frontice.

At the time of the invitation to Cooke in 1845, Robert Crichton Wyllie (1798-1865) was serving as Kamehameha III's Minister of Foreign Affairs. He was born in Hazelbank, Scotland and, after cruising the world, had arrived in Honolulu in 1844. Gerrit Parmele Judd (1803-1873) was serving as Kamehameha III's Secretary of State for Foreign Affairs at the time of the *America*'s arrival. He was born in Paris, New York and had arrived with the 3rd Company of missionaries but had left the service of the church to join Kamehameha in 1842. The children who were possibly in attendance at the Palace that night included:

> Moses Kekuaiwa, son of Kekuanaoa and Kinau, born 7/20/1829, adopted by Kaikioewa, and presumptive Governor of Kaua`i.
> Lot Kamehameha, brother of Moses, born 12/11/1830, adopted by Hoapili and presumptive Governor of Maui.

> Alexander Liholiho, brother of Moses and Lot, born 2/9/1834, adopted by the King(Kamehameha III), and his heir apparent.
> Victoria Kamamalu, sister of Moses, Lot, and Alexander, born 11/1/1838, successor of her mother as Premier.
> William Charles Lunalilo, son of Kanaina and Kekauluohi (acting Premier), born 1/31/1835.
> Bernice Pauahi, daughter of Paki and Konia, born 12/19/1831, adopted by Kinau.
> Abigail Maheha, daughter of Namaile and Liliha, born 7/10/1832, adopted by Kekauonohi.
> Jane Loeau, half-sister of Abigail, born 12/5/1828, adopted by Kaukauali`i.
> Elizabeth Kekauiau, daughter of La`anui and Oana Ana (daughter of John Rives), born 9/11/1834.
> Emma Rooke, daughter of Naea and Kekela (Fanny– daughter of John Young), born 1/2/1836.
> Peter Young Kaeo, son of Kaeo and Lahilahi (Jenny– daughter of John Young), born 3/4/1836.
> James Kaliokalani, son of Pa`akea and Keohokalole, born 5/29/1835, adopted by his grandfather, Aikanaka.
> David Kalakaua, brother of James, born 11/16/1836, adopted by Ha`aheo(Konia).
> Lydia Kamakaeha (Lili`uokalani), sister of James and David, born 9/2/1838, adopted by Paki and Konia.
> Polly Pa`a`aina, daughter of Henry Lewis and Kekela, born 1833, adopted by John I`i.
> John Pitt Kinau

[46] *Pacific Commercial Advertiser*, July 31, 1869, p. 3.

[47] *Hawaiian Gazette*, August 4, 1869.

[48] Cleghorn, Archibald. Diary – entry for Wednesday, July 28, 1869. Located in the Hawai`i State Archives (Microfilm -MFL 46, Reel 1).

In typically brief fashion, Cleghorn's entry doesn't begin to capture the rest of the story. The Duke's visit also gave rise to the sad unfulfilled love between Nancy Wahinekapu Sumner and a member of the Duke's party, Lord Charles Beresford documented by family member John Kaha`i Topolinski in "Nancy Sumner, Hawaiian Courtlady" *The Hawaiian Journal of History*, Volume 15, 1981, pp. 50-58; and the fact that Queen Victoria had written Queen Emma in April 1869 of her son's impending visit to Honolulu and that Queen Emma had begun to remodel her home 'Hanaiakamalama' by adding a room in anticipation of the Duke's arrival. Unforutnately, the room was not completed in time for his use but was named in his honor as the "Edinburgh" room once completed a few weeks after his departure. (see: Rhoda E.A. Hackler. "My Dear Friend": Letters of Queen Victoria and Queen Emma," *The Hawaiian Journal of History*, Volume 22, 1988, p. 120).

[49] *Punch Bowl*, August, 1869, p. 9.

[50] "J. F. Farquharson," *Piping Times*, vol. 50, No. 11, August, 1998, pp. 52-55.

[51] The diary is in a scrapbook compiled by J. F. Farquharson which continues to be in his family. Carol Knight and her sister Beverly Biddlecombe of Banham, Norwich, Norfolk, England own the scrapbook. Through their good will and that of Michael Knight, Carol's husband, this material was made available to the author.

In his diary, J. F. Farquharson described his time in Hawai`i:

Hilo Bay. Sandwich Islands 21ˢᵗ July 1869
In the afternoon the Duke came aboard at 6 pm and the governor of the town came on board and said goodby.

We got up anchor immediately after they left the ship and steamed out about 6:30 pm. I enjoyed myself so much and got lots of curios. We was out of sight of the island at 10 pm.

Hilo Bay To Honolulu Sandwich Islands 22nd July 1869

We steamed all night and sighted an island next morning at daylight we passed it and sighted Honolulu at 10 am. There were some small Bonny mountains on our way up between these two islands. We sighted the town and was anchored at 5 pm. The English Consul came aboard and arranged for a landing tomorrow.

Thursday, 23 July

We landed at 10 am and the sea forgottten and went all to a small house that had been arranged for us. There were no servants that knew anything we had to manage for ourselves. And get cooking things ready as the Duke wanted lunch. We was busy till very late.

24th Friday

We was all very busy. I went for a walk and returned when dark. It was a very dusty day.

25th Saturday

I did not go out. it was very hot and we had a dinner in the evening. I could not sleep all night for fleas.

26th Sunday

We was very quiet all day. The Duke went on board and I went out for a walk after dinner. Very hot day.

27th Monday

This was a great day with the natives and the King gave a dinner in the evening and I had to go and wait on him and play afterwards. There were some old Scotishmen there.

28th Tuesday

Very hot day. There was a Ball at the Palace given by the King. I played several times. I got home at 2 am – and very tired.

29th Wednesday
> We left the shore at 10 am in the steam launch and the Duke and the English Consul came in the boat along with guardsmen, the footman, and myself – got on board at 11 and got dressed and the King and Queen came on board at 2 and left at 4 and was saluted. They were accompanied by a lot of natives. We came on shore again 5 o'clock and had dinner.

30th Thursday
> We gave a dinner ourselves to the King and Queen....15 sat down. It went off very well and I played after dinner – very hot day.

31st Friday
> Very hot day. I went out riding along with some men had a splendid horse...Smith and I rode to the tops of the mountains but the others would not go. I never saw such a sight...It was splendid. We went and saw a native feast and returned again in the evening.

1st August – Sunday (somehow J.F. loses a day)
> A very hot day – the Duke did not go on board and we are all anxious looking for the English mail. She arrived at 5 o'clock in the afternoon and brought no English letters. She came from San Francisco, America.

2nd Monday
> We left Honolulu and came aboard at 11 am. We got up steam and left the harbor by six o'clock.....Lots of people to see us leave.

Some of the Hawaiian language newspapers of that time also carried accounts of the Duke's visit – see:

> *Ke Au Okoa*, Iulai 29, 1869.
> *Ke Au Okoa*, Augate 5, 1869.
> *Ka Nupepa Kuokoa*, Iulai 24, 1869.

[52] J. F. Farquharson Diary (noted above).

[53] *Hawaiian Gazette*, Wednesday, October 5, 1870, p. 2.

[54] Notice appearing in the *Pacific Commercial Advertiser*, Saturday, September 24, 1870, and in the *Hawaiian Times*, Tuesday, September 27, 1870, p. 2.

[55] The Passenger Index File in the Hawai`i State Archives identifies Mr. and Mrs. Alfred H. Havell as being English and arriving in Honolulu on March 14, 1870, from Sydney, Australia. They left Honolulu on November 19, 1870, bound for San Francisco. Notices about Mr. Havell and his music business and performances appear in the *Pacific Commercial Advertiser* – see:

> July 2, 1870, p. 3 – Business notice
> July 30, 1870, p. 2 – Correspondence File; from Havell to the members of the Hawaiian Lodge, No. 21, F & A.M.
> August 20, 1870, p. 2 – Performance notice
> October 8, 1870, p. 2 – Performance notice

[56] *Pacific Commercial Advertiser*, Sat., August 20, 1870, p. 3.

[57] Notice appearing in the *Hawaiian Gazette*, October 5, 1870, p. 2.

[58] *Pacific Commercial Advertiser*, "Notes of the Week," June 18, 1870, p. 3.

Pacific Commercial Advertiser, "Notes of the Week," June 25, 1870, p. 2.

Hawaiian Gazette, June 22, 1870, p. 2.

Hawaiian Gazette, June 29, 1870, p. 3.

[59] *Pacific Commercial Advertiser*, "Notes of the Week," June 25, 1870, p. 2.

[60] *Honolulu Advertiser*, "History From Our Files," Friday, October 4, 1940.

[61] *Honolulu Star-Bulletin*, "Waimea Lauds Cook Memory in Ceremonies," August 16, 1928, p. 1.

The official publication of the Royal Marines, the *Globe and Laurels* for Dec. 1928 states:

On Thursday, August 20th we arrived off the island of Kauai. A seaman guard was landed under the command of Lieut.-Comdr W.S. Green, R.N., to commemorate the discovery of Kauai by Captain Cook. we left in the evening for the Island of Kaawaloa (Kealakekua, Kona) arriving on Friday in time to assist in further celebrations (page 299).

The author "A.J.W." is almost certainly from the H.M.S. *Cornwall* but unfortunately makes no mention of the bagpiper.

[62] *Honolulu Advertiser*, "Kauai Honors Captain Cook," August 17, 1928, p. 1.

This account is also found in:

Taylor, Albert P. (Librarian, Archives of Hawai`i). Captain Cook *Sesquicentennial – Hawaii – 1928*, Captain Cook Sesquicentennial Commission and the Archives of Hawaii, Honolulu, 1929, p. 19.

[63] *The Garden Island*, "Simplicity Marks Local Celebration for Capt. Cook," August 21, 1928, p. 8.

[64] *Honolulu Star-Bulletin*, "Swords Rattle in Scabbards As Cook Sesqui Play is Rehearsed," July 7, 1928, p. 2.

[65] *Honolulu Advertiser*, "Hawaii is Dramatized in Play of Capt. Cook Produced at Hamohamo," August 21, 1928, pp. 1-2.

[66] Most of Stevenson's Hawai`i writings have been published. *See:*
Stevenson, Robert Louis (edited by A. Grove Day. *Travels in Hawaii*, University of Hawai`i Press, Honolulu, 1973.

[67] Sir Harry Lauder's brief visits to Hawai`i were described in Hawai`i's major newspapers of the day:

> *Pacific Commercial Advertiser*, "Lauder Sings Honolulu Song," October 10, 1914, p. 9.
> *Pacific Commercial Advertiser*, "Harry Lauder will Sing in Honolulu for Red Cross Fund," April 2, 1918, 2nd Section, p. 1.
> *Honolulu Star-Bulletin*, "Sir Henry Lauder to be Welcomed by City," April 12, 1919, p. 7.
> *Pacific Commercial Advertiser*, "Welcome Staged for Harry Lauder," April 13, 1919, p. 1.
> *Honolulu Star-Bulletin*, "To Harry Lauder" (poem), April 14, 1919, p. 3.
> *Pacific Commercial Advertiser*, "Honolulans Make Today Lauder Day with Much Aloha," April 14, 1919, p. 8.
> *Honolulu Star-Bulletin*, "Man Who Lost Son Grasps Lauder's Hand," April 15, 1919, p. 3.
> *Pacific Commercial Advertiser*, "Honolulu Happier, Lauder Fund Richer," April 15, 1919, p. 1.
> *Pacific Commercial Advertiser*, "Lauder is Told Success of Visit," April 17, 1919, p. 1.
> *Pacific Commercial Advertiser*, "Lauder Arrives this Morning to be Rotary Guest," October 21, 1919, p. 1.

See also section about Sir Harry Lauder in:

Hackler, Rhoda E.A. (Editor). *The Story of Scots in Hawai`i*, The Caledonian Society of Hawai`i, Honolulu, November 2000, pp. 163-165.

[68] For accounts on the Prince's visit see:

Pacific Commercial Advertiser, " Prince of Wales, guest of City for 1 Day Only...,"April 13, 1920, p. 1.

Honolulu Star-Bulletin, April 13, 1920, p.1.

Pacific Commercial Advertiser, "Prince Displays keen Interest in Island's History...," April 14, 1920, p. 1.

Honolulu Star-Bulletin, April 14, 1920, p. 1.
Pacific Commercial Advertiser, "Prince Radios Governor – He is Looking Forward to Second Hawaiian Visit," April 15, 1920, p. 1.

Pacific Commercial Advertiser, August 28, 1920, p. 1.

Honolulu Star-Bulletin, August 28, 1920, p. 1.

Pacific Commercial Advertiser, August 29, 1920, p. 1.

Honolulu Star-Bulletin, August 29, 1920, p. 1.

Pacific Commercial Advertiser, "Battle Cruiser *Renown*'s Officers are Men who have seen Great War Service," August 30, 1920, p. 2.

Honolulu Star-Bulletin, August 30, 1920, p. 2.

Pacific Commercial Advertiser, September 1, 1920.

Pacific Commercial Advertiser, September 2, 1920.

[69] *Pacific Commercial Advertiser*, "Battle Cruiser *Renown's* Officers are Men who have seen Great War Service," August 30, 1920, p. 2.

[70] *Pacific Commercial Advertiser*, "Royal Visitor finds Beach Honolulu's Greatest Asset," April 14, 1920, p. 1.

[71] *Pacific Commercial Advertiser*, " Century of Civilization in Hawaii Depicted...," April 14, 1920, pp. 1-2.

[72] *Pacific Commercial Advertiser*, "Many Descendants of Missionaries Figure in Today's Pageant-Drama," April 13, 1920, p. 2

Chapter 3. Social Acceptance Achieved

[1] *Pacific Commercial Advertiser*, "The Clubs of Honolulu," March 30, 1901, p. 16.

[2] "Club Life in Honolulu," *Hawaiian Journal of History*, Honolulu, 1902.

[3] From "Constitution and Bye-Laws of the Scottish Thistle Club of Honolulu, H.I.," Organized in April 27, 1891 – document is located in the Hawaiian Historical Society Library, Honolulu.

[4] *Pacific Commercial Advertiser*, "Burns' Anniversary – Celebrated in Honolulu in the 18th Century," January 26, 1892, p. 2.

[5] *Evening Bulletin*, "Scots Will Honor Memory," January 23, 1902.

6 *Pacific Commercial Advertiser*, "Scots Pay Highest Tribute to Memory of Robt Burns," January 25, 1902.

7 *Evening Bulletin*, January 25, 1902, p. 8.

8 *Honolulu Star*, January 25, 1902, p. 8.

9 *Pacific Commercial Advertiser*, January 26, 1907, p. 3.

10 *Evening Bulletin*, "Scots Do Honor to the Great Poet," January 26, 1907, p. 5.

11 *Pacific Commercial Advertiser*, "Weird Power of Scottish Pipes," January 25, 1908.

12 *Evening Bulletin*, "Sons of Scotland Honor Robbie Burns," January 27, 1908, p. 3.

13 *Pacific Commercial Advertiser*, January 28, 1917, p. 2.

14 *Pacific Commercial Advertiser*, "Tribute Paid to Scotland's Poet...," January 26, 1921, 2nd Section, p. 1.

15 *Honolulu Advertiser*, January 25, 1928, p. 9.

16 *Honolulu Advertiser*, January 26, 1928, Front Page.

17 *Honolulu Advertiser*, January 26, 1929, p. 5.

18 *Honolulu Advertiser*, "Scots Celebrate Poet's Birthday...," January 25, 1930, p. 4.

[19] *Honolulu Advertiser*, "Scots will Honor Burns at Dinner," January 25, 1934, p. 2.

[20] *Honolulu Advertiser*, "Local Scots Honor Famed Poet...," January 26, 1934, p. 4.

[21] *Mid Pacific Country Club at the Turn-Seventy Five Years of Progress, 1926-2110*. Mid-Pacific Country Club, Kailua, HI, 2001, p. 30.

[22] Donald MacKay obituary – *Honolulu Advertiser*, "Donald MacKay Services Set," November 30, 1965, p. A10:1; and

Donald Rae MacKay obituary – *Honolulu Advertiser*, " D.R. MacKay Dies; Founded VW Here," April 10, 1965, p. A8:7.

[23] Account in interview with Aggie Wallace in the 'Scot in Hawaii' oral history project located in the Hawaiian Historical Society Library, Honolulu – MS 325.1 C12 #22 WALLACE (parts 1 and 2); Interviews conducted 9/28/1976 and 6/13 & 27/1979.

[24] Account in interview with Aggie Wallace in the *Honolulu Advertiser*, "Pipe Dream Come True," August 5, 1976, p. B-1.

[25] Account in interview with Aggie Wallace in the 'Scot in Hawai`i' oral history project located in the Hawaiian Historical Society Library, Honolulu – MS 325.1 C12 #22 WALLACE (parts 1 and 2). Interviews conducted 9/28/1976 and 6/13 & 27/1979.

[26] *Honolulu Advertiser*, "Birthday of Poet Burns is Observed," January 26, 1950, p. 3.

[27] *Honolulu Advertiser*, "Bagpipes, Dancers Honor Bobby Burns" (photo), January 26, 1951, p. 1.

[28] *Honolulu Advertiser*, January 26, 1965, p. 1.

[29] *Honolulu Star-Bulletin*, January 21, 1967, p. 8.

[30] Dorrance, William Henry and Francis Morgan. *Sugar Islands; the 165-Year Story of Sugar in Hawai`i*, Mutual Publishing, Honolulu, 2000, p. 176.

[31] References to Burns Nights are found in the Hilo Tribune as early as 1895 (*Hilo Tribune, January 31, 1895, p.*).

See also:

Account in interview with Margaret Burso in the 'Scots in Hawai`i' oral history project located in the Hawaiian Historical Society Library, Honolulu – MS 325.1 C12 #4 BURSO.

[32] *Hilo Tribune*, "In Honor of Burns," January 31, 1905, p. 1.

[33] *Hilo Tribune*, "Burns Club Entertainment," January 30, 1906, p. 2.

[34] *Evening Bulletin*, "Hilo Scots Program," January 26, 1907, p. 7.

[35] *Maui Times*, "Burns Dinner is Great Success," January 30, 1932, p. 1.

See also:

Maui Times, "Banquet Jan 25 to Honor Burns," January 16, 1932, p. 1.

[36] *Honolulu Star-Bulletin*, "The Irish and Hawaii," March 17, 1962, p. 3.

See also:

Honolulu Star-Bulletin, "Scot and Irish Roots Deep in Hawn Soil," February 19, 1985, p. Historical Section, II- 34.

Honolulu Advertiser, "Ireland – Hawaii have Lots in Common," March 12, 1986.

Conrad, Agnes. "The Irish in Hawai`i," Presented at the Hawaii Heritage Center Annual Meeting on March 30, 1996

A presentation about some of the Irish who found their way to Hawai`i's shores.

Glazier, Michael (editor). *The Encyclopedia of the Irish in America*, University of Notre Dame Press, Indiana, 1999. – See section contributed by Agnes Conrad on "Hawaii," pp. 378-379.

An expanded version of Agnes Conrad's "The Irish in Hawai`i" noted above.

[37] *Pacific Commercial Advertiser*, "Concerning St. Patrick's Day," March 20, 1869.

[38] *Pacific Commercial Advertiser*, "Saint Patrick's Day," March 14, 1868, p. 2.

[39] *Bennett's Own*, " St Patrick's Day," Vol. 1, No. 27, Honolulu, March 22, 1870, p. 4.

[40] *Maui Times*, "St. Patrick's Day Ball," March 28, 1903, p. 3

See also:

Maui Times, "Makawao News Item," March 25, 1911, p. 6.

[41] For accounts of memorable Honolulu St. Patrick's Days see:

Honolulu Advertiser, "Parade Led Off by O'Fasi," March 18, 1971, p. B1.

Honolulu Advertiser, "7 Streakers in St. Patrick's Day Parade," March 18, 1974, p. A5.

Honolulu Star-Bulletin-Advertiser, "Parade Enough to Make Dublin Turn Green with Envy," March 18, 1979, p. A3.

Honolulu Advertiser, "How Al Castro Got to Watch St. Patrick's Day Parade," March 18, 1987, p. A3.

[42] *Honolulu Advertiser*, "St. Patrick's Day Parade in Waikiki," March 17, 1970, p. B-7.

[43] *Honolulu Star-Bulletin-Advertiser*, "The Hawaii Pipe Line to the Emerald Isle," March 16, 1986, p. C1.

[44] *Honolulu Star-Bulletin*, "Highland fling on the Big Island," October 6, 1973, p. A-6.

See also:

Hawaii Tribune Herald, "Hawaii – Scotland Mingle at First Waimea Games," October 7, 1973, p. 13.

Honolulu Star-Bulletin, "A Highland Fling," March 28, 1980, p. B-1.

Honolulu Star-Bulletin, "Joys of Tradition," March 30, 1980, p. A3.

Honolulu Advertiser, "Highland Fling," March 28, 1983, p. A3.

Honolulu Advertiser, "Honolulu Highlanders," March 24, 1986, p. A3.

Honolulu Advertiser, March 27, 1992, p. C2.

Honolulu Star-Bulletin, "Weekend Report – Dressed to Kilt,"

[45] Most of the major pipe bands in the world have web sites. An excellent resource to find pipe band web sites is 'Montie's List of Pipe Band Web Pages' which was established in 1996 by Montie Derby when he was a member of the Celtic Pipes and Drums of Hawai`i. Montie Derby now resides in Nebraska. See: http://incolor.inetnebr.com/bagpipe/thelist.html

Another excellent web site for bagpipe information has been developed by Bob Dunsire and is regarded as the 'biggest and the best in the piping world' by many pipers. See: http://www.bobdunsire.com/cgi-bin/ultimatebb.cgi

[46] See: Lerwick, Pipe Major R.W. *The Pipe Major's Handbook*, Canada, 1980.

[47] Interview conducted by the author with Pipe Major Lawrence Coleman in November 1995.

[48] Account in interview with Aggie Wallace in 'Scots in Hawai`i' oral history project located in the Hawaiian Historical Society Library, Honolulu – MS 325.1 C12 #22 WALLACE (parts 1 and 2).

[49] *IBID*

[50] *IBID*

[51] Hobbs, Betsy. "Scots – Hawaiians Hail the Chief," *Paradise of the Pacific*, Honolulu, December 1956, pp. 32-33/98.

[52] Interview conducted by the author with David Furumoto on February 20, 2000.

[53] *Honolulu Advertiser*, "A Pipe Dream Come True," August 5, 1976, p. B-1.

[54] *IBID*

[55] *Honolulu Advertiser*, "A. J. Frappia of Honolulu Pipes and Drums Practices Bagpiping on his Punchbowl Condo Roof," August 5, 1976, p. B1.

[56] *Honolulu Advertiser*, "Bagpipe Player Agnes Hendrix Dies," July 16, 1981, p. B4.

[57] *Honolulu Star-Bulletin-Advertiser*, "The Hawaii Pipe Line to the Emerald Isle," March 16, 1986, p. C1.

[58] Personal interview with David Furumoto, February 20, 2000.

[59] For articles and photos on the Celtic Pipes and Drums of Hawai`i see:

Honolulu Star-Bulletin, "HPD Pipe Band will Salute Marines in St. Patrick's Day Parade," March 14, 1991, p. B1. "Featured Band," *The Police Piper*, July/August, 1992, p. 7.

"Honolulu Police Pipe Band Pose for History," *The Blue Light*, September/October, 1992.

Honolulu Advertiser, "Piping Up for Scottish Week" (photo), March 28, 1993, p. A4.

Honolulu Star-Bulletin, "Members of the Celtic Pipes and Drums of Hawaii Piping Under the *Rigging of the Falls of Clyde*" (photo), March 30, 1993, p. A3.

Honolulu Star-Bulletin, "Larry Coleman Tunes his Bagpipes at Iolani Palace for St. Andrews Cathedral Concert" (photo), April 2, 1993, p. A4.

Honolulu Advertiser, "Pied Piper," April 6, 1995, p. B1 Celtic Pipes and Drums Newsletter, vol. 1, No. 1, Spring 1995.

Honolulu Advertiser, Sister Roberta's Funeral Notice, April 9, 1996, p. A3.

"The Honolulu Police Pipe Band," *The Blue Light*, August, 1996.

"Celtic Pipes and Drums of Hawaii – Honolulu Police Pipe Band," *The Piping World*, August/September 1996, pp. 28-29.

"25th Hosts First DeRussy Tattoo," *Hawaii Army Weekly*, February 13, 1997.

Honolulu Advertiser, "Haunting Pipes call Hawaiian to Distant, Foreign Tradition," March 17, 1998, p. B3.

Honolulu Advertiser, A. J. Frappia's Funeral Notice, p. B2.

Honolulu Star-Bulletin, "An Exec Trek" (photo), March 9, 1999.

Honolulu Star-Bulletin, "Bagpipe Lovers Gather this Weekend," April 1, 1999, p. B1.

The Korea Times, "St. Patrick's Day Parade Marchers," March 19, 2000, p. Front Page.

[60] *Honolulu Star-Bulletin*, "Isle Man Earns World Renown in Bagpiping," October 28, 2002, p. A3.

[61] *Honolulu Star-Bulletin*, "Proud Pipers," August 4, 2002,

[62] *Maui Time Magazine*, "Maui's Millennium Marchers," August 1, 2000.

[63] Interview with Mrs. Florence Hall MacIntyre in oral history project on the Scots in Hawai`i. Transcription is in the Hawaiian Historical Society Library, Honolulu – MS 325.1 C12 #14 MACINTYRE.

[64] Hedemann, Nancy Oakley. *A Scottish-Hawaiian Story – The Purvis Family in the Sandwich Islands*, Virginia, 1994.

An in-depth story of a Scottish-Hawaiian family.

See also:

McGowan, William. *Bagpipes and Grass Skirts*, University of Hawai`i Press, Honolulu, 1944.

A short account of Scot culture found along the Hamakua Coast of the island of Hawai`i.

[65] Account in interview with Margaret Burso in "Scots in Hawai`i" oral history project located in the Hawaiian Historical Society Library, Honolulu – MS 325.1 C12 #4 BURSO.

[66] Personal correspondence with the author from Roy Forbes (son of Robert Forbes), Hilo, Hawai`i; January 27, 2004.

The photo of Robert Forbes with a group of businessmen wearing 'See Hawaii First' ribbons has an interesting history recounted in an article by Kent Warshauer in the *Hawaii Tribune Herald*, "Hilo Hotel Headstone Mystery Fnally Uncovered," March 14, 2004, p. F1:

> ...This Honolulu practice of discouraging tourist travel to Hilo and the volcano was based on the short-sighted policy that tourists would stay in Honolulu and spend their money there instead of Hilo. On Jan. 11, 1913, Zeno K. Meyers, president of the Honolulu-base Promotions Committee, offered a $50 reward to any Hilo resident who could show that a Honolulu business had knocked Hilo tourism. The Promotions Committee then named a representative Lorrin A. Thurston, to outline a plan to attract tourists to Hilo using advertising, photographs and brochures. Thurston revealed his plan to Hilo residents at a meeeting held Jun. 25, 1913. At a meeting of the Honolulu Ad Club on July 23 1913, it was decided to travel to Hilo and "See Hawaii First." On Aug. 16, 1913, members of the club left Honolulu on the Steamer Mauna Kea bound for Hilo. Members of the Hilo Board of Trade met the Honolulu Ad Club at the Hilo docks and accompanied them on a tour of the Hamakua Coast by railroad, an overnight visit to the Volcano House, and a luncheon given in their honor at the

Hilo Hotel prior to their return to Honolulu that afternoon. At the banquet held at the Hilo Hotel on Aug. 18, 1913, a hammer was ceremoniously buried on the front lawn of the hotel symbolizing the 'Knocker's Hammer.' On Sept 26, 1913, it was announced that a granite headstone had been erected over the buried hammer, donated by the Honolulu Ad Club and presented to the Hilo Board of Trade.

Today the granite headstone is in the Hilo offices of the Hawaii Island Chamber of Commerce. The photo depicting Robert Forbes and the 'See Hawaii First' group must have been taken during the visitation described above.

[67] Account in interview with Robert Bruce in "Scots in Hawai`i" Oral History Project located in the Hawaiian Historical Society Library, Honolulu – MS 325.1 C12 #3 BRUCE.

[68] Personal correspondence with author from Shelley Anne Cost Chaffee (daughter of James Peter Cost), January 11, 2004.

Illustrations
and
Photographs

iii   Bagpipes in Paradise – Pipe Major A. J. Frappia plays for Visitors on Waikiki Beach (1980s), *Honolulu Star-Bulletin* Photo.

vii   Saved by a Bagpipe by Stanley Berkeley. *Chatterbox*, London, 1896, pp. 385-386.

A Highland bagpiper was one evening going from a village to a neighboring town, having only collected a few coppers after playing all day. On his way he asked a boy to show him the nearest way to the town which he wished to reach. The boy told him to go across some fields, which he pointed out to him, and which would bring him to a road leading directly to the town. After the bagpiper had got to the middle of the second field, he noticed a bull coming at full speed towards him. He had heard that some animals liked music, so he took out his bagpipe and began playing. The bull stopped as soon as he heard the music, and seemed much pleased, but at each attempt of the man to escape the bull's anger returned. It became evident that he must either play all night, or be gored by the bull; but, presently, help came in the shape of the farmer with his dog, who drove the bull off, and so rescued the poor bagpiper from his dangerous position (p. 386).

viii   Bagpipes; An Uncommon Instrument – A Young Humanitarian, *Punch, or the London Charivari*, London, January 1, 1887, p. 6.

2   Types of Bagpipes: (top)Great Highland Bagpipe (post card – 1906)/Caucases Bagpipe(postcard-nd)/(bottom)Bagpipe Seller, Charing Cross (postcard-nd).

3   Bagpipe illustration from: *The Highland Bagpipe and its Music*, Edinburgh, 1997, p. 11.

4   A Roman Bagpiper by J. Gilbert. *The Illustrated London News*, London, June 8, 1861, p. 539.

   Of a more substantial and sterling quality than many that we have mentioned...is Gilbert's fine Rembrandtish figure of "A Roman Bagpiper"...All who have seen the original in the streets of the Eternal City will recognize the accuracy of the study, both as to the physiognomy and the expression, the wild flow of the hair, and the picturesque equipment of the figure. The grand chiaroscuro which surrounds it renders the picture doubly impressive. This may be pronounced one of the happiest national studies which Mr. Gilbert's fertile pencil has produced (p. 540).

8   The Queen At Balmoral – Waking Her Majesty – Her Majesty the Queen (Victoria) is awakened every morning by the strains of the Royal bagpipes played beneath her bedroom. The music generally lasts from eight to nine o'clock. *The Graphic*, London, November 11, 1882, p. 515-516.

10 British Military Regiment – Pipers and Pipe Majors – (top) Pipe Major, Royal Scots Fusiliers (Oilette-Raphael Tuck & Sons); Pipe Major, Seaforth Highlanders (Oilette-Raphael Tuck & Sons Postal #9356); (bottom) Piper, The Gordon Highlanders (Oilette-Raphael Tuck & Sons Postal #9884); Piper, The Scots Guards (Oilette-Raphael Tuck & Sons Postal #8625).

11 Pipers and Pipe Majors (cont.) – (top) Cameron Highlanders; (bottom) Piper, Argyll and Sutherland Highlanders (Oilette-Raphael Tuck & Sons Postal #9937); Pipe Major, "Black Watch" (Valentine's "Valesque" series).

12 Pipers and Pipe Majors (cont.) – (top) Pipers, Royal Highlanders, the Black Watch (Valentine's Series); (bottom) Pipers, 2nd Black Watch. South African Kit (E.F.A. "Military" Series); An Athole Highlander (J.R. Russell, Edinburgh).

16	The Drummers: Grenadier Guards – Side Drummer(post card – Tuck#9366)/Seaforth Highlanders–Drum Major(post card – Tuck#8533/Drummer, Seaforth Highlanders(post card – Millar & Lang National Series)/ Drummers, Seaforth Highlanders(post card – Millar & Lang National Series)
17	(top) Royal Household Guards – Capt Sam Nowlein in command at Iolani Palace – 1890s; Hawai`i State Archives P.C. Neg. No. 167 – Military. (bottom) same title, Hawai`i State Archives Neg. No. 16,619.
23	Amateurs with the Highland Bagpipes by Evelyn Hardy. *The Illustrated London News*, London, September 28, 1889, p. 407.

      1. Cockney tourists have donned the kilt; they buy a set of bagpipes.
      2. And bear them off in triumph.
      3. Attempt to play: Chanters and drones get rather mixed.
      4. Directions: Ye'll jist pit a guild blaw intil them, set them under one arm, an' gie them in a wheeze.
      5. Unearthy scream
      6. Sudden collapse.
      7. It knocks him down.
      8. Rescued from suffocation.
      9. "No more of the bagpipes for me!"

24	The Highland Piper (in the General Exhibition of Water-Colour Drawings) by J. Richardson. *The Illustrated London News*, London, April 29, 1865, p. 413.
25	Highland Games at Aboyne, Aberdeenshire. *The Illustrated London News*, London, September 23, 1871, p. 281.

An illustration is given of the Highland sports and exercises of athletic skills which took place, on the 31st ult., on the Green of Aboyne, in Aberdeenshire, under the patronage of the Marquis of Huntly. Prizes were bestowed for the best performances, and the honours of the championship were also to be gained. Among

Lord Huntly's tenantry the prizes for throwing the hammer, for "putting" the stone, for the hurdle race, and for dancing were valiantly contested. The championship of bagpipe music was adjudged to his Lordship's piper, Cameron; the champion at throwing the light hammer was John George, who threw it 99 ft; the best-dressed Highlander in his national costume, was John McHardy; in tossing the caber, John Moir excelled all others, and John Joss in putting the stone; while John Cumming was the champion at dancing Highland reels...(p. 282).

26 The Prince of Wales in the Highlands: A Torchlight Dance at Mar Lodge by 'our special agent.' *The Illustrated London News*, London, October 16, 1880, p. 392.

27 The Court in the Highlands – the Queen and the Prince of Wales Going to the Gillies' Ball, Abergeldie Castle. *The Graphic*, London, October 16, 1880.
Depicted are Her Majesty, the Prince of Wales, the Princess of Wales, and the Duke of Hesse.

28 Sword Dance of Boys of the Royal Caledonian Asylum, at Westbrook Park, Goldalming. *The Illustrated London News*, London, October 8, 1881.

29 The Queen Keeping Halloween at Balmoral. Engraving by S. Stacey, nd.

30 Highland Pipers Practicing in Hyde Park. *The Graphic*, London, June 28, 1890, p. 726.

31 The Coming of Age of Lord Warkworth: The Garden Party at Alnwick Castle by John Charlton. *The Graphic*, May 21, 1892, p. 601.

In our last issue we published portraits of the Duke of Northumberland, Earl Percy, and Lord Warkworth, on the occasion of the coming of age of the Duke's grandson. The festivities continued at Alnwick Castle all last week, and on the first day presentation of addresses, a banquet to 1,246 of the Duke's tenants, and a grand display of fireworks took place. On the second day a garden party was given to the tenantry on the estate and the tradesmen of the town, with their wives and families, and on the Thursday a Country Ball was given, to which some 500 guests were invited. The Duke of Argyll, the Marquess of Lorne, the Bishop of Newcastle, and Lord Armstrong were among the house-party (p. 602).

32 Lord Archibald Campbell and his Pipers Marching through the Pass at Glencoe by Lockhardt Bogle. *The Graphic*, London, September 21, 1895, p. 345.

The Inverary Pipe Band, which consists of ten pipers and three drummers, was instituted about six years ago by Lord Archibald Campbell. For some years the band has accompanied Lord Archibald to Oban to perform at the Gaelic Mod, which is very similar to the Eisteddfod of Wales. This year they arranged an excursion through Glencoe, the famous pass where the Macdonalds were massacred by a band of men under Campbell of Glenlyon in 1692. The proposed march was therefore reported to be much resented by the inhabitants of the name of Macdonald residing in the Glen, and was discussed as a subject of great interest by the papers. It is believed by some that Lord Archibald meant by the march to commemorate the massacre, and, indeed, in every possible way, his motives for the march were misconstrued, whereas it was arranged simply to give the members of the band an outing and an opportunity to admire the magnificent scenery of Glencoe. Before the excursion started on its journey several threatening letters were received by Lord Archibald, which held out the prospect of a second Massacre of Glencoe if he insisted on carrying out the intended march. On Monday, September 9, the members of the Fife Band, with Lord Archibald and his daughter, Miss Elspeth Campbell, started from Inverary at eight in the morning, and reached Achnacloich about noon, where they went on board the steamer Ossian, and sailed up Loch Etive in perfect weather to the stirring strains of the band, which began to play, much to the delight of those assembled on shore to watch and listen.

At Loch Etive Head Pier a coach and carriage awaited the party, when then drove down the sandy roads to Dalness. The proprietress of Dalness is Mrs. Stuart, a descendant of the Macdonalds of Glencoe, and an enthusiastic Highland lady.

The party drove down to her hospitable mansion, where they partook of luncheon, after which the men played on the green in front of the house opposite a field where Highland cattle were grazing, and these no sooner heard the sound of the pipes than they tossed up their shaggy heads and ran excitingly up to the fence to be nearer the players, in whom they seemed to take quite a human interest. The party then resumed their seats in their various carriages and drove on to King's House, where they were joined by other carriages. All along the route, after this, relays of people augmented the procession till it was a difficult matter for the carriages to make their way, especially as evening had now set in and the Glen was shrouded in gloom.

Near Invercoe Bridge the men descended from the coach, and began the march escorted by a large crowd, who, instead of showing the least resentment, were most cordial in their reception of Lord Archibald and greatly enjoyed the splendid inspiriting playing of his men. A halt was made under some trees, and here the Pallachulish and Glencoe choirs, with a number of torch bearers, joined the party and sang some Gaelic songs, after which the procession resumed its march to the green opposite Invercoe House, the residence of Sir Donald Smith, now proprietor of Glencoe. Here they halted and played and sang at intervals, surrounded by a large crowd of people who had come long distances to witness Lord Archibald's march through Glencoe (p. 345).

33 The Queen's Long Reign: A Celebration at Dublin Castle. *The Graphic*, London, March 20, 1897, p. 345.

In celebration of the Diamond Jubilee of the Queen's reign, the Lord-Lieutenant of Ireland, Earl Cadogen, held a state banquet in St. Patrick's Hall, Dublin Castle, last Saturday. Gentlemen selected to represent the thirty-two counties of Ireland were present, and the company numbered upwards to 250. After the banquet a torchlight tattoo was held on an elaborate scale in the Lower Castle Yard, as a special compliment to the Lord-Lieutenant and Countess Cadogen, by the troops of the garrison. The bands of six regiments, as well as those of the Dublin Metropolitan Police and the Royal Irish Constabulary, took part in the tattoo. The march past of the Pipers of the Scots Guards was the most effective part of this imposing spectacle.

34 An Old Highland Custom: Celebrating a Marriage Outside the Brides House by A. G. Small. *The Graphic*, London, 1899.

> Most of the old customs connected with Highland weddings are fast disappearing, but although it is becoming more and more the fashion for couples to be married in church, after the English manner, yet in some of the less frequented parts of Scotland the marriage ceremony is still celebrated in the bride's house as of yore, and there are many old churches in which to this day no marriage has ever taken place. The marriage ceremony is usually conducted in the open air, in front of the bride's home, and is as simple as one would expect from the life and surroundings of the Highland peasant. The minister first prays and reads a portion of the Scriptures, generally seasoned with a piece of good advice delivered in a homely and outspoken manner, and the couple then join hands and answer the questions of the Marriage Service. The ceremony then is complete, the guests flock round to congratulate the lucky pair, and the pipers strike up and march them off to the bridegroom's home.

35 The Gran Hieland Bagpipes, the Pride O' the Land by Arthur Garratt. *The Graphic*, London, Christmas Number, 1917, p. 13.

39 Mounted Pipers for the Highland Regiments – What Might Happen at the First Parade. *The Graphic*, December 28, 1889, p. 773.

> 1. "Quiet! He's as quiet as a thousand lambs."
> 2. But, C'est le premier skirl.
> 3. Qui Coule.
> 4. Nevertheless, he really was quiet...and when he understood it was meant for music,
> 5. Appeared even to enjoy it.

40 Amusements in the Camp of the London Scottish, Wimbleton. The Illustrated London News, London, July 15, 1871, p. 44.

41   A Highland Soldier's Wedding – Chairing the Bridegroom. *Harper's Bazar*, New York, April 8, 1876, p. 237.

A wedding in a Scotch regiment creates no little stir. The bridegroom (who doubt obtains leave of absence for a few days to carry out his purpose) is seized upon by his comrades on his return to barracks, and, despite his struggles and entreaties, hoisted, with little or no ceremony, on a throne improvised by placing a chair upon a barrack-room table top, and thus carried on his comrades' shoulders round the barrack square, escorted by a cheering and derisive and ever-swelling crowd. A piper, or perhaps corps of pipers, headed by a mock drum-major (who would vie in absurdity of costume...), wielding probably a regulation mop and handle by way of baton, leads the way. Every body turns out to greet the procession, the women and children appearing particularly active on these occasions. Finally the victim – or, rather, happy man – is deposited at the door of the canteen, which he is expected to enter, and there to treat his late tormentors, who then are most hearty in their congratulations, and drink, with considerable gusto, health and happiness to the bride and bridegroom. The bride, of course, has no part in the proceedings.

Our drawing represents the wedding of a man in the Princess Louise's Argyleshire Highlanders, at Sterling castle, and is from a sketch by a captain in that regiment (p. 237).

42   The Halloween Dinner of the London Scottish Volunteers – Bringing in the Haggis by Lockhardt Bogle. *The Graphic*, London, October 31, 1891, p. 513.

...Sir Charles R. McGrigor, Bart., treasurer to the institution, the other day kindly entertained all the children at his seat, Westbrook Park, New Godalming, in Surrey. Our illustration of this pleasing subject represents the sword-dance performed in Highland fashion by two of the boys of the Royal Caledonian Asylum School. They have not lost their national agility in the course of an education received in London, though it is denied to these youngsters, for the present, to tread their native heather; but we have no doubt they have been taught to do well, and to

maintain the honour of their country, as so many good Scochmen do, in all parts of the world.

43 The Queen at Aldershot: Military 'Tattoo' and Tourchlight Procession, Wednesday, July 11. *The Illustrated London News*, London, August 4, 1894, p. 129.

44 Queen Victoria Loved the Pipes – The Queen at the Birthday Parade of the 2nd Scots Guards at Windsor: The March Past by W. Small. *The Graphic*, London, May 27, 1899, p. 665.

45 The Zulu War: Embarkation of the 91st Highlanders at Southampton – "Good-Bye." *The Illustrated London News*, London, March 1, 1879, np.

46 En Route to the Zulu War: The Mess Piper of the 91st on Board the *Pretoria*. *The Illustrated London News*, London, May 3, 1879, p. 425.

> *...The last Illustration of the Zulu war to be noticed in this week's publication, is a sketch by our Special Artist on board the* Pretoria, *during the passage of the 91st Highlanders from Capetown to Natal. The mess piper of that regiment was accustomed daily to sound a loud musical summons at the officers' dinner-time; but whether it was the "Roast Beef of Old England," or "Cauld Kail at Aberdeen," we are not precisely informed (p. 426).*

47 The Zulu War: The 91st (Princess Louise's) Highlanders Leaving the *Pretoria* at Durban by Melton Prior. *The Illustrated London News*, April 26, 1879, p. 401.

48 The Zulu War: The 91st Regiment Leaving Camp at Durban for the Front. *The Illustrated London News*, London, May 3, 1879, p. 413.

> *Our Special Artist, Mr. Melton Prior, sent us an Illustration of the 91st (Princess Louise's Highlanders), at Durban on March 19, two days after landing from the steamship* Pretoria, *starting from the camp to join Lord Chelmsford's army on the Tugela, for the advance to the relief of Ekowe. It was between ten and eleven in the morning when they left the camp, with their band*

playing a lively tune, all in the highest spirits, and encouraged with hearty cheers from the blue jackets of the Naval Brigade, who were shortly to follow and join them in their march through Zululand, as well as from the assembled crowd of Durban people. The regimental colours were carried by two of the officers. An address of welcome had been prepared by the Scottish residents of Durban, and was presented to the 91st in the camp there. Major Bruce had the men drawn up in order for the reception of those who came as a deputation from their fellow-countrymen of North Britain. He responded to the address with a brief and soldier-like speech, thanking the Scotchmen of Natal, and expressing a hope that the 91st would do their duty. So in fact they did, in the fight of April 3 at Gingihlovo which we related last week, and by which the safety of Colonel Pearson and the garrison of Ekowe was secured (p. 426).

49   The Evacuation of Zululand: The 21st Royal Scots Fusiliers on the March Homewards. *The Illustrated London News*, London, October 11, 1879, p. 341.

50   Troops for South Africa – The Eve of Departure. *The Illustrated London News*, London, January 15, 1881, p. 57.

...The dispatch of troops from Portsmouth and Woolwich to South Africa has been continued with great activity; three transports left the Thames on Tuesday. We give an Illustration of the scene at the mess-table of a Highland regiment, "On the Eve of Departure" (p. 86)

51   The Rival Pipers from a Sketch taken at the Rawul Pindi Durbar by an Officer of the Seaforth Highlanders. *The Graphic*, London, May 23, 1885, p. 505.

52   The King's Own Scottish Borderers Leaving the Citadel, Cairo, Egypt, En Route for India. *The Graphic*, London, January 18, 1890, p. 77.

53   The Highland Brigade on the March. *Chatterbox*, 1897.

A Company of Highland soldiers on the march, accompanied, of course, by the Sergeant Piper and his men, is a very inspiring sight; the music, though rather ear-piercing to those not accustomed to it, being very attractive to the various inhabitants of a great city, more especially to those persons who are of the same social standing as the soldiers themselves. The writer of this remembers to have watched the passing of a Highland Brigade down the steep slopes of the Castle Hill, Edinburgh, on their way to Granton, where they were to embark for London on their way South. It was a heart-stirring sight, but withal a somewhat melancholy one, many of the men being accompanied by their female relatives, some of them weeping and clasping the disengaged hand of their dear one, while they whispered words of tender farewell.

One old woman was especially noted, whose trembling limbs could scarcely keep pace with the men as they tramped along, and whose sad eyes were ever and anon turned upon a sun-browned young fellow, who seemed afraid to look at his old mother lest he should lose a little of the manly composure which he was striving hard to maintain. The officer in charge was conveniently blind to many tender farewells, which passed between his men and the groups of sad-eyed women who walked along with them. Indeed, discipline was much relaxed, and very properly so; for these men would not all return to their native land, and who could tell which of them was destined to find a soldier's grave in the far-off land to which they were going?

Ah! war, which seems such a grand thing in the eyes of the young and inexperienced, is indeed one of the saddest necessities of this life, and makes one long for the time when we are told that men shall beat their swords into ploughshares, and their spears into pruning hooks, and learn the trade of war no more.

The Highland Brigade has ever taken a worthy place in the annuals of our country, particularly so during the Crimean War, when under the command of Sir Colin Campbell, one of the bravest soldiers and most skillful generals of modern times, it was chiefly instrumental in the splendid repulse of the Russians at Balaclava, as well as in the victory of the Alma. D.

54 The Storming of the Dargai Ridge by the Gordon Highlanders: Piper Findlater Continuing to Play though

Wounded in Both Legs, *The Illustrated London News*, Supplement, April 2, 1898.

Portrayal of Piper George Findlater of the 1st Battalion Gordon Highlanders, wounded in both legs, playing on his comrades fighting for the heights of Dargai in India in 1897. Findlater played the tune Cock of the North and was awarded the Victoria Cross for his actions.

55   Highland Pipers Playing the Canadian Scottish in Ypres: Heroic Canadians Honoured by their British Comrades on their reurn from the Fight at Langemarck by R. Caton Woodville. *The Illustrated London News*, London, May 8, 1915, p. cover.

Commendations, congratulations, compliments have been showered on the heroic Canadians of the Ypres-Langemarck battle, from the highest personages of the realm and from the ends of the Empire all over the world – yet nothing probably has so appealed to the men themselves as did the reception that the wearied survivors received, as they tramped through the ruins of Ypres on their return from the fight, from their British comrades in arms. The regiments at the moment in reserve in the town turned out in crowds, and lined the streets, cheering themselves hoarse in their enthusiastic admiration of what the Canadians had done. To rouse still further the martial enthusiasm of the moment, the pipers of a Highland regiment, as the Canadian Scottish came in, were sent to welcome them, and headed them through the streets, playing them into camp.

56   World War I – Black Watch Pipers Playing to the Captives of Longueval (Official War Photographs, Crown Copyright Series III, No. 21); Highlanders Pipe themselves back from the Trenches (Official War Photographs, Crown Copyright Series I, No. 2); The Black Watch Returning to Camp (Daily Mail Official War Pictures, Crown Copyright Series 15, No. 114); postcards.

57   Armee Anglaise (Edition L.D. Brux); Les Fetes de La Victoire, 14 Juiliet 1919 (Levy Fils Du Cue, Paris); Liege-Revue Canadienne (no id); postcards.

68	Decorated Gate across King Street at Richards Welcoming King Kalakaua Home after his trip around the World – Note countries visited on posts including 'Scotland.' Hawai`i State Archives, Kalakaua Collection.
78	(top) King Kamehameha III and wife Queen Kalama ca. 1850 – entertained Piper MacIntyre at the Palace. Bishop Museum Photo, Neg No. CP 114,512-xs 34745.
	(bottom) Palace of Kamehameha III after drawing ca. 1854 – Palace where Piper MacIntyre played in 1845, Bishop Museum Photo, Neg. No. CP 99493.
81	(top) National Maritime Museum, Greenwich, London – File correspondence DR No. 12218 / File Ref: H01/2592 dated June 29, 2001 – Ship Plan – "inboard Profile 1861 ZAZ1865; scale 1:48. This ship was originally classified as a batttleship of the 3rd Rate but in 1835 was reduced in armament and was redefined as a Frigate of the 4th Rate carrying 50 guns. The diagram presented is of the *H.M.S. America*' s sister ship *H.M.S. Vindictive*. *See also:* Lyon, David. *The Sailing Navy List*, Conway Maritime Press, 1993. (description of sailing ships including the *H.M.S. America*)
	(bottom) National Maritime Museum, Greenwich, London – Photograph Collection, Repro ID N5341 – *H.M.S. Galatea* 60.30.1859.
84	(left) Donald MacKay, Piper to the Prince of Wales and, on the right, J.F. Farquharson, Piper to the Duke of Edinburgh, photographed at Balmoral Castle in 1876, *Piping Times*, Vol. 50, No. 11, August, 1998, p. 53.
	Oval Insert: Photo of J.F. Farquharson from his journal and provided to the author by Michael and Carol Knight.
89	(top) British troops land at Waimea, Kaua`i on August 16, 1928 in commemoration of the 150th year of Capt. James Cook's arrival. (bottom) British troops in foreground with American detachment on the left in Waimea town for the

Cook commemoration ceremony. Hawai`i State Archives, Captain Cook Collection, #44a(top) and b(bottom).

100   Donald MacKay at the Mid-Pacific Club House-1931; photo provided by Carol Commeford.

104   Young Piper Aggie Wallace, Ross family photo.

105   Young Piper Aggie Wallace Leading the Labor Day Parade, 1938, Ross family photo.

107   Pipe Major Aggie Wallace and Piper Sandy Gair with 'Moki' at the Burns Night Dinner given by the Caledonian Society, 1965, Ross family photo.

109   Celtic Pipes and Drums of Hawai`i performs at Burns Night Dinner (1996), Author's Collection.

(leading band) Drum Major Bill Hart; (front row) Pipe Sgt. John "Doc" Sheedy, Pipe Corporal Montie Derby; (second row) Pipe Corporal Craig Ross, Gary Kanaya ; (third row) Dave Reid, Dan Quinn; (fourth row) Pat Roberts, Hardy Spoehr; (fifth row) Drummer Marilyn Giese; (sixth row) Bass Drummer Bonnie Graff; (last row) Drum Sgt. Alan Miyamura.

112   Kaua`i's First Burns Night Celebration, Waimea, Kaua`i, 2002, Author's collection.

(top)'Serving the Haggis': left to right – David Walker from Edinburgh (cousin to Kaua`i's David Walker), Lawrence Coleman (Celtic Pipes and Drums of Hawai`i),Chef;

(bottom)David Walker and Family.

115   Dr. John 'Doc' Sheedy – St. Patrick's Day, 2000, Celtic Pipes and Drums of Hawai`i photo.

116   St. Patrick's Day Parade, Honolulu – 1980, Drum Major Bill Morrison, *Honolulu Advertiser* Photo.

118   The Royal Scots Pipe Band trained by Agnes Wallace at the 1st Highland Games in Waimea, Hawai`i (1973),

Hawaiian Historical Society, Photograph Collection, 'Scots in Hawai`i' Series:

(Front row – left to right) Tom Burdick, Roberta Jones; (Back row – left to right) Drum Major Bill Morrison, Bob Cent, David Guthries; two brothers Mark and Mike ?; Bass Drummer/Piper David Furumoto, ?.

122   British Army Pipe Bands: (top) Pipes and Drums of the Seaforth Highlanders (Valentine & Sons – Regimental Pipe Band Series – Conrad Leigh); (middle) Pipes and Drums of the Argyll and Sutherland Highlanders (Valentine & Sons – Regimental Pipe Band Series – Conrad Leigh); (bottom) Pipes and Drums of the Queen's Own Cameron Highlanders (Valentine & Sons – Regimental Pipe Band Series – Conrad Leigh).

123   British Army Pipe Bands: (top) Pipes and Drums of the Gordon Highlanders (Valentine & Sons – Regimental Pipe Band Series – Conrad Leigh); (middle) Pipes and Drums of the Royal Scots (Valentine & Sons – Regimental Pipe Band Series – Conrad Leigh); (bottom) Pipes and Drums of the Black Watch (Valentine & Sons – Regimental Pipe Band Series – Conrad Leigh).

126   Description of the Hawai`i Tartan

128   Hawai`i's First Pipe Band – 1940 (Aggie Wallace – far left. Donald MacKay – far right. Rae Commeford, Donald MacKay's nephew – on his right); photo provided by Carol Commeford

130   (top) Aggie Wallace plays at USO Camp Show, Schofield Barracks, 1942; (bottom) Fellow Piper Sgt. Bill Gillespie, U.S. Marine Corps, plays at USO show at Ford Island, 1945, Ross family photos.

132   (top) Piper Aggie Wallace greets the Clan MacLeod Chieftain, Dame Flora MacLeod, at the Honolulu Airport in 1955, Hawaiian Historical Society, Photograph Collection, Scots in Hawai`i Series;

This same photo of Dame MacLeod's arrival at the Honolulu International Airport with Piper Aggie Wallace appeared in the *Honolulu Advertiser*, "Honolulu Scots Welcome Chieftain," February 9, 1955, A8:1.

(bottom) Piper Aggie Wallace with her Royal Scots dancers in 1950s. Hawaiian Historical Society, Photograph Collection, Scots in Hawaii Album, p. 45.

138 Honolulu Pipes and Drums Piper Kanoe Miller, 1st piper of Native Hawaiian ancestry – 1987. Photo provided by Kanoe Miller.

141 (top) Noted Piper Kathy Kinderman and Pipe Major Jacob Kaio, Jr. at the performance 'Aloha Kekokia'(2000), author's photo. (bottom) Noted Piper Andrew Wright with Drum Major Kevin Richards and his wife at Burns Night Dinner (2000), author's photo.

144 Combined bands of the Pipes and Drums of the Atlantic Watch and the Celtic Pipes and Drums of Hawai`i play on the *U.S.S. Missouri*, 2003; author's photo.

147 Photograph of Robert Anderson, possible Honolulu's first resident piper. Hawaiian Historical Society Photograph Collection, Scots in Hawai`i Series.

150 (top) William Forbes; (bottom) Robert Forbes – Ribbons on their chests say "See Hawaii First." Both pipers were Hilo residents; photo taken in the early 1900s; Roy Forbes Family Photo.

161 Pipe Major Aggie Wallace and the Royal Scots, 1954; Ross family photo:

(Left to right) PM Aggie Wallace; Pipers Bill Davidson, Sandy Lauchlin, Bill Savage, George Parker, E. Petrongilli (all pipers are members of the 25th Division, Artillery, Schofield Barracks); Dancers: Sandy Ross and May Louise Mulvehill.

162 PM Aggie Wallace and the Royal Scots at the home of Mrs. Finlay Ross for the Burns Tea given by the Daughters of the British Empire of Hawai`i, 1957; Ross family photo.

PM Aggie Wallace – most of the members of the band are the same as noted in the former photo.

165   Honolulu Pipes and Drums, 1970s, Author's Collection.

(Left to right – front row) ?, ?, Rick Shuman, John Johnson, ?, ?, Drum Major Bill Morrison; (back row) Honolulu Mayor Frank Fasi, Pipe Major Charles Anderson, Dr. Rob Knudson, A. J. Frappia, ?, ?, Bob Cent.

166   Honolulu Pipes and Drums, 1970s, Author's Collection. Pipe Major Charles Anderson

167   Honolulu Pipes and Drums, 1970s, Author's Collection.

(Left to right) George MacRae, Lawrence Coleman, Steve, A. J. Frappia, unidentified.

168   Honolulu Pipes and Drums aka Johnnie Walker Pipes and Drums – 1970s, Author's Collection.

(Front row – left to right) Rick Shuman, John Johnson, ?, ?; (back row) Pipe Major Charles Anderson, A. J. Frappia, ?, Johnnie Walker, Drum Major Bill Morrison, ?, ?, Bob Cent.

169   (left) Drum Major Bill Morrison, (right) Pipe Major A. J. Frappia, Honolulu Pipes and Drums, 1970s, Author's Collection

170   Honolulu Pipes and Drums, Pipe Major A. J. Frappia – 1970s, Author's Collection.

(Left to right – front row) Pipe Major A. J.Frappia, Dick Markoff, George Maclellan, Larry Samuels, David Siegel, Drum Major John Patella; (back row) Rick Shuman, ? Anderson, George MacRae, Sandy ?.

171   Honolulu Pipes and Drums, Drum Corps – 1980s, Author's Collection.

George MacRae, Drum Major John Patella, Scotty Dawson, ? Anderson, ?, Mark ?.

172   Honolulu Pipes and Drums, Bass Drummer Stuart Cowan – 1980s, Author's Collection.

173 Honolulu Pipes and Drums, Pipe Major David Furumoto –1980s, *Honolulu Advertiser* Photo.

174 Honolulu Pipes and Drums, Pipe Major David Furumoto – 1980s, Author's Collection.

Marching by Honolulu Community College; Drum Major?; (Left to right – front row) Pipe Major David Furumoto, Cora Dargan, Paul Lynch; (second row) A. J. Frappia, Bass Drummer Stuart Cowan, Jim Crisafulli; (third row) ?, Doug Macaulay; (back row) Mayor Frank Fasi

177 Shamrock Pipe Band, Pipe Major Lawrence Coleman – 1980s, *Honolulu Star-Bulletin* Photo.

Top: (Left to right) Pipe Major Lawrence Coleman, Barry Cronin, Glenn Wheaton

Bottom: (Left to right) Pipe Major Lawrence Coleman, Dr. John Sheedy, Charles Ireland, Paul Lynch, Scotty Dawson, unidentified, Shannon O'Hannigan

178 Shamrock Pipe Band, Pipe Major Lawrence Coleman – 1980s Author's Collection.

(up front) Drum Major Jamie McCormick; (front row) Pipe Major Lawrence Coleman, Jean Smith, Dr. John Sheedy; (second row) Glenn Wheaton, ?, Barry Cronin

181 Celtic Pipes and Drums of Hawai`i, Pipe Major Lawrence Coleman – Aloha Week Parade – 1993, Author's Collection.

(front row) PM Lawrence Coleman, Montie Derby, Glenn Wheaton, PM Emeritus A. J. Frappia; (second row) John "Doc" Sheedy, Dave Reid, Tina Berger, Frank Talamantes; (back row) Tenor Drummer Dave Graham, Bass Drummer Hardy Spoehr, and Hunter McEuen.

182 Celtic Pipes and Drums of Hawai`i, Pipe Major Lawrence Coleman, 1990s, Author's Collection.
March of Dimes Executive's Walk, 1996: Drum Major Bill Hart; (front row) PM Lawrence Coleman, Tina Berger,

unknown; (second row) Patrick Roberts, Hardy Spoehr; (back row) Bass Drummer Ron Graff (half hidden).

183   Celtic Pipes and Drums of Hawai`i, Pipe Major Jacob Kaio, Jr., 1990s, Author's Collection.

184   Celtic Pipes and Drums of Hawai`i, Pipe Major Dan Quinn, St. Patrick's Day, March 19, 2002, *Honolulu Star-Bulletin* Photo.

PM Dan Quinn; (front row) Daniel Eisen, Howard Levy – partially hidden, Dan Sinclair; (second row) Patrick Roberts, Frank Talamantes.

185   Celtic Pipes and Drums of Hawai`i aka Honolulu Police Pipe Band, Pipe Major Lawrence Coleman, 1990s, Author's Collection.

(front row) Bass Drummer Bill Burgess, ?, John K, Shannon O'Hannigan; (back row) Pipe Major Lawrence Coleman, ?, Bill Hart, Charles Ireland, Merle, ?, Jean Smith, ?, Drum Major Joe O'Hannigan, Dr. John Sheedy, ?, ?, ?, Bruce Middleton, A. J. Frappia.

186   Celtic Pipes and Drums of Hawai`i aka Honolulu Police Pipe Band, Founding Members Pipe Major Emeritus A. J. Frappia and Police Chief Douglas Gibb, 1990s, Author's Collection.

187   Celtic Pipes and Drums of Hawai`i aka Honolulu Police Pipe Band, Pipe Major Lawrence Coleman – Note Hula Dancer Debbie Nakanelua-Richards in white mu`umu`u – first hula dancer to dance to the pipes, Central Union Church Concert, 1997, Author's Collection.

(front row) Drum Sgt. Alan Miyamura, Matt Enderton, Bonnie Graff, unknown, Brian Overby, Ron Graff, John Beebee (second row) PM Lawrence Coleman, Dancer Carol Brown, Dave Mackay, Tina Berger, Les Enderton, Rob Knudson, Dancer Debbie Nakanelua-Richards, Hardy Spoehr, Drum Major Bill Hart; (third row) Kevin Richards,

Dan Quinn, Dave Graham, Gary Kanaya, Patrick Roberts, Dave Reid.

188 Celtic Pipes and Drums of Hawai`i aka St. Andrews Pipe Band, Pipe Major Lawrence Coleman, 1993, Author's Collection.

Drum Major Bill Hart; Flag Bearer unknown; (front row) A. J. Frappia (partially hidden), John "Doc" Sheedy, PM Lawrence Coleman; (second row) ?, Charles Ireland; (third row) ?, Bruce Middleton; (back row) drummers – ?.

189 Celtic Pipes and Drums of Hawai`i aka Honolulu Fire Pipes and Drums, Pipe Major Lawrence Coleman, 4th of July Parade, 1998, Author's Collection.

Drum Major Kevin Richards; (front row) PM Lawrence Coleman, Tina Berger, Hardy Spoehr, Patrick Roberts, Dan Quinn; (second row) Dave Mackay, Frank Talamantes, Susan Yamamoto, Les Enderton; (third row) – last column Elizabeth Kent.

190 Celtic Pipes and Drums of Hawai`i aka Honolulu Fire Pipes and Drums, Pipe Major Dan Quinn, 4th of July Parade, 2000, Author's Collection.

(front row) Drum Major Kevin Richards, Sandy Rose, Gene Marcus, Laurie Yagi; (second row) Tomiko Salz, Tina Berger, Elizabeth Kent; (third row) Erin Brown, Andy Grandinetti, Daniel Eisen, Alicia Delos Reyes, Joe Miller, Dave Mackay, Frank Talamantes, Patrick Roberts, Hardy Spoehr, Alan Miyamura, Buck Buchanan, Dan Quinn.

191 Celtic Pipes and Drums of Hawai`i aka Honolulu Fire Pipes and Drums, Pipe Major Dan Quinn, March 5, 2004. Photo by Bill Melemai.

(standing) Alan Miyamura, Mike Hudgins, Hardy Spoehr, Dan Sinclair, Frank Talamantes, Rick Cuthbertson, Howard Lavy. (sitting) Tina Berger, Andrew Grandinetti, Stu Cowan, Tomika Salz, Sita Seery, Laurie Yagi, Dan Quinn.

195 Hawaiian Thistle Pipe Band, Pipe Major Jacob Kaio, Jr., 2001, web site photo.

196 Hawaiian Thistle Pipe Band, Pipe Major Jacob Kaio, Jr. 2003, Brian Overby Photo.

(front row) Bonnie Graff, Alison Sherwood, (back row) Pipe Major Jacob Kaio, Jr., Ian Styan, Craig Dolack, Brian Overby, Pat McGuigan, Susan Yamamoto.

199 Pipe Major 1st Lt. Justin Stodghill, U.S. Marine Corps, Craig Kojima Photo (appeared in the *Honolulu Star-Bulletin*, 8/04/02).

203 Pipe Major John Grant, Maui Celtic Pipes and Drums, 4th of July 2003 (Hamish(Jim) Douglas-Burgess Photo).

(front row) Pipe Major John Grant, Will McBarnet, Hamish (Jim) Douglas-Burgess, Pipe Sergeant James Brent; (second row) Roger McKinlay Pleasanton, John Impey, Mike MacDougall; (back row) Drum Sergeant Peter Della Croce, bass drummer Bradley Salter.

276 (left to right) Charles H. Judd, King David Kalakaua, W.N. Armstrong during their trip around the world, 1881, Bishop Museum Photo, Neg. No. CP 58992.

277 Places Kalakaua Visited: (top) Edinburgh Castle – Changing of the Guard; (bottom) Edinburgh Castle – The Esplanade; postcards.

278 Places Kalakaua Visited: Loch Lomond (Valentine Series); Holyrood Palace (Edinburgh); postcards.

335 Drum Major Kevin Richards, Celtic Pipes and Drums of Hawai`i, 2000, author's collection.

345 Sandy Takes the Floor. *Punch, or the London Charivari*, June 1, 1889, p. 258.

"A Song of the Scotch Local Government Bill, (Some way after Sir Walter Scott)"

> *Pibroch of Donnel Dhu, Piper of Pipers,*
> *Wake they wild voice anew, Scare Saxon vipers!*
> *Come away! come away! Hark to the summons!*
> *Come in your war-array Into the Commons!*
> *` Come with the swagger of Argyle the cocky.*
> *The war-pipe will stagger the unionists rocky.*
> *Work chanter and reed, Like that marvellous man,*
> *Macphairson Clonglocketty Angus M'Clan!*
> *Leave untinded the "links" For the Commons' wild welter;*
> *The Speaker e'en shrinks, As you go it a pelter.*
> *As the great Mace you near, Your for enlarges,*
> *Suggestive of fighting-gear, Broadswords and targes.*
> *Sandy now takes the floor, Faith, and he fills it,*
> *"Progress" shall be no more Unless he wills it.*
> *Out, patient John, and out pat the belated!*
> *Scots for their turn about O'er long have waited.*
>
> and
>
> Mr. Punch's Notes. – The March Past of Correct Time. Punch, or The London Charivari, April 6, 1889, p. 158.

Back Cover:

> Painting on canvas – Bishop Museum Archives, Honolulu. The Accession label notes:
>
> *Landscape painting (oil) by Princess Victoria Kaiulani, probably during her schooling in Europe (England or Scotland) bought by donor at auction 1910-11 (Cleghorn Estate). Inscribed on reverse "For Papa from his loving child – V.Y.K."*

Appendix 1

King David Kalakaua's Trip to Scotland (1881)

Scotland Itinerary

Tue, Sept. 6, 1881:
- London area – AM
- Visits the Prince and Princess of Wales at Marlborough House
- Leaves London – Via Midland Express (train) – PM

SCOTLAND

Wed, Sept. 7, 1881:
- Arrives Glasgow – (St. Enoch's Station) – AM
- Guest of William Rennie Watson
- Visits foundry of Messrs Mirrlees, Tait & Watson
- Visits shipyard of John Elder & Sons (Fairfield)
- Attends banquet at Corporation Galleries
- Spends the night at Watson residence

Thu, Sept. 8, 1881:
- Stays in the Glasgow area
- Travels to Balloch by special train
- Tours Loch Lomond – lands at Tarbet
- Carriages from Tarbet to Arrochar to Finnait
- Tours Loch Long – lands at Grennock
- Returns to Glasgow
- Attends dinner and party with Watsons
- Spends the night at Watson residence

Fri, Sept. 9, 1881:	> Leaves Glasgow (Queen Street Station) – AM
	> Arrives Edinburgh (Waverly Street Station) – AM
	> Guest of R. A. Macfie-Dreghorn Castle
	> Visits Edinburgh Castle (tour given by Col. Macpherson, C.B., commanding the Royal Highlanders (Black Watch – bagpipers present)
	> Visits Parliament House
	> Visits Holyrood Palace
	> Visits Register House
	> Attends lunch at the New Club
	> Visits Council Chamber (entertained by pipers of the Royal Highlanders (Black Watch))
	> Visits St. Giles Cathedral and University of Edinburgh
	> Attends banquet at Dreghorn Castle (haggis played in by bagpiper(s))
	> Spends night at Dreghorn Castle
Sat, Sept. 10, 1881:	> Stays in the Edinburgh area
	> Visits Queens Park
	> Attends ceremony at Free Mason's Hall (receives Grand Knight Cross of the Order)
	> Visits Charlotte Square
	> Confers Literary Order of Kapiolani on Mrs. Bishop at RR Station
	> Leaves Edinburgh (Caledonian Railway Station) – PM

England

> Arrives Rufford Hall
> Guest of Sir Thomas Hesketh
> Spends night at Rufford Hall (home of Sir Thomas Hesketh – near Ormskirk, Lancashire)

Sun, Sept. 11, 1881:	>	Stays at Rufford Hall
	>	Rest and Relaxation
Mon, Sept. 12, 1881:	>	Leaves Rufford Hall – AM
	>	Arrives Liverpool, ENGLAND (Exchange Station) – AM
	>	Guest of W. B. Forwood (Mayor) and Mr. Jarmon (Hawaiian Consul)
	>	Visits St. George's Hall
	>	Visits Free Library (Picton Reading Room)
	>	Visits Art Gallery
	>	Attends lunch with Mayor
	>	Visits docks and tours the river
	>	Visits Exchange News Room
	>	Attends dinner at Town Hall (Mayor host)
Tue, Sept. 13, 1881:	>	Leaves Liverpool for New York on S.S.Celtic

Newspaper Accounts of the Trip

(1) *Edinburgh Courant*, Edinburgh, Scotland
- > Wednesday, September 7, 1881, p. 5
- > Friday, September 9, 1881, p. 5
- > Saturday, September 10, 1881, p. 4
- > Monday, September 12, 1881, p. 5

(2) *Glasgow Herald*, Glasgow, Scotland
- > Monday, September 5, 1881, p.
- > Thursday, September 8, 1881, p. 4
- > Friday, September 9, 1881, p. 6 & p. 7
- > Saturday, September 10, 1881, p. 4

> Monday, September 12, 1881, p. 4
> Tuesday, September 13, 1881, p. 5

(3) *Pacific Commercial Advertiser*, Honolulu, Hawai`i
> October 29, 1881, p. 2

(4) *The Bailie*, Glasgow, Scotland
> Wednesday, September 14, 1881, volume XVIII, 1880-1881 (published "for the proprietors by A.F. Sharp & Company, 14 Royal Exchange Square, Glasgow")

During his visit to Scotland, the King met with a number of people who had ties to Hawai`i. In Glasgow, he was hosted by William Renny Watson, an engineer by training but, also, a wealthy politician. He was a partner in the firm Mirrlees, Tait and Watson, a major manufacturer of machinery used in Hawai`i's sugar industry. Watson had visited Hawai`i months earlier, arranging the sale of machinery to plantation owners. Years after the King's visit to Glasgow, Watson moved to Hawai`i and started the Hawaiian Sugar Company on lands leased from Gay and Robinson on the island of Kaua`i.

The stop in Glasgow also included a visit to the shipyards of John Elder which over the years built a number of ships for the inter-island trade.

In Edinburgh, the King was hosted by Robert A. Macfie, another wealthy businessman, who was an investor in the Kilauea Plantation on Kaua`i. At a banquet later in the day at Macfie's Dreghorn Castle at least two of the invited guests had Hawai`i ties. One of these guests was John Purvis of Kinaldy, Fife. He had two sons, William H. and Robert W., who owned and operated Kukuihaele Plantation on the Hamakua Coast on Hawai`i. Another member of the family was Edward Purvis who lived on Kaua`i and who eventually became the King's Vice-Chamberlain. The other guest was the noted author Isabella Bird who had written *Six Months in the Sandwich Islands* and who had married Dr. John Bishop. Later in his visit, the King presented Mrs. Bishop with the 'Literary Order of Kapi`olani' for her work as an author.

> NOTE: Much of this information is found in the recent publication edited by Rhoda Hacker and published by the Caledonian Society of Hawai`i entitled *The Story of Scots in Hawai`i*, Honolulu, 2000 (See pages 88-92).
>
> The story of the Purvis family is documented by Nancy Hedemann in her recent publication *A Scottish-Hawaiian Story: The Purvis Family in the Sandwich Islands*, Honolulu, Oakley Press, 1995.

The following newspaper accounts have been reproduced as printed. There are a number of spelling and grammatical errors in the text which the author has maintained in the copy.

W. Judd, King David Kalakaua, W. A. Armstrong
On Their Trip Around The World (1881)

Some Places Visited By King Kalakaua In Scotland

Edinburgh Castle – Changing The Guard

Edinburgh Castle – The Esplenade

Loch Lomond and Ben Lomond

Holyrood Palace, Edinburgh

EDINBURGH COURANT.

EDINBURGH COURANT.

EDINBURGH, SCOTLAND Wednesday, September 7, 1881

The King Of The Sandwich Islands

King Kalakaua, of the Sandwich Islands, is to arrive in Glasgow this morning, attended by his chamberlain, Colonel Judd, and suite; and will be received by Mr. William Rennie Watson, who will conduct the illustrious stranger over the city. During his visit the King will be the guest of Mr. Watson, at 16 Woodlands Terrace. Tonight his Majesty will be entertained to dinner by the Lord Provost and magistrates in the Corporation Galleries, and a representative assembly have also been invited to honour his Majesty. It has been arranged by Mr. Watson that on the following day, should the weather prove favourable, the King will sail up Loch Lomond in the specially-chartered steamer Prince Consort, along with a company of ladies and gentlemen. A special train from Queen Street will convey the King, his suite, and Mr. Watson's guests to Balloch. The King will take his departure tomorrow night or Friday morning for Edinburgh, where as formerly mentioned, he will be the guest of Mr. R. A. Macfie of Dreghorn. On Friday it is expected that the King will visit the Castle and other places of interest in the city, and at two o'clock his Majesty will be entertained at a cake and wine luncheon by the Corporation in the Council Chambers.

According to "Men of the Time" David Kalakaua, King of the Sandwich or Hawaiian Islands, was born in 1838. He belongs to one of the highest families in the islands. When King Kamehameha V died in 1872 there were two candidates for the vacant throne – David Kalakaua and William Lunalilo. The latter was elected by a plebiscitum, which was confirmed by the Legislature. Lunalilo died within a twelvemonth, and Kalakaua again put forward his claims. A legislature specially convened for this purpose elected him in February 1874; but the validity of this election was contested by Queen Emma, widow of Kamehameha IV, who died in 1863. Queen Emma was the daughter of a native chief by an English woman. She was adopted by Dr. Rooke, an English physician on the islands, and before her marriage with Kamehemeha was known as Emma Rooke. The dispute threatened to result in a civil war, the adherents of Emma hoping that the British Government would refuse to acknowledge Kalakaua, who was presumed to be hostile to European influence in the islands; but in June 1874 Queen Victoria sent a letter to Kalakaua congratulating him upon his accession, and his right was then admitted. He is well educated, of exemplary habits, and dignified manners, and speaks English with fluency.

When the unfortunate Captain Cook visited the Sandwich Islands in 1778, little more than a century ago, each island of the group had a king of its own. In the closing years of the century, however, Kamehameha I, who has been styled the Napoleon of the Pacific, by force of arms, consolidated the group into a single kingdom, which he placed under the protection of George III in 1810. He died in 1819, and was succeeded by Lilolilio (Liholiho), who adopted on his accession the name of Kamehameha II. Under his reign idolatry was abolished, the idols were everywhere destroyed, and American missionaries commenced their labours in the islands, which are no wholly Christian. Kamehameha II and his Queen visited England, and after a short residence in the country, both died in London in July 1824. In reference to this event, a recent correspondent in the Times says: – "It may be worth recording the fact that just fifty-seven years ago, Miss Berry tells us that 'their savage Majesties' of the Sandwich Islands visited England, and were lionized over London. Miss Berry records the fact that she met them at Mr. Canning's house, and describes their person and their dress, which would seem to have seriously embarrassed their movements. Lord Byron adds that they lived very much on fish, and were particularly fond of oysters. They resided at Osborne's hotel in the Adelphi, where their bill appears to have amounted to no greater sum on an average than about 17s. a head for their food, which consisted of poultry, fish, and fruit. It is said that the once popular song of the King of the Cannibal Islands was composed apropos of the above royal visit. The royal pair, however, did not long survive, both dying in the Adelphi in July 1824 from an attack of measles and inflammation of the lungs, and they were buried under the parish church of St. Martin's-in-the-Fields." Prior to 1838, the Government was a despotism, but in 1840 King Kamehameha III granted a constitution consisting of king, assembly of nobles, and representative council, based on that of Great Britain. In 1843 the independence of the Hawaiian Kingdom was formally declared by the French and English Governments, and is now universally recognized. Kamehameha IV acceded to the throne in 1854, and died as already stated in 1863.

Edinburgh Courant, Wednesday, September 7, 1881, page 5

EDINBURGH COURANT.

EDINBURGH, SCOTLAND   Saturday, September 9, 1881

The King Of The Sandwich Islands

Yesterday morning, King Kalakaua, accompanied by Mr. Watson and a party of friends, left Queen Street Station at 9:30, by special train for Balloch. Here the steamer Prince of Wales, which had been specially chartered for a sail up Loch Lomond, was waiting, and on the party getting on board she steamed off, amidst the cheers of those who had been assembled on the pier to see his Majesty. The morning was not the best for seeing the beauties of the loch, but the sale(sic) was on the whole an enjoyable one. After sailing up the loch the King and his suite crossed over to Arrochar, where they joined Mr. Pearce's yacht, and in her came up the Clyde to Greenock, from whence the party returned to Glasgow per rail.

King Kalakaua is to arrive at the Caledonian Railway Station, Princes Street, today, either by the train which leaves Glasgow at 8:45 A.M. or 9:50 A.M. He will be received at the station by Mr. R.A. Macfie of Dreghorn. It is expected that his Majesty will first visit the Castle, and from thence proceed to the Parliament House. The party, after being shown through the different buildings, will then visit Holyrood Palace. These visits, it is expected, will be overtaken before two o'clock, when his Majesty will be received by the Lord Provost and the Magistrates at a service of cake and wine in the Council Chambers. That being over, arrangements have been made for a drive, possibly round Arthur's Seat. The party will afterwards proceed to Dreghorn Castle, the residence of Mr. Macfie, where extensive preparations have been made for the royal visit. A temporary entrance hall has been fitted up in an attractive manner. The floor and steps are covered with red cloth, and on the walls are displayed large trophies of flags, with various devices in the center of each. Several fine evergreen plants are ranged along each side of the building, giving quite a lovely appearance to the scene. Decorations have also been erected at the two lodge gates which lead to the castle. Over each an arch made of evergreens and heather has been placed, in the center of which are printed the words, "God save King Kalakaua." In addition to this, the Sandwich Islands for of welcome, "Aloha," has been neatly brought out with leaves on one of the arches. On reaching the castle his Majesty will be received by a company of friends who have been invited by Mr. Macfie. In all probability the King will receive a Masonic deputation in a private house at Walker Street tomorrow forenoon.

Other places of interest throughout the city will, according to present arrangements, be visited. His Majesty is expected to leave Edinburgh in the course of tomorrow afternoon for Manchester or Liverpool, whence he sails next week for home.

Edinburgh Courant, Friday, September 9, 1881, page 5

EDINBURGH COURANT.

EDINBURGH, SCOTLAND   Saturday, September 10, 1881

The King Of The Sandwich Islands In Edinburgh

King Kalakaua left Glasgow yesterday morning by train at ten minutes to ten o'clock, and arrived at the Waverley Station at a quarter past eleven. His Majesty was met at the station by Mr. R. A. Macfie of Dreghorn, whose guest he is at Dreghorn Castle, during his brief stay in this district. The royal party – consisting of his Majesty; Mr. R. A. Macfie of Dreghorn; Colonel the Hon. Hastings Judd, chamberlain to his Majesty; Colonel Macfarlane; Mr. Robert Follett Synge, representing the Foreign Office; Sir Thomas M'Clure, Bart., M.P., Vice Lieutenant of County Down; and Mr. Reid, Queen's and Lord Treasurer's Remembrancer – then drove in two open carriages to the Castle, where they were received by Colonel Macpherson, C.B., commanding the Royal Highlanders (Black Watch). His Majesty King Kalakaua carried a magnificent bouquet, which was presented to him on his alighting at the Waverley Station by Miss. Macfie, grand-daughter of R. A. Macfie. The royal party were then shown by Colonel Macpherson over the various points of interest within the Castle, visiting in succession the Crown Room and Regalia, and Queen Mary's Room. An inspection was next made of the time-gun, the working of which was explained to the distinguished visitors. Thence the party proceeded to the Mons Meg Battery, and Queen Margaret's Chapel adjoining. After having been entertained at the officers' mess, his Majesty and party left the Castle about twelve o'clock. A guard of honour, consisting of 100 men of the Black Watch, under the command of Captain Eden, had been paraded shortly before eleven o'clock, to receive his Majesty on arrival; but in consequence of the showery weather which prevailed, this formality was dispensed with, and the royal party made their tour of the historical fortress very much as ordinary visitors, of whom there were a goodly number in the Castle at the time. His Majesty, in proceeding through the Castle, courteously returned the salutes of both soldiers and civilians.

After leaving the Castle, the royal party proceeded to the parliament House Buildings, which were successively inspected. Among the many interesting documents contained in the Advocates' Library, his Majesty had an opportunity of examining the original manuscript of "Waverley." Holyrood Palace was thereafter visited, with the numerous historically interesting objects in which his Majesty evinced deep interest. Driving by Regent road, the royal party next visited the Register House, which he inspected very minutely, and manifested great interest in. At one o'clock he went to the New Club, where he was to have been entertained to luncheon by Mr. Purvis of Kinaldy. Mr. Purvis, however, was unable to be present through a steamboat detention, and the honours were done by Colonel Craigie Halkett.

Banquet In The Council Chambers

At two o'clock, his Majesty the King of Hawaii was entertained to a cake and wine banquet in the Council Chambers. The square and staircases leading to the Council Chambers were decorated with palms, tree ferns, and exotics, and the band and pipers of the Royal Highlanders (Black Watch) played a selection of music during the proceedings.

Sir Thomas Jamieson Boyd, Lord Provost, presided; Treasurer Harrison was croupier; and among those present were – Lord Belhaven; Lord Deas; Admiral Sir Alexander Milne, Bart.; Professor Sir Wyville Thomas; Mr. J. Dick Peddie, M.P.; Dr. Henderson, Provost of Leith; Mr. Keir, Provost of Musselburgh; Mr. Hunter, Provost of Portobello; Colonel Macpherson, Black Watch; Professor Archer; Archbishop Strain; the various Consuls; the Magistrates and Town Council; Mr. Skinner, Town-Clerk; Mr. Harris, Depute Town-Clerk.

Apologies were intimated from Lord Moncreiff, the Lord Advocate; Sir William Baille; Sir Noel Paton, R.S.A.; Sir William Johnston, Lord Provost of Glasgow; Colonel Preston, C.B.; Major-General Anderson, C.B.; Colonel Thomson; Mr. Duncan M'Laren; Rev. Dr. Cameron Lees; Mr. Charles Morton, Crown Agent; &c.

His Majesty, on entering the chamber, was received with loud applause, every one present standing. After a service of cake and wine, the Lord Provost said – *I am sure we are all delighted to see here today his Hawaiian Majesty, King Kalakaua, who has honoured us with his presence, and in the name of the Corporation of this ancient city, and of the people, generally, I give his Majesty a cordial welcome to the capital of Scotland. Since his Majesty's arrival in this country, our attention has been drawn more than formerly to the kingdom of Hawaii, over which his Majesty rules, consisting of the rich, interesting, and beautiful chain of the Sandwich Islands, in the centre of the Pacific Ocean; and especially we are pleased to think of the vast progress in civilisation(sic) which their people have made during the present century. In the last seven years, when his Majesty has been King, further progress has been made, and during that time great material prosperity has been also experienced in a largely increased revenue. From what we know of the islands in former times, well may those who pay them a visit be greatly struck with what they see. Honolula(sic)(sic), the metropolis and principal seaport of the group, and which occupies so convenient a position in the great thoroughfares of the vast pacific, is quite a place of active commercial* enterprise. It has its shops and its warehouses and public buildings. The churches stand out prominently. Then there are comfortable hotels, and newspapers for the breakfast table. And Honolula(sic), besides being the centre of trade, is also the seat of Government, and in it there are consuls from Great Britain, from America, and from many other countries throughout the world. Then the Ministry is composed of persons who are responsible for their actions; and there is a Legislature which passes laws affecting natives and people of other countries alike, without respect of persons. I am not here, however, either to describe these charming islands of Polynesia, or to make a speech, but to express the great pleasure we experience in his Majesty honouring us with a visit, and to give him in your name a most cordial and hearty welcome to Edinburgh. I have now the honour to propose that we should drink to the health of King Kalakaua, and wish him much happiness and every blessing. We must all greatly admire the public spirit and love of his people's good shown in his thus going through the world in their best interests. I trust his Majesty will enjoy his short visit among us; and of this I am sure that, go where he may, he will now here see a more beautiful city, or a more quiet and orderly people. (Loud applause).

His Majesty in reply said – *My Lord Provost, my Lords, and gentlemen – I feel deeply gratified for the manner in which you have drank my health. I must thank the Lord Provost for having given us such a vivid account and description of my country. I am sure that my people will feel very much gratified by your expressions of esteem towards them and towards myself. (Applause.) What the Lord Provost has said in regards to the improvements in my country is quite true. (Applause.) We have advanced a little, but not so much, perhaps, as he has described just at this moment. I appreciate most highly the sentiments that he has given utterance to, in regard not only to myself, but also to my country. (Applause.) Edinburgh can boast of its literary institutions, of its science and art, and of its statues, ancient monuments, and historical places of note, and I can verify the boast from what I have seen today. I only regret that my brief stay will not allow me to enjoy very long your hospitalities.* (Loud applause.)

Lord Deas proposed "The health of the Lord Provost," and the toast was drank with enthusiasm.

The Lord Provost, in reply, said – *It was one of the privileges connected with the hard work consequent upon his office, to receive visitors of distinction; and, as he had before, it had afforded him great pleasure in having King Kalakaua among them today.* (Applause.)

The proceedings shortly afterwards terminated, the whole assemblage rising and cheering as his Majesty left the room.

After leaving the Council Chambers, his Majesty and party drove to Dreghorn Castle, which was reached shortly before four o'clock. As stated yesterday, extensive preparations had been made for welcoming the royal guest and his suite – spacious entrance hall, laid with crimson cloth, and decorated all round with trophies of flags, with various devices in the centre of each, having been improvised. Here his Majesty was received by a large number of friends invited by Mr. Macfie. Tea having been served, a garden party was held, at which about two hundred persons were present. The wet weather, however, greatly interfered with the arrangements, and a projected game at lawn tennis had to be abandoned. In the evening his Majesty was entertained to dinner, among those whose for whom covers were laid being – His Majesty King Kalakaua; Colonel the Hon. Charles Hastings Judd, Chamberlain to his Majesty; Colonel Macfarlane, A.D.C.; Mr. R. Follett Synge, in attendance on his Majesty during his stay in the United Kingdom; the Right Hon. Sir Thomas J. Boyd, Lord Provost of Edinburgh and lady Boyd; Sir Thomas M'Clure, Bart., M.P., and Lady M'Clure; Sir Peter Coates, the Lord Advocate; Mr. Peter M'Legan, M.P.; Mr. J. Dick Peddie, M.P.; Major Campbell of Tullyveolan; Mr. J. J. Reid, Queen's and Lord Treasurer's Remembrancer; Mr. J. Purvis of Kinaldy; Dr. Bishop and Mrs. Bishop; Mr. George Collie, Hatton House, and Mrs. Collie; Mr. and Mrs. J. W. Macfie; and Mr. David J. Macfie of Borthwickhall. A number of national dishes entered into the evening's menu – the haggis being played in and around the Castle. From the time of the arrival of his Majesty at the Castle, the Hawaiian ensign floated from one of the towers.

As at present arranged, his Majesty and party will leave Dreghorn Castle this afternoon and drive round by Roslin, where the different points of interest in the district will be visited. On the return journey the party will pay a visit to Craigmillar Castle, thereafter going round the Queen's Drive. About noon the Royal Botanic Gardens will be reached, the magnificent palm-house being the special object of attention. A conclave of the Knights of the Red Cross of Constantine is to be held in the Freemasons' Hall at 12:45 P.M., when the Earl of Kintore will confer the Grand Cross of the Order on his Majesty. He is afterwards to lunch with Dr. Bishop, Walker Street. His Majesty leaves Edinburgh by the train starting from the Caledonian station today at 2:25 P.M. He goes on a visit to Sir Thomas Hesketh, Rufford Hall, and from thence, on Monday, proceeds to Liverpool, where he will dine with the Mayor. His Majesty sails for America on Tuesday, en route for Honolulu.

Edinburgh Courant, Saturday, September 10, 1881, page 4

EDINBURGH COURANT.

EDINBURGH, SCOTLAND   Saturday, September 12, 1881

The King Of The Sandwich Islands In Edinburgh

On Saturday, after breakfast, King Kalakaua walked in the grounds of Dreghorn Castle, and in commemoration of his visit planted two maple trees, naming them after Jenny Cowan Scott Macfie and Robert Andrew Scott Macfie, grand-children of Mr. Macfie of Dreghorn, and niece and nephew of Mr. Cowan, M.P. About a quarter to twelve his Majesty took his departure from Dreghorn Castle, a piper playing through the reception hall to his carriage. As his Majesty drove off, the assembled servants gave a hearty farewell "Aloha!" which his Majesty courteously acknowledged. The royal party – consisting of the King, Colonel the Hon. Hastings Judd, Chamberlain; Colonel Macfarlane, A.D.C.; Mr. Robert Follett Synge; Mr. and Mrs. Macfie of Dreghorn; Lady M'Clure; and Dr. Bishop – drove in two carriages, by way of Hunters' Tryst avenue and Comiston, to Fairmile Head toll, at which they turned towards Edinburgh. They drove by the Borestone at Morningside, and proceeding along by the Grange Cemetery, passed into the Queen's park at the Messrs Nelson's works. Driving to Samson's Ribs, the party returned to the higher drive, went round Arthur Seat by Dunsappie, and passing Holyrood (where the guard turned out and presented arms as the King's party passed), proceeded by Regent Road to the Freemasons' Hall via St Andrew Square. For almost the first time during his Majesty's brief stay here, the sun shone brilliantly, and the city looked at its best. The atmosphere being clear, the party had the pleasure of witnessing the magnificent view which the Queen's Drive commands in all directions, and here, we believe, the King expressed regret that he had not been able to allow himself more time in Scotland.

King Kalakaua was expected at noon in the Royal Botanic Gardens, and preparations were made for his planting a Thuga Giganta (gigantic arbor vitae of California). Professor Dickson, regius keeper; Professor Balfour, ex-regius keeper; Mr. J. Sadler, curator; and Mr. Isaac Anderson Henry of Hay Lodge, awaited the arrival of his Majesty, and a number of people loitered about the gardens in the hope that they might see the illustrious stranger. Between twelve and one o'clock, however, a telegram was received from Mr. R. A. Macfie of Dreghorn, stating that King Kalakaua was so much fatigued that he would have to forego the pleasure of visiting the gardens.

Ceremony In Freemasons' Hall

The Freemasons' Hall was reached about one o'clock, and his Majesty, as he entered, was respectfully saluted and loudly cheered. The object of the visit was to attend a special meeting of the Grand Conclave of Scotland of the Order of the Red Cross of Constantine, which had resolved to confer on his Majesty the rank of Knight Grand Cross of the Order. There was a large attendance of brethren, among those present being the following members of the Grand Council, viz.: – Captain John Crombie, Aberdeen, Grand Senior General, Acting Grand Sovereign in the unavoidable absence of the Earl of Kentore; James Crichton, Grand Junior General, Acting Grand Viceroy; Robert S. Brown, Grand Recorder; James Dalrymple Duncan, Glasgow, Grand Standard-Bearer; James B. Mercer, Past Grand Chancellor; and the following members of the Grand Senate, viz.: – William Milne; Captain A. M. Bruce; James Melville; Sir Molyneux H. Nepean, Bart.; Francis law; and F. W. Roberts; also William Mann, S.S.C.; P. G. Warden; D. Murray Lyon, Grand Secretary, Grand Lodge of Scotland; Chancellor Alexander Henry; G. S. Ferrier; J. Fleming; P. R. Haddow; W. Hamilton; J. H. M. Bairnsfather, S.S.C.; &c. &c.

His Majesty was received by the Grand Recorder, and by the Grand Secretary of the Grand Lodge of Scotland, Brother D. Murray Lyon, by whom he was conducted to the ante-room, where he signed the attendance book of the Grand Council, and the Visitors' Book of the Grand Lodge of Scotland. The Conclave was opened under the presidency of Captain John Crombie. His Majesty having been introduced to the Conclave, and received under the arch of steel, the Acting Grand Sovereign, addressing his Majesty, then said – *The members of the Grand Imperial Council of Scotland are very much gratified at having the pleasure of meeting your Majesty here today, and conferring on you the highest honour they have it in their power to bestow; and they have desired me to convey to your Majesty their grateful sense of your courtesy in allowing your name to be added to the roll of Knights Grand Cross of Scotland. I regret exceedingly that the Grand Sovereign of the Order, the Right Hon. the Earl of Kintore, has been prevented from attending and personally conferring this distinction upon you. As your Majesty's time is very limited, and as we heartily concur in every word said by the Lord Provost of Edinburgh at the meeting yesterday, I shall only detain you to say that we all join – and very Freemason in Scotland when he reads of the event today will join – in earnest and heartfelt prayer to our Omnipotent Ruler, the great Architect of the universe, that every blessing and happiness may attend your Majesty through life, that you may have a safe and pleasant return to your kingdom, that your reign there may be long and prosperous, and that you may continue to take a warm interest in manifest a zeal for, and be a credit and ornament to the craft we love so dearly.*

The King was then presented with a copy of the statutes of the Council, which he pledged himself to obey. The Acting Sovereign, in investing him with the Grand Cross, further said – *In the name and by the special authority of the Grand Council of the Order, I now invest you with the jewel of a Knight Grand Cross of the Imperial Council of Scotland; and may I venture to express the hope that the jewel and the patent, which the Grand Recorder will forward in a few days, may sometimes recall to your mind your visit to Scotland, where thousands of Freemasons who have never seen your Majesty's face, but know your great talents as a Mason, and the high position you have attained in the craft, extend to your Majesty their fraternal feelings of esteem and love, and will be highly gratified to find that those feelings are reciprocated by your Majesty?* The Acting Viceroy, Brother James Crichton, in appropriate terms, then offered his Majesty honorary membership of the Edinburgh Conclave, No. 1.

His Majesty, in graciously intimating his acceptance of these honours, referred to the cordial reception he had met with during his visit to Scotland. No honour which he had received would be more appreciated than that which had been conferred upon him by the Grand Council. He would ever retain a lively recollection of his visit to the Freemasons' Hall, and it would give him great pleasure to convey to the brethren in Honolulu, of whom there was a large number, an account of the hearty reception he had received from the Grand Imperial Council of Scotland. He had also much pleasure in accepting the honorary membership of the Edinburgh Conclave No. 1, which he regarded as an additional Masonic tie between himself and this country, so famous for in Masonry. (Applause.)

His Majesty then signed the roll of membership in Conclave No. 1. After the ceremony his Majesty's health was drunk with great enthusiasm, and afterwards his Majesty departed amid the acclamations of the assembled brethren. Among those who had the honour of being introduced to his Majesty were – William Mann, S.S.C., Past Senior Grand Warden of the Grand Lodge of Scotland; Sir Molyneux Nepean, Bart.,; Councillor Henry; and Dr. Loth, who presented a copy of his work on the Ancient and Accepted Scottish Rite. Before his departure his Majesty graciously accepted the portraits of Sir Michael Shaw Stewart, Grand Master Mason of Scotland; and of the Earl of Kintore, Grand Sovereign of the Red Cross Order. His Majesty also accepted a copy of "The Grand Lodge of Scotland Galop," by Francis Law. Letters of apology were received from the Earl of Kintore, Grand Sovereign; Capt. Charles Hunter, Grand Viceroy; the Rev. T. N. Wannop, Grand High Prelate; J. H. Balfour, W.S., Grand Marshall; and Col. J. Todd Stewart, Glasgow, Grand Chamberlain.

As on his arrival, the departure of his Majesty from the Freemasons' Hall was witnessed by a large crowd, who again raised a hearty cheer.

Departure Of The King

After leaving the Freemasons' Hall, his Majesty drove by way of Charlotte Square (where he obtained a view of the Prince Consort statue) to the residence of Dr. Bishop, 12 Walker Street. Here his Majesty was entertained at luncheon, the other members of the company being Sir Thomas and Lady M'Clure; Mr. and Mrs. Macfie of Dreghorn; Col. the Hon. Hastings Judd, Chamberlain to the King; Colonel Macfarlane, A.D.C.; and Mr. Robert Follett Synge, representative of the Foreign Office in attendance upon his Majesty. After luncheon the King drove to the Caledonian Railway Station, and proceeded at 2:25 P.M. in one of the London and North-Western royal saloon carriages for Rufford hall, the seat of Sir Thomas Hesketh. The carriage was attached to the ordinary train by the west coast route, but, through the liberality of the railway company, was to be run special from Preston to avoid his Majesty being detained waiting an hour and a half at the station there. The arrangements for the departure of the train were superintended by Mr. Irons, stationmaster. The King was received at the station by the Lord Provost; and amongst others who accompanied his Majesty to the platform were Sir Thomas and lady M'Clure; Mr. and Mrs. Macfie; and Dr. and Mrs. Bishop. A large crowd assembled at the station, and, respectfully saluting his Majesty on arrival, gave him a hearty cheer on leaving. His Majesty courteously acknowledged the enthusiasm of the crowd, and seemed specially touched by the "Alohas" and "Hurrahs" which were raised as the train moved off from the platform. The King before leaving entered into conversation with several of the ladies and gentlemen on the platform, and expressed himself highly pleased with the heartiness of the reception given to him in Scotland. He was, it may further be mentioned, particularly gratified with the respect everywhere shown to him while driving about, hats being everywhere lifted by pedestrians on his Majesty being recognized.

The King's Tour

King Kalakaua, of whom we gave a short sketch several days ago, has undertaken his present tour with the view of making himself generally acquainted with the state of civilization in various countries of the world, and introducing such reforms into his own dominions as might be suggested by him. He proceeded first to Japan, and then to China, Siam, and India from which he came on to Italy. When there he came direct from Rome to this country to see the royal volunteer review at Windsor.

Remaining in London for a few weeks, he received distinguished honours from the royal family, the City companies, and private individuals of rank and fashion. He subsequently returned to the Continent, visiting Brussels, Vienna, and other large cities, and latterly Paris, to which he went with the special object of seeing the President of the French Republic. From Paris he returned again to this country, where he has latterly met with a hearty reception in Glasgow, as well as in Edinburgh. This morning his Majesty proceeds to Liverpool, where the Mayor is to devote the day in showing the King the docks and public works, and preside in the evening at a farewell banquet in his Majesty's honour. The King will sail tomorrow in one of the White Star steamers for New York, and, after spending a few days in the Eastern States, proceed to California, sailing from San Francisco for home. During his absence the Government is being conducted by the Princess Likelike, the heir-apparent to the throne.

The impression formed by the King by those who have had the opportunity of conversing with him is one of a very favourable character. His manner and deportment are, it is said, those of a thoroughly well-bred gentleman. He is very affable, while retaining the natural dignity befitting his position. Possessed of remarkable conversational powers, he expresses himself well in English with a slight foreign accent. He is acute in his criticisms, which manifest culture and originality of thought, and when speaking of his travels shows that he is keen-sighted, and has received impressions which are not likely to be lost in furthering the comfort and happiness of the people over whom it is his lot to rule.

A Hawaiian Honour

King Kalakaua has conferred on Mrs. Bishop (formerly Miss. Bird), authoress of "Six Months in the Hawaiian Archipelago," the Literary Order of Kapiolani, with the jewel and decoration, including a miniature of Queen Kapiolani. The Order is one which the King himself instituted, and its latest recipient is one who by her writings has done much to interest the inhabitants especially of Great Britain and America, not only in the Hawaiian Islands, but also in Japan and other foreign countries. We believe that a fourth edition of "Six Months in the Hawaiian Archipelago" has just been issued.

Edinburgh Courant, Monday, September 12, 1881, page 5

The Glasgow Herald.

`Upoho Uka Nui `O Kekokia – 𝄞 – 297

The Glasgow Herald.

99th YEAR, No. 212   PUBLISHED DAILY   Price ONE PENNY

KING KALAKAUA'S VISIT TO GLASGOW. – We are informed by Mr. George Gray Macfarlane that King Kalakaua will reach Glasgow on Wednesday morning, and will be entertained by the Lord Provost that evening to dinner in the Corporation Galleries.

The Glasgow Herald, September 5, 1881, page 4

The Glasgow Herald

99th YEAR, No. 215 — PUBLISHED DAILY — Price ONE PENNY

The King Of The Sandwich Islands In Glasgow

His Majesty King Kalakaua of the Sandwich Islands is just now a visitor to our city. Attended by Colonel Judd and Colonel Macfarlane, His Royal Highness left London on Tuesday Evening after having visited the Prince and Princess of Wales at Marlborough House, and traveling by the Midland express reached St Enoch's Station at nine o'clock yesterday morning. King Kalakaua was received Councillor W. Renny Watson, whose guest he will be during his stay in the West, and immediately on arrival the royal party drove to Mr. Watson's residence, 16 Woodlands Terrace. While there the Hon. the Lord provost called and paid his respects to the King. During the forenoon His Majesty and suite, under the guidance of Councillor Watson, visited the extensive foundry establishment of Messrs Mirrlees, Tait & Watson in Scotland Street, driving thence to the shipbuilding yard of Messrs John Elder & Co. at Fairfield. After luncheon the visitors were at one or two places in the centre and East end of the city, honouring the flower show in the City Hall by their presence.

Corporation Banquet To The King

In the evening His Majesty King Kalakaua was entertained to a banquet in the Corporation Galleries. The Hon. the Lord Provost presided, and was supported on the right by His Majesty King Kalakaua, Colonel Judd, Colonel Macfarlane, Sir James Watson, Dean of Guild Mirrilees, Captain Freeman, Captain Garland, 71st Regiment; Provost Campbell, of Greenock; Principal Douglas, Mr James King of Levernholm, Mr W. Rae Arthur, Mr M. Connall; and on the left by Rev. D. Ramage, Lieutenant Rouchersky and Lieutenant Miasnikoff, of H.I.M.'s Ship Peter the Great ; Councillor W. R. Watson, Sir William Collins, Deacon-Convener M'Onie, Mr R. A. Macfie, Provost M'Kean, of Paisley; Mr Peter Cloustos, Mr Wm. M'Ewan, Mr Richard Hobson, Dr Scott-Orr; while the croupiers were Bailie Laing, Bailie Thomson, and Bailie M'Onie; and around the tables, in addition to members of the Magistracy and the Town Council, were Sir Peter Coates, Mr William Pearce, Mr J. H. Stoddart, Mr David Rowan, Mr Charles Irwin, Mr F. Wicks, Mr John Carrick, Mr Andrew Cunningham, Mr W. West Watson, and Mr James Nicol.

Grace having been said by the Rev. Dr Ramage, the company partook of a recerche dejeuner, purveyed by Messrs Ferguson & Forrester; and at the conclusion of the excellent repast, Principal Douglas returned thanks.

The Hon. CHAIRMAN then said it was usual on such occasions ton intimate the names of those who had been invited and were unable to attend. They were – The Duke of Argyll, the Earl of Shaftesbury, the Earl of Glasgow, Lord Provost of Edinburgh, Sir Edward Colebrook, Sir Michael Shaw-Stewart, Sir William Thomson, Mr Anderson, M.P.; Dr. Cameron, M.P.; Mr A. Orr-Ewing, M.P.; Mr Charles Tennant, M.P.; Colonel Hamilton, M.P.; Mr J. C. Bolton, M.P.; Mr Helms, M.P.; Mr J. A. Campbell, M.P.; Sheriff Clark, Mr Crum-Ewing, Mr James Campbell, Principal Caird, and Mr John Burns. One could well understand, his Lordship said, that those noblemen who were members of the House of Peers and those gentlemen who were members of the House of Commons might well be excused from attending after the work of such a busy session. (Applause.) The other gentleman had, no doubt, sufficient reason for being absent from this meeting, and he was sure from the expressions of regret in their letters that if they had not been otherwise engaged they would have been present. Gentlemen, I have much pleasure in proposing the health and offering a hearty welcome to His Majesty the King of Hawaii. (Loud and prolonged cheers.) It is very seldom that the City of Glasgow is honoured by the visit of a crowned head – even our own sovereign only comes to us at very rare intervals, only on occasions when there is something specially to attract Her Majesty, certainly not for the purpose of seeing the city itself. I am afraid your Majesty will be rather disappointed with what we have got to show you here, and that you are not likely to come back to us again. Contrasting the atmosphere of Glasgow with the pure air of your native country ours must suffer much in comparison. I have not had the advantage which my brother magistrate the Lord Mayor of London, has enjoyed of visiting your dominions, but I have the good fortune to know one member of my Town Council who has, and from him I have had the most glowing accounts of the delightful climate and beautiful land which owns your away. (Applause.) I had I must own some doubts of the account he gave me of it, and so I sought out the last book that gives any information on the subject, and in it I find even a stronger statement than Councillor Watson gives. The Writer says: – "The Kingdom of Hawaii is in its way an earthly paradise, washed by the soft blue waters of the pacific Ocean, and exposed to mild and balmy zephyrs. The very people have a holiday look, never appearing oppressed by overwork, but rather light hearted pleasure-seekers. Mounted on their ponies, they gallop about merrily over the white sands, or disport themselves heedlessly in the still whiter yeast of the surging billows. No less charming than the sea-shore is the scenery further inland, where, between green hills, the purling streams often flow invisibly in their deep rocky channels, where the gigantic trees spread their rich leafy branches in all directions – where the banana, bread-fruit, guava, and cocoa-nut offer such an overflow of delicious drink and substantial savoury food that this bright little Eden seems exempt from the common doom 'In the sweat of thy face shalt thou east bread.'" When I read that to you I am almost inclined to say in the words of Claude Molnette after he had described the Lake of Come to the Lady of Lyons, "Now, do you like the picture?" (Applause.) I find also that there are extensive tracts of beautiful land and fine pasturage, that the upland slopes of the mountains are clothed with dense forests, and lower down are vast plains and sugar plantations, that several of the islands are well supplied with rivers, but of course they are necessarily small, as even the largest island has only an area of 2,500,000 acres. There are eight islands of consequence in all, with a superficial area of 6,000 square miles; and it appears to me, from all that I can read or hear about them, that the exception of the absence of metals, all else is in ample abundance. The commerce of the islands is increasing in a most extraordinary manner; but, considering their capabilities, it may be said to be still in its infancy. There can be no doubt but that there is a great future of the Kingdom of Hawaii. (Loud applause.) The sugar plantations have increased enormously the late years, as is evidenced by the produce; for whilst in 1862 only 3,000,000 pounds of sugar were produced the last year's product amounted to upwards of 60,000,000 pounds. Of course there are other products, but sugar, coffee, and rice are the principal. In early times each of the eight islands had its own king; but under Kamehameha 1, the islands were formed into one kingdom. In 1810 King Kamehameha wrote to George III., desiring to acknowledge the King of Great Britain as his sovereign, and to place the islands under British protection, an offer which was accepted, and I believe, continued till 1843, when the independence of the Hawaiian kingdom was declared by the French and British Governments. Since 1840 the Government has been on the model of our own, namely, King, Lords, and Commons, and the result, as we might expect is that good order prevails everywhere, His Majesty ruling over a happy and contended people. (Loud cheering). The first missionaries to Hawaii came from the United States, in 1820. The nation had just cast off the religion of their ancestors, and so were in a favourable position to adopt Christianity. Since that time great progress has been made, and now it is the proud boast of their teachers that the Hawaiian people are ahead of all those western nations which pride themselves on their civilisation in the proportion to the total population of those who can read and write. In 1861 an English Bishopric was established in Honolulu, the capital of the kingdom, and now wherever there are inhabitants there are schools and chapels. The Kanakas, as the natives are called, are admitted the finest and most intelligent race of the pacific. In our Glasgow Royal Exchange there is the statistical director of Hawaii. I have also seen their newspapers – of course they are printed in English, which I understand almost everyone speaks there, and, indeed, is the language in which at least all business transactions are conducted. I might enlarge upon the advancement of the nation in everything, that recommends it to us if time permitted, but it would be thought by His Majesty to be rather singular that in commercial Glasgow an auience (audience) should require to be instructed in the importance of the kingdom over which he reigns. No doubt the western seaboard of the United States has the largest intercourse, but Hawaii is on the direct Pacific route from San Francisco to Australia and New Zealand, and is, indeed, the stopping place of steamers on that now well-frequented passage. I am sure I can truly say to His Majesty that it is felt by us as representing the city of Glasgow to be a great privilege to have had the opportunity of showing His Majesty any little attention which may have been in our power, and to express to him our desire, which we believe to be the earnest desire of the whole nation, that those cordial relations which have hitherto subsisted betwixt the Government of this country and his own may continue as long as the nations exist. (Loud cheers).

His Majesty KING KALAKAUA, who was enthusiastically received, in replying said – My Lord Provost and gentlemen, I must thank you all for the kind manner in which you have received and drunk my health. I feel very much flattered at the demonstration and expression of good-fellowship and feeling that has been displayed towards me tonight. Most thankful do I feel to the Lord Provost for having given so long a description of the condition, resources, and prosperity of my kingdom. There is nothing, I think, I can say beyond what he has said, which is all quite true, and indicates that he has read up a good deal regarding the country. I may add this, however, that at the first construction of our kingdom we had the advice and assistance of the people of Scotland – that is to say, we have had Scotsmen in the administration of the Government. (Applause.) Since the first construction of our Government as a political body we have had Scotsmen at the head of the judicial work, which is the highest, the most reliable, and the most important department in the political organization of my kingdom; and in almost all the other departments there seems to be a Scotsman always at the head. (Loud applause). We have not only Scotsmen at the head of affairs, but we have a Caledonian Club and a St George's Club, both organized by Scotsmen. In fact, of the members of my family a Scotsman is one. (Loud applause.) Besides our political connection we have been very much indebted to the people of Scotland, not only for their connection in commerce, but for supplying us with machinery, which has been the means of adding a great deal to the prosperity of my kingdom – (applause) –not only machinery for the manufacture of sugar, but also for steamships in bringing commerce and navigation to my country; and in that we are indebted to two or three gentlemen who are present tonight – Mr Pearce of the firm of Messrs Elder & Son – (loud applause) – also to Messrs Mirrlees, Tait & Watson – (applause) – and to the firm of Messrs Macfarlane, and I may say to many more I do not know at present. (Applause.) indeed, taking it all in all, I have more or less to acknowledge our indebtedness to Scotland and to the Scotch people. (Loud applause.) With these few words I would like to thank you again for having granted me that great privilege and honour of being invited to such an assembly of distinguished and wise men I see before me. (Loud and continued applause.)

The Hon. CHAIRMAN submitted the toast of the health of "The Prince and Princess of Wales and the other members of the Royal Family," which was drunk with enthusiasm.

Mr JAMES KING proposed the toast of "The Army, Navy, and Reserve Forces."

Liet. ROUCHERSKY, of the Russian navy, replied on behalf of the Navy, and Capt GARLAND, of the British Rrmy, on behalf of the Army.

Sir WILLIAM COLLINS proposed "The Houses of Parliament," and

Sir JAMES WATSON gave the toast of "The Clergy of Scotland."

Rev. Dr RAMAGE replied for the latter, and submitted the sentiment "Increased Concord among the Nations," which was responded to warmly.

Mr PETER CLOUSTON proposed the health of "The Lord Provost and Magistrates of Glasgow."

The Hon. CHAIRMAN replied, and the company afterwards adjourned to another portion of the Galleries, where views at Honolulu and other places in their guest's domains were exhibited.

It has been arranged by Mr Watson that to-day the King will sail up Loch Lomond in the specially-chartered steamer Prince Consort, along with a company of ladies and gentlemen. A special train from Queen Street at 9:30 a.m. will convey the King, his suite, and Mr. Watson's guests to Balloch, and after sailing up the Loch the King and his suite will cross over to Arrochar, where they will join Mr. Pearce's yacht, and in her come up the Clyde to Glasgow. The King will take his departure to-morrow morning for Edinburgh, where, as formerly mentioned, he will be the guest of Mr R. A. Macfie of Dreghorn. it is expected that the Ding will visit the Castle and other places of interest in the city, and at two o'clock His Majesty will be entertained at a cake and wine luncheon by the Edinburgh Corporation in the Council Chambers.

The Glasgow Herald, September 8, 1881, page 4

The Court

Sir E.J. Reed, K.C.B., M.P., and Mr. Robert Follet Synge, of the Foreign Office, arrived at the Grand Hotel yesterday morning. Mr. Synge is in attendance on His Majesty the King of the Sandwich Islands.

The Glasgow Herald, September 9, 1881, page 6

The Glasgow Herald.

99th YEAR, No. 216   PUBLISHED DAILY   Price ONE PENNY

King Kalakaua's Visit to Glasgow

Yesterday morning His Majesty King Kalakaua, accompanied by Mr. W. Renny-Watson and a party of friends, left Queen Street station, Glasgow, by special train for Balloch. At this point the steamer Prince of Wales was awaiting the party to covey them up Lochlomond. This portion of the journey was much enjoyed by His Majesty, who was able to view the beauties of the loch under the most favourable conditions. After partaking of luncheon the party landed at Tarbet, where they were met by Mr. Caird of Finnart, who kindly placed his carriage at the disposal of His Majesty. The party drove across to Arrochar, and on the way stopped at the little churchyard where the remains of the Macfarlanes are said to rest. The spot seemed specially interesting to the King's aide–de-camp, Colonel Macfarlane, and, that gentleman remained so long examining the ancient monuments that His Majesty jocularly asked him whether he meant to leave his remains there. On reaching Arrochar the party drove down the side of Loch Long to Finnart, where they joined the yacht of Mr. Wm. Pearce of Messrs John Elder & Co. Sailing down Loch Long, the yacht took a turn opposite Blairmore, and then crossed in order to show His Majesty the entrance to the Firth. After this the yacht was headed for Princes' pier, Greenock, which was reached about five o'clock. The King then entered the special train which the Glasgow and South-Western Company had in waiting and Glasgow was reached about six o'clock. In the evening Mr. Watson entertained His Majesty to dinner, and to which the Lord Dean of Guild and Mrs. Merrilees and Mr. and Mrs. Caird, of Finnart, and a number of private friends were invited. His Majesty expressed expressed himself thoroughly pleased with the excursion, and made special mention of the pleasure which he experienced while cruising about on Loch Lomond. We understand the King will leave Glasgow by the ten o'clock express from Queen Street, and that he will be met at Edinburgh by Mr. R.A. Macfie, of Dreghorn, and at whose house he will reside during his stay in the metropolis.

The Glasgow Herald, September 9, 1881, page 7

The Glasgow Herald.

99th YEAR, No. 217 — PUBLISHED DAILY — Price ONE PENNY

King Kalakaua, of the Sandwich Islands, left Glasgow yesterday morning for Edinburgh, where he visited the Castle, Holyrood Palace, and other places of interest, and was entertained to cake and wine by the Lord Provost and Magistrates. In the evening, a diner party was given by Mr Macfie of Dreghorn Castle in honour of His Majesty, who will leave Edinburgh to-day for Rufford Hall, where he will be the guest of Sir Thomas Hesketh. From thence he goes to Liverpool, and will sail for Honolulu on Tuesday.

King Kalakaua In Edinburgh

After a brief stay in Glasgow, King Kalakaua arrived at the Waverly Station, Edinburgh, yesterday morning at 11.40, having traveled in a saloon carriage by the ordinary fast train from Queen Street Station. his Majesty was attended by Colonel the Hon. Hastings Judd, Chamberlain to His Majesty, and Mr Robert Follett Synge, Her Majesty's representative from the Foreign Office. On the train drawing up the Royal visitor was received by Mr R. A. Macfie of Dreghorn Castle, Sir Thomas M'Clure, M.P. for Londonderry County; Dr Bishop, Mr Paton, stationmaster; and Mr Carswell, C.E., engineer of the North British Railway. Before His Majesty entered Mr Macfie's carriage that gentleman's grand-daughter presented him with a beautiful bouquet of flowers with the word "Aloha," the Hawaiian for welcome, neatly wrought out in flowers on the top. The party immediately drove off to Edinburgh Castle, where they were received by Colonel Macpherson, of the 42d Highlanders. On leaving the Castle the party drove to Parliament House and inspected the Advocate's Library, and from thence, accompanied by Mr J J. Reid, the Queen's Remembrancer, proceeded to Holyrood Palace and were shown through the Royal apartments, the picture gallery, the Chapel Royal, and other places associated with the earlier times of Scottish history. From Holyrood His Majesty drove by Regent road to the Register House and seemed much interested by the description given him of the nature of the work conducted there. Thence he proceeded along Princess Street to the New Club, where he was to have been the guest of Mr Purvis of Kinaldy. That gentleman, however, had been detained by an accident and, in his absence, Colonel Craige-Halkett entertained His Majesty and party.

Reception At The Council Chamber

From the Club King Kalakaua, accompanied by Colonel Judd, Mr Synge, and Mr R. A. Macfie, proceeded to the Council Chamber, where His Majesty was received by the Right Honourable Sir Thomas J. Boyd, Lord Provost, and the Magistrates. Cake and wine were provided, and among the guests present, besides the members of Council, were Lord Belhaven, Lord Deas, Sir Jas. Gardiner Baird, Bart.; Admiral Sir Alexander Milne, Bart.; Professor Sir Wyville Thomson, Mr J. Dick-Peddie, M.P.; Dr Henderson, Provost of Leith; Mr Keir, Provost of Musselburgh; Mr Hunter, Provost of Portabello; Professor Archer, Archbishop Strain, the various Consuls, Mr Skinner, Town-Clerk; Mr Harris, Deputy Town-Clerk, &c. Among those from whom apologies for absence were received were the Right Hon. the Lord-Advocate, Right Hon. the Lord Provost of Glasgow, Lord Moncreiff, Sir Noel Paton, Sir Wm. Bailie, Bart.; Sir Wm. Johnston, Colonel Morrison, Colonel Preston, C.B.; the Rev. Dr Lecs, and others.

The LORD PROVOST. in proposing the health of King Kalakaua, said – I am sure we are all delighted to see here to-day His Hawaiian Majesty, King Kalakaua, who has honoured us with his presence – (applause) – and in the name of the Corporation of this ancient city and of the people generally I give His Majesty a cordial welcome to the capital of Scotland. Since His Majesty's arrival in this country our attention has been drawn more than formerly to the kingdom over which His Majesty rules, consisting of the rich, interesting, and beautiful group of the Sandwich Islands, in the center of the Pacific Ocean; and especially we are please to think of the vast progress in civilisation which their people have made during the present century. (Hear, hear, and applause) In the last seven years, when His Majesty has been King, further progress has been made, and during that time great material prosperity has been also experienced in a largely increased revenue. From what we know of these islands in former times, well may those who pay them a visit be struck with what they see there now. Honolulu, the metropolis and principal seaport of the group, is quite a place of active commercial enterprise. It has its shops, its warehouses and public buildings, and its churches. Then there are comfortable hotels, and newspapers for the breakfast table. (Applause.) And Honolulu, besides being this centre of trade, is also the seat of Government, and in it there are Consuls from Great Britain, from America, and from many other countries throughout the world. Then the Ministry is composed of persons who are responsible for their actions, and the Legislature passes laws which affect natives and people of other countries alike, without respect of persons. I am not here, however, either to describe these charming islands of Polynesia or to make a speech, but to give His Hawaiian Majesty, in your name, a most cordial and hearty welcome to Edinburgh. I have now the honour to propose that we should drink to the health of King Kalakaua, and wish him much happiness and every blessing. We must all greatly admire the public spirit and love of his people's good which has been shown by His Majesty thus going through the world in their best interests. (Applause.) I trust His Majesty will enjoy his short visit among us and of this I am sure that, go where he may, he will nowhere see a more beautiful city or a more quiet and orderly people.

The toast was warmly honoured.

HIS MAJESTY, who was received with cheers, said – My Lord Provost, my Lords, and Gentlemen, I feel deeply gratified at the manner in which you have drank my health. I must thank the Lord Provost for having given so vivid a description of my country. I assure you my people will feel very much gratified with the expression of esteem you have conferred upon me to-day. (Applause.) What the Lord Provost has said in regard to the improvements in my country is quite true. We have advanced a little, but not so much perhaps as he has described. I appreciate very highly the sentiments he has expressed in regard not only to myself but also to my country. (Applause.) Edinburgh can boast of its literary institutions, its sciences, its arts – and I can verify all her boast from what I have seen to-day – be: statues, her ancient monuments, and her historical places of note. (Applause.) I only regret that my short stay in Edinburgh will not allow me to enjoy very long the hospitalities which you have to-day shown your willingness to give me. (Applause.)

LORD DEAS proposed "The health of the Lord Provost," and expressed himself indebted to his Lordship for enabling him to be present at so interesting a meeting.

The LORD PROVOST suitably replied, and the proceedings terminated. The band and pipers of the 42d Highlanders were stationed in the quadrangle, and played a selection of music.

Immediately after leaving the Council Chamber King Kalakaua and party visited St Giles Cathedral and the University, and then drove to Dreghorn Castle, where in the evening a dinner party was given by Mr Macfie in honour of His Majesty. Weather permitting His Majesty will to-day visit Roslin and inspect the Chapel, and on returning to Edinburgh will drive to the Botanic Gardens. In the afternoon he is expected to leave Edinburgh for Rufford Hall, where he will be the guest of Sir Thomas Hesketh. Thence he goes to Liverpool, where he will be entertained to dinner by the Mayor; and from Liverpool His Majesty sails on Tuesday for Honolulu.

The Glasgow Herald, September 10, 1881, page 4

`Upoho Uka Nui `O Kekokia

The Glasgow Herald.

King Kalakaua In Edinburgh

His Majesty, the King of Hawaii, before leaving Edinburgh on Saturday, was the principal actor in an interesting ceremony which took place in the Free Masons' Hall. On leaving Dreghorn Castle, where he was the guest of Mr. Macfie, His Majesty, accompanied by Sir Thomas and Lady M'Clure, Mr. and Mrs. Macfie, Colonel Judd, Colonel Macfarlane, A.D.C., and Dr. Bishop proceeded to Edinburgh by Morningside, and drove through the Queen's park, and thence to the Free Masons' Hall in George Street. Here a grand conclave of the Knights of the Red Cross of Constantine had assembled to confer the dignity of the Knight Grand Cross of the Order on His Majesty. King Kalakaua having been received by the Recorder of the Order, Brother R.S. Brown, and Brother Murray Lyon, the conclave was opened under the presidency of Captain John Crombie, Aberdeen, Acting Grand Sovereign, in the absence of the Earl of Kintore. His Majesty was introduced to the conclave by the Sovereign, who presented him with a copy of the constitution of the order and the Star of the Knight Grand Cross. Brother Crombie's remarks were supplemented by the Acting Viceroy, Sir Knight James Crichton, who offered His Majesty the rank of honorary membership of the Edinburgh Conclave No. 1. King Kalakaua in reply referred to the cordial reception he had met with in this country, and said he appreciated no honour that had been conferred on him more than that he had now received. He would ever retain a lively recollection of his visit to the Freemasons' Hall, and to the meeting of the Grand Conclave. He accepted the honorary membership of the Edinburgh Conclave No. 1, and would regard it as an additional tie between himself and this country, so famous in masonry. Before leaving, His Majesty accepted portraits of Sir Michael Shaw Stewart, Grand Master of Scotland; and of the Earl of Kintore, Grand Sovereign of the Red Cross Order. The King then went by way of Charlotte Square (where he obtained a view of the Prince Consort statue) to the residence of Dr. Bishop, 12 Walker Street. Luncheon having been partaken of, the King drove to the Caledonian Railway Station, and proceeded at 2:25 p.m. in one of the London and North-Western Royal saloon carriages for Rufford Hall, the seat of Sir Thomas Hesketh, Bart. The King was received at the station by the Lord Provost; and amongst others who accompanied His Majesty to the platform were Sir Thomas M'Clure,

Bart., M.P., and Lady M'Clure; Mr. and Mrs. Macfie of Dreghorn, and Dr. and Mrs. Bishop. A large crowd assembled at the station, and gave His Majesty a hearty cheer on leaving. His Majesty has conferred on Mrs. Bishop (Miss. Bird), authoress of "Six Months in the Hawaiian Archipelago," the Literary Order of Kapiolanie (sic), with the jewel and decoration and miniature of Queen Kapiolanie (sic), which is an Order instituted by His Majesty.

The Glasgow Herald, September 12, 1881, page 4

`Upoho Uka Nui `O Kekokia – 𝄞 – 311

The Glasgow Herald.

99th YEAR, No. 219 — PUBLISHED DAILY — Price ONE PENNY

KING KALAKAUA IN LIVERPOOL. – The King of the Sandwich Islands paid a visit to Liverpool yesterday. He arrived at Rufford Park, the seat of Sir Thomas Hesketh, on Saturday night, and yesterday morning he left by train for the Exchange Station, Liverpool, reaching there at noon. The King was received by the Mayor (Mr W. B. Forwood) and the Hawiian (sic) Consul (Mr Jamon), and was taken to St George's Hall, the Free Library, the Picton Reading-Room, and the Art Gallery. After being entertained by the Mayor at luncheon he went to the river in the Dock Board tender *Alert*, accompanied by Mr T. D. Hornby, chairman of the Mersey Dock Board, and subsequently he visited the Exchange News-Room. In the evening His Majesty was entertained by the Mayor at dinner at the Town Hall. He leaves for New York today in the White Star steamer *Celtic*.

The Glasgow Herald, September 13, 1881, page 5

The Glasgow Herald.

| 99th YEAR, No. 220 | PUBLISHED DAILY | Price ONE PENNY |

KING KALAKAUA. – King Kalakaua left Liverpool for New york yesterday by the White Star steamer *Celtic*.

The Glasgow Herald, September 14, 1881, page 7

`Upoho Uka Nui `O Kekokia – 313

THE BAILIE

THE BAILIE

Chance throws us among strange bedfellows. Such must have been Mr. Pearce's opinion at the banquet to King Kalakaua in the Corporation Galleries last Wednesday evening, when he found himself "sandwiched" between Councillor John Neil and Mr. Irwin, of Govan Parochial Board fame. In a manner neglected by the powers at the head of the room, "the greatest shipbuilder in the world" evidently felt quite at home, and chatted away gaily with "Johnny," who proved to be a most attentive listener.

Another grouping, not less interesting in a way, was that of Councillor Jackson and his editorial chief, Mr. Stoddart of the Herald.

— o —

The very lengthy menu card of the Kalakaua banquet, drawn out in elegant French, must have puzzled not a few of our municipal rulers, of whom the company was mainly composed; and many must have been the appeals to the waiters for the plain English of this, that, and the other dish. The dinner itself was a chef d'oeuvre of the culinary art, and the fact that the eating lasted over two hours is an eloquent testimony to the number and variety of the courses provided by Messrs Ferguson & Forrester. And the wines! Ma conscience! To one or two present, indeed, the dinner and its accompaniments was as trying to their stomachs as the card had been to their brains, and it is reported that an ex-occupant of the civic chair had to beat a hasty retreat from the table.

The chief fun of the evening, however, was provided by the magic lantern which the Corporation provided by the magic lantern which the Corporation provided for the delectation of the King of the Sandwich Islands!

— o —

Disregarding the warnings of the past, Granny has been going in for unknown tongues again. The other day she talked about a *recerche* (sic) *dejeuner* having been given to King Kalakaua in the evening! We shall presently have the "Tuscan Tongue" trotted out once more?

The Bailie, September 14, 1881, page 5

PACIFIC COMMERCIAL ADVERTISER

PACIFIC COMMERCIAL ADVERTISER

HONOLULU, HAWAII   October 29, 1881   WHOLE NO. 1326

TUESDAY, SEP. 6 – In the afternoon His Majesty accompanied by the officers of his staff, paid a farewell visit to their Royal Highnesses the Prince and princess of Wales at Marlborough House. Among those who have called upon the King at Claridge's, during this last visit to London; have been Count Steenbock, Mr. W.W. Follett Synge, late Her Majesty's Commissioner in the Hawaiian Islands, Mr. A. Hoffnung, Baroness Burdett Coutts and Mr. Burdett Coutts Bartlett, Lieutenant General Sir Dighton Probyn and Colonel Teesdale of the Prince of Wales' household, to express thanks, His Excellency M. d'Antas, Portuguese Minister; Manley Hopkins, Consul-General; R.W. Janlon, Vice Counsul, for Hawaii in London, Dr. H.J. Billing and Lieutenant W.M. Synge, R.A., Mr. R.F. Synge, was relieved from attendance on His Majesty until after the funeral of his uncle, General Synge, who died two days ago, but he will join the King again in Scotland. At half past 9, His Majesty and suite left St. Pancras station by Midland express for Glasgow.

The King In Glasgow
(*Scottish American Journal*, New York)
A Warm Tribute To Scotsmen

On the 7th Sept. the King of the Sandwich Islands visited Glasgow. He was met by Councillor W. Renny Wilson, and by him was escorted through several of the leading shipbuilding yards and other works. In the evening the King was entertained at dinner by the Magistrates. Lord Provost Uro presided, supported by a distinguished company. In responding to the toast of his health the King said: –

"My Lord Provost and Gentlemen, – I must thank you all for the kind manner in which you have received and drank my health. I feel very much flattered at the demonstration and expression of good fellowship and feeling that has been displayed towards me tonight. Most thankful do I feel to the Lord Provost for having given so long a description of the condition, resources, and prosperity of my kingdom. There is nothing, I think, I can say beyond what he has said, which is all quite true, and indicates that he has read up a good deal regarding my country. I may add this, however, that at the first construction of our kingdom we had the advice and assistance of the people of Scotland – that is to say, we have had Scotsmen in the administration of the Government. (Applause.) Since the first construction of our Government as a political body we have had Scotsmen at the head of the judicial work, which is the highest, and most reliable, and the most important department in the political organization of my kingdom; and in almost all the other departments there seems to be a Scotsman always at the head. (Loud applause.) We have not only Scotsmen at the head of affairs, but we have a Caledonian Club and a St. George's Club, both organized by Scotsmen. In fact, of the members of my family a Scotsman is one. (Loud applause.) Besides out political connection we have been very much indebted to the people of Scotland, not only for their connection in commerce, but supplying us with machinery, which has been the means of adding a great deal to the prosperity of my kingdom – (Applause.) – not only machinery for the manufacture of sugar, but also for steamships in bringing commerce and navigation to my country; and in that we are indebted to two or three gentlemen who are present tonight – Mr. Pierce, of the firm of Messrs. Elder & Son – (loud applause) – also to Messrs. Mirrlees, Tait & Watson – (applause.) – and to the firm of Messrs. Macfarlane, and I may say to many more I do not know at present. (Applause.) Indeed, taking it all in all, I have more or less to acknowledge our indebtedness to Scotland and the Scotch people. (Loud applause.) With these few words I thank you again for having granted me this great privilege and honor of being invited to such an assembly of distinguished and wise men as I see before me. (Loud and continued applause.)

On the following day King Kalakaua visited Loch Lomond, and enjoyed a trip on the Clyde from Arrochar to Glasgow. On the 9th he left for Edinburgh, where he was warmly received by the Lord Provost and municipal officers, and under their pilotage visited the many objects in the city.

The King Of The Sandwich Islands In Edinburgh
The Scotsman

On Saturday, after breakfast, King Kalakaua walkin(sic) in the grounds of Dreghorn Castle,* and, in commemoration of his visit, planted two maple trees, naming them after Jenny Cowan Scott Macfie and Robert Andrew Scott Macfie, of Dreghorn, and niece and nephew of Mr. Cowan, M.P. About a quarter to twelve His Majesty took his departure from Dreghorn Castle, a piper playing through the reception hall to the carriage. As His Majesty drove off, the assembled servants gave a hearty farewell "aloha," which His Majesty courteously acknowledged. The Royal party – consisting of the King, Colonel the Hon. Hastings Judd, Chamberlain; Colonel G.W. Macfarlane, A.D.C.; Mr. Robert Follett Synge; Mr. and Mrs. Macfie, of Dreghorn; Lady M'Clure; and Dr. Bishop – drove in two carriages by way of Hunters Tryst avenue and Comiston, to Fairmile Health toll, at which they turned towards Edinburgh. They drove by the Borestone at Morningside, and proceeded along by the Grange Cemetery, passed into the Queen's park at the Messrs. Nelson's works. Driving to Samson's Ribs, the party returned to the higher drive, went around Arthur Seat by Dunsapple, and passing Holyrood (where the guard turned out a presented arms as the King's party passed) proceeded by Regent Road to the Freemasons' Hall via St. Andrews Square. For almost the first time during His Majesty's brief stay here, the sun shone brilliantly, and the city looked at its best. The atmosphere being clear, the party had the pleasure of witnessing the magnificent view which the Queen's Drive commands in all directions; and here, we believe, the King expressed regret that he had not been able to allow himself more time in Scotland.

King Kalakaua was expected at noon in the Royal Botanic Gardens, and preparations were made for his planting a Thuja Gigantea (gigantic arbor vine of California). Professor Dickson, regius keeper; Prof. Balfour, ex-regius keeper; Mr. J. Sadler, curator; and Mr. Isaac Anderson Henry, of Hay Lodge, awaited the arrival of His Majesty, and a number of people loitered about the gardens in the hope that they might see the illustrious stranger. Between 12 and 1 o'clock, however, a telegram was received from Mr. R.A. Macfie, of Dreghorn, stating that King Kalakaua was so much fatigued that he would have to forego the pleasure of the Gardens.

Ceremony In Freemasons' Hall

The Freemasons' Hall was reached about 1 o'clock, and His Majesty, as he entered, was respectfully saluted and loudly cheered. The object of the visit was to attend a special meeting of the Grand Conclave of Scotland of the Order of the Red Cross of Constantine, which had resolved to confer on His Majesty the rank of Knight Grand Cross of the Order. There was a large attendance of brethren, among those present being the following members of the Grand Council, viz.:– Captain John Crombie, Aberdeen, Grand Senior General, Acting Grand Sovereign in the unavoidable absence of the Earl of Kintore; James Crichton, Grand Junior General, Acting Grand Viceroy; Robert S. Brown, Grand Recorder; James Dalrymple Duncan, Glasgow, Grand Standard Bearer; James B. Mercer, Past Grand Chancellor; and the following members of the Grand Senate Viz: William Milne, Captain A.M. Bruce, James Melville, Sir Molyneux H. Nepean, Bart.; Francis Law., and F.W. Roberts; also

William Mann, S.S.C., P.G. Wardon; D. Murray Lyon, Grand Secretary, Grand Lodge of Scotland; Councillor Alexander Henry, G.S. Ferrier, J. Fleming, P.R. Haddow, W. Hamilton, J.H.M. Bairnsfather, S.S.B.; etc., etc.

His Majesty was received by the Grand Recorder, and by the Grand Secretary of the Grand Lodge of Scotland, Brother D. Murray Lyon, by whom he was conducted to the anteroom, where he signed the attendance book of the Grand Council, and the Visitors' Book of the Grand Lodge of Scotland. The Conclave was opened under the presidency of Captain John Crombie. His Majesty having been introduced to the Conclave, and received under the arch of steel, the Acting Grand Sovereign, addressing His Majesty, then said: " The members of the Grant Imperial Council of Scotland are very much gratified at having the pleasure of meeting your Majesty here today, and conferring upon you the highest honor they have it in their power to bestow; and they have desired me to convey to your Majesty their grateful sense of your courtesy in allowing your name to be added to the roll of Knights Grand Cross of Scotland. I regret exceedingly that the Grand Sovereign of the Order, the Right Hon. the Earl of Kintore, has been prevented from attending and personally conferring this distinction upon you. As your Majesty's time is very limited, and as we heartily concur in every word said by the Lord Provost of Edinburgh at the meeting yesterday, I shall only detain you to say that we all join – and every Freemason in Scotland when he reads of the event of today will join-in earnest and heartfelt prayer to our Omnipotent Ruler, the Great Architect of the Universe, that every blessing and happiness may attend your Majesty through life, that you may have a safe and pleasant return to your Kingdom that your reign there may be long and prosperous, and that you may continue to take a warm interest in, manifest a zeal for, and be a credit and ornament to the craft we all love so dearly." The King was then presented with a copy of the statutes of the Council, which he pledged himself to obey. The Acting Sovereign, in investing him with the Grand Cross, further said: "In the name and by special authority of the Grand Council of the Order, I now invest you with the jewel of a Knight Grand Cross of the Imperial Council of Scotland; and may I venture to express the hope that the jewel and the patent, which the Grant Recorder will forward in a few days, may sometimes recall to your mind your visit to Scotland, where thousands of Freemasons who have never seen your Majesty's face, but know your great talents as a Mason, and the high position you have attained in the craft, extend to your Majesty their fraternal feelings of esteem and love, and will be highly gratified to find that those feelings are reciprocated by your Majesty?" The Acting Viceroy, Brother James Crichton, in appropriate terms, then offered His Majesty honorary membership of the Edinburgh Conclave, No. 1.

His Majesty, in graciously intimating his acceptance of these honors, referred to the cordial reception he had met with during his visit to

Scotland. No honor which he had received would be more appreciated that that which had been conferred upon him by the Grand Council. He would ever retain a lively recollection of his visit to the Freemasons' Hall, and it would give him great pleasure to convey to the brethren in Honolulu, of whom there was a large number, an account of the hearty reception he had received from the Grand Imperial Council of Scotland. He had also much pleasure in accepting the honorary membership of the Edinburgh Conclave, No. 1, which he regarded as an additional Masonic tie between himself and this country, so famous in Masonry. (Applause.)

His Majesty then signed the roll of membership of Conclave No. 1. After the ceremony His Majesty's health was drunk with great enthusiasm, and afterwards His Majesty departed amid the acclamations of the assembled brethren. Among those who had the honor of being introduced to His Majesty were – William Mann, S.S.C., Past Senior Grand Warden of the Grand Lodge of Scotland; Sir Molyneux Nepean, Bart.; Councillor henry; and Dr. Loth, who represented a copy of his work on the Ancient and Accepted Scottish Rite. Before his departure His Majesty graciously accepted the portraits of Sir Michael Shawl Stewart, Grant Master Mason of Scotland; and of the Earl of Kintore, Grand Sovereign of the Red Cross Order. His Majesty also accepted a copy of "The Grand Lodge of Scotland Galop" by Francis Law. Letters of apology were received from the Earl of Kintore, Grand Sovereign; Capt. Charles Hunter, Grand Viceroy; the Rev. T.N. Wannop, Grand High Prelate; J.H. Balfour, W.S., Grand Marshall; and Col. J. Todd Stewart, Glasgow, Grand Chamberlain.

As on his arrival, the departure of His Majesty from the Freemasons' Hall was witnessed by a large crowd, who again raised a hearty cheer.

Departure Of The King

After leaving the Freemasons' Hall, His Majesty drove by way of Charlotte Square (where he obtained a view of the Prince Consort statue) to the residence of Dr. Bishop, 12 Walker street. Here his Majesty was entertained at luncheon, the other members of the company being Sir Thomas and Lady M'Clure, Mr. and Mrs. Macfie, of Dreghorn, Colonel the Hon. Hastings Judd, Chamberlain to the King, Colonel G.W. Macfarlane, A.D.C.; and Mr. Robert Follett Synge, representative of the Foreign Office in attendance upon His Majesty. After luncheon the King drove to the Caledonian Railway Station, and proceeded at 2:25 p.m. in one of the London and North-western royal saloon carriages for Rufford Hall, the seat of Sir Thomas Hesketh. The carriage was attached to the ordinary train by the west coast route, but, through the liberality of the railway company, was to be run special from Preston to avoid His

Majesty being detained waiting an hour and a half at the station there. The arrangements for the departure of the train were superintended by Mr. Irons, stationmaster. The King was received at the station by the Lord Provost; and amongst others who accompanied His Majesty to the platform were Sir Thomas and Lady M'Clure, Mr. and Mrs. Macfie, and Dr. and Mrs. Bishop. A large crowd assembled at the station, and, respectfully saluting His Majesty on arrival, gave him a hearty cheer on leaving. His Majesty courteously acknowledged the enthusiasm of the crowd and seemed especially touched by the "Alohas" and the "Hurrahs" which were raised as the train moved off from the platform. The King before leaving, entered into conversation with several ladies and gentlemen on the platform, and expressed himself highly pleased with the heartiness of the reception given to him in Scotland. He was, it may further be mentioned, particularly gratified with the respect everywhere shown him while driving about, hats being everywhere lifted by pedestrians on His Majesty being recognized.

> * DREGHORN CASTLE. – The following description of the Castle, written by Prof. Frank W. Damon, we clip from the *Friend* of July: – "The Castle of Dreghorn stands on cugying slopes of Pentlands, an hour or so from Edinburgh. It is a fine spacious edifice, partly covered with ivy, with tower and turrets and arches, strong and stately, and gray without and bright with all cheer and home-beauty within. It has seen the Pentlands changing from brown and green for something like two hundred Springs. Glorious Stretches of woodland lead you off on either side, while down the murmuring stream in the hallow below sweep away the greenest of the meadows, with here and there stately drooping trees and varied with wandering white-wooled sheep and capering lambs. Passing down the long drive you come to the ancient "Lodge," with its stone turrets half smothered in a wealth of the richest ivy. Still farther on are the cottages of the tenantry and the village of Collington down in the valley or clinging amid the trees to the hillside. And what a magnificent reach of country spreads itself out before you on every side. There in the foreground, like some mighty gulf of tendered green, lighted by bursts of splendid April sunshine, and deepened by the shadows of drifting clouds, lies a superb forest ridged, village dotted plain. And there beyond this, where the sun comes out and the clouds part at its coming, may be seen still, motionless in its verdant setting, like a silver mirror the Firth of Forth in the distance."

Arrival At and Departure From Liverpool

This morning His Majesty proceeds to Liverpool, where the Mayor is to devote the day in showing the King the docks and public works, and preside in the evening at a farewell banquet in his Majesty's honor. The King will set sail tomorrow in one of the White Star steamers for new York, and, after spending a few days in the Eastern States, proceed to California, sailing from San Francisco for home. During his absence the Government is being conducted by the Princess Liliuokalani, the heir apparent to the throne.

The impression formed of the King by those who have had the opportunity of conversing with him is one of a very favorable character. His manner and deportment are, it is said, those of a thoroughly well-bred gentleman. He is very affable, while retaining the natural dignity befitting his position. Possessed of remarkable conversational powers, he expresses himself well in English with a slight foreign accent. He is acute in his criticisms, which manifest culture or originality of thought, and when speaking of his travels shows that he is keen sighted, and has received impressions which are not likely to be lost in furthering the comfort and happiness of the people over whom it is his lot to rule.

(For fuller particulars in relation to His Majesty's visit to Liverpool, see our European correspondent's letter, No. 66.–ED. P.C.A.)

A Hawaiian Honor

King Kalakaua has conferred on Mrs. Bishop (formerly Miss. Bird) authoress of "Six Month's in the Hawaiian Archipelago," the Literary Order of Kapiolani, with the jewel and decoration, including a miniature of Queen Kapiolani. This order is one which the King himself initiated, and its latest recipient is one who by her writings has done much to interest the inhabitants of Great Britain and America in the Hawaiian Islands.

The King At Liverpool – Departure For New York. Letter No. 66

London, September 14.

Yesterday the King bade farewell to Europe, and sailed from Liverpool for America.

On Monday morning, Sep. 12th, His Majesty and suite (Mr. Synge, Colonel Judd, Colonel Macfarlane, and Herr Von Ochlhaffen) left Rufford Park (the seat of Sir Thomas Hesketh) by train, for Liverpool, and arrived at the the Exchange Station of the Lancashire and Yorkshire Railroad at noon. The King was received by the Mayor, Mr. W.B. Forwood; the Hawaiian Consul, Mr. Janion; the Hawaiian Commissioner, Mr. Hoffnung, and other officials. A large crowd had assembled at the station, who greeted the King on his arrival with hearty British cheers. The Mayor placed four State carriages at His Majesty's disposal for himself and his suite, and then drove to St. George's Hall, where the King was tendered the hospitality of the city of Liverpool by the Mayor. Visits were then paid to the Free Library, the Picton Reading Rooms, and the Walker Art Gallery. After inspecting the prominent buildings, His Majesty was entertained by the Mayor at luncheon at the Town Hall, a number of public men of Liverpool being also present. In the afternoon the King and attendants made a trip up the Mersey on the Dock Board tender Alert, specifically placed at his disposal by Mr. T.D. Hornby, chairman of the Mersey Dock Board, who, with a large number of invited guests, accompanied His Majesty. A band on board performed a musical selection during the excursion, and many of the vessels in the river raised their bunting in honor of the King. On his return from the river trip, His Majesty paid a visit to the Commercial Chambers and the Exchange New Rooms, and then drove to the North-western Hotel, where apartments had been prepared for the royal party. In the evening His Majesty honored the Mayor with his presence at a State dinner at the Town Hall. On this occasion the King wore the Star of the Order of St. Michael and St. George, and the Grand Cross of Kamehameha I. Colonel Macfarlane (having just received his promotion and appointment) wore his new order as Knight Companion of the Kamehameha Order; and Colonel Judd's breast was resplendent with the numerous decorations conferred on him by foreign rulers. The toasts to the health of King Kalakaua, and to the prosperity of his Kingdom, was received with great enthusiasm; and His Majesty replied in his usual appropriate and felicitous manner.

Tuesday, Sept. 13th, the King and his suite were conveyed in the Mayor's State carriage from the hotel to the landing stage, where an immense crowd had assembled to witness his departure from Old England. The Mayor drove down to the landing to bid adieu to the King, who expressed his gratification with his reception in Liverpool. A special tender took the King out to the White Star steamship Celtic, Captain Gleadell. His Majesty was accompanied to the steamer by Mr. R.W. Janion (Hawaiian Consul), and Mrs. and Miss. Janion, Mr. Hoffnung, Mr. Watson of Glasgow, Mr. Macfie of Edinburgh, Sir Thomas Hesketh, Mr. Synge, Mr. Spreckels, Mr. W.L. Carpenter (who was also his fellow passenger on the City of Sydney from Honolulu to San Francisco in

January last), and a large number of ladies and gentlemen. Mrs. Janion and several other ladies presented the King with beautiful bouquets of flowers. On board of the Celtic's special accommodations had been made for His Majesty. The captain's room on the spar-deck amidships had been reserved, and tastefully fitted up as a royal sitting room and parlor; and the sleeping apartment, which is the first stateroom forward of the saloon, had been richly decorated. Among those who took leave of His Majesty on board of the Celtic was the Right Rev. Dr. Staley, for nearly ten years Bishop of Honolulu (in 1861-70), during which period (says the Times) Kalakaua, then highest chief in the Kingdom, was intimately associated with the Bishop in planting a branch of the Church of England in the Islands. "King Kalakaua (I still quote from the above paper) was its most distinguished lay member, grudging neither labour nor means in his devotion to the Church, in which he was confirmed and married by the Bishop Staley."

After a last farewell, the tender returned with all non-passengers, and just before 1 o'clock the steamer started on the voyage across the ocean, the Royal Standard of Hawaii floating proudly from the main masthead.

Brigham.

Pacific Commercial Advertiser, October 29, 1881, page 2

Appendix 2

Newspaper Account of Piper MacIntyre Playing for
Kamehameha III (1845)

`Upoho Uka Nui `O Kekokia – 331

THE POLYNESIAN

PUBLISHED WEEKLY, AT HONOLULU, OAHU, HAWAIIAN ISLANDS

| J. JARVIS, EDITOR. | Saturday, November 1, 1845 |

Court News

The Honorable Captain Gordon, of H.B.M.'s ship *America*, attended by three of his officers, and with the British Consul General, paid a friendly visit to the king last Tuesday.

His Majesty took occasion to express the pleasure he felt in making the acquaintance of the gallant captain as the brother of the Earl of Aberdeen, who had shown so much attention to his commissioners in London, and all whose communications had been so king and friendly, and requested the captain to make known to the noble Earl his sentiments of esteem.

The King added that he was much obliged to her grace the Duchess of Somerset, Sir Augustus d'Este, the Earl of Selkirk, the Right Honorable Edward Ellice, and other distinguished personages who had befriended his commissioners.

The gallant captain very courteously replied that he would have an opportunity of writing soon, and would make His Majesty's sentiments known to the Earl of Aberdeen.

Musical Soiree At The Palace – The Honorable Capt. Gordon, of H.B. M.'s ship *America*, had the kindness to send on shore, on Wednesday evening, for the entertainment of the king, his fine band, composed of about twenty well-trained musicians of an excellence in their art fat beyond any thing that had ever before been heard in Honolulu. MacIntyre, his Scotch Piper, struck up the wild and exciting strains of old Scotch martial airs, at half past 6 o'clock, and the band commenced soon afterwards, beginning with the national anthem, alternating with the piper in some very select and well executed pieces of music, till about 10 o'clock, when the national anthem was repeated, and the musicians retired.

His Majesty, desirous that others as well as himself, should partake of an entertainment which so seldom offers on his Islands, ordered that notice should be given to the principal residents and their families. Although the evening was cold, damp and stormy, there was a greater assemblage of the elite of Honolulu than had ever before been witnessed on any other similar occasion. Distinctions of nation, party and family, seemed to be lost in the general harmony and hilarity which prevailed.

To this, in no small degree, contributed the kind affability to all, of the King and Queen, the very courteous and polite bearing of the gallant Captain himself, and the pleasing influences which fine music never fails to produce.

After the missionary families had retired, dancing commenced with the reel of Tulloch-gorum, played by the piper; quadrilles, &c, followed to the music of the band.

MacIntyre, the Scotch Piper, in the romantic garb of Caledonia, was an object of great and universal interest. He played round the drawing rooms repeatedly during the evening, measuring his steps to to the time of the air that he was playing. The bagpipes and every article of his attire down to his dark kilt, garter, dirk, hose and buckles, excited the curiosity of the company. The good humored Highlander had often to stop to allow some part of his dress and equipment to be examined.

The piper belongs to Argyleshire, but he wore on the occasion the Gordon tartan, with silver buckles and shoulder ornaments richly chased. The Scotch cap and eagle's feather formed his head dress.

The kind courtesy to the King and chiefs of the honorable Capt. Gordon, upon this occasion, has reanimated the never forgotten impressions left by the earlier British navigators; and we know it was much appreciated by their Majesties, the King and Queen.

The foreigners of rank present were the Hon. Captain Gordon, with several of his officers, H.B.M.'s Consul General, the Consul of France with his lady, the Consul of the United States with his lady, and Mr. Marshall, the Consul for Peru.

Among those connected with the King's government present, were the following, viz: – the Premier of the Kingdom, with his lady, Parki(sic.. Paki), and other chiefs with their ladies, Dr. and Mrs. Rooke, Alexander, the heir apparent and the other young chiefs of both sexes, together with all His Majesties Ministers, Mrs. Judd, with three Misses Judd, Mrs. Richards and the two Misses Richards, Mr. Paty, the Collector of Customs and his lady, and a numerous staff of the King's officers, Mr. Hopkins, and Mr. Sea, the High Sheriff.

Among the ladies we remember, were – Mrs. Brewer, Mrs. Cooke, Mrs. Carter, Mrs. Castle, Miss Corney, Misses Chamberlain, Mrs. Dowsett, Miss E. Dowsett, Mrs. Domines, Mrs. Damon, Mrs. Diamond, Misses French, Mrs. Grimes, Mrs. Hoyer and daughter, Mrs. Hall, Mrs. Hitchcock, Mrs. Knapp, Miss Ogden, Mrs. Ricker, Mrs. Rogers, Mrs. Stevens, Mrs. Sumner, junior, Miss Whitney.

Among the gentlemen, we noticed the Rev. Mr. Armstrong, Mr. Brewer, jr., Mr. Brown, jr., Mr. Boardman, Dr. Blume, Mr. Carter, Mr. Cooke, Mr. Chamberlain, Rev. Mr. Damon, Mr. Douglass, Mr. French, Mr. Gillman, Mr. Gleason, Mr. Grimes, Mr. Hooper, Rev. Mr. Hitchcock, Mr. Hitchcock, Mr. hall, Capt. Hoyer, Mr. Hellrung, Mr. Janion, Captain Meek, Mr. Marpillero, Mr. Punchard, Mr. Reynolds, Mr. Rhodes, Mr.

Robinson, Mr. Rogers, Mr. Stevens, Mr. Suwerkroop, Captain Snow, and many others whose names were not familiar to us. The rooms were so crowded, that it is possible others were present whose names have escaped out notice.

The Polynesian, November 1, 1845

Appendix 3

Pipe Majors and Drum Majors
of Hawai`i's Pipe Bands

Drum Majors and Pipe Majors of Hawai`i's Pipe Bands

	Royal Scots		Honolulu Pipes & Drums aka: Johnny Walker Band aka: Budweiser Pipe Band *Royal Stewart Tartan*	
	Pipe Major	Drum Major	Pipe Major	Drum Major
1950's	Aggie Wallace			
1960's	Aggie Wallace			
1970	Aggie Wallace			
1971	Aggie Wallace			
1972	Aggie Wallace	Bill Morrison		
1973	David Furumoto	Bill Morrison		
1974	David Furumoto		Charles Anderson	Bill Morrison
1975	David Furumoto		Charles Anderson	Bill Morrison
1976	David Furumoto		David Guthries	Bill Morrison
1977	David Furumoto		David Guthries	Bill Morrison
1978	David Furumoto		A. J. Frappia	Bill Morrison
1979	David Furumoto		A. J. Frappia	Bill Morrison
1980	David Furumoto		A. J. Frappia	John Patella
1981	David Furumoto		David Furumoto	John Patella
1982			David Furumoto	John Patella
1983			David Furumoto	John Patella
1984			David Furumoto	John Patella
1985			David Furumoto	Ken Merrit
1986			Barbara Macaulay	Ken Merrit
1987			Barbara Macaulay	Ken Merrit
1988			Tom Campbell	Harry Murray
1989			Tom Campbell	Harry Murray
1990			Tom Campbell	Harry Murray

	Royal Scots		Honolulu Pipes & Drums aka: Johnny Walker Band aka: Budweiser Pipe Band *Royal Stewart Tartan*	
	Pipe Major	Drum Major	Pipe Major	Drum Major
1991			Glenn Stewart	Harry Murray
1992			Alexander Causey	Harry Murray
1993			Alexander Causey	Harry Murray
1994			Col. Richard Adams	
1995			Col. Richard Adams	
1996			Col. Richard Adams	
1997			Craig MacDonald	
1998			Craig MacDonald	
1999			Craig MacDonald	

	Shamrock Pipe Band *Irish Saffron Tartan*		Celtic Pipes & Drums of Hawai`i aka: Honolulu Police Pipe Band aka: St.Andrews Pipe Band aka: Honolulu Fire Pipes & Drums *Black Watch Tartan*	
	Pipe Major	Drum Major	Pipe Major	Drum Major
1985	Lawrence Coleman	Jamie McCormick		
1986	Lawrence Coleman	Jamie McCormick		
1987	Lawrence Coleman	Jamie McCormick		
1988	Lawrence Coleman	Jamie McCormick	Lawrence Coleman	Joe O'Hannigan
1989			Lawrence Coleman	Joe O'Hannigan
1990			Lawrence Coleman	Bill Hart
1991			Lawrence Coleman	Bill Hart
1992			Lawrence Coleman	Bill Hart
1993			Lawrence Coleman	Bill Hart
1994			Lawrence Coleman	Bill Hart
1995			Lawrence Coleman	Bill Hart
1996			Lawrence Coleman	Bill Hart
1997			Lawrence Coleman	Bill Hart
1998			Lawrence Coleman	Bill Hart

	Shamrock Pipe Band *Irish Saffron Tartan*		Celtic Pipes & Drums of Hawai`i aka: Honolulu Police Pipe Band aka: St. Andrews Pipe Band aka: Honolulu Fire Pipes & Drums *Black Watch Tartan*	
	Pipe Major	Drum Major	Pipe Major	Drum Major
1999			Jacob Kaio, Jr..	Kevin Richards
2000			Jacob Kaio, Jr..	Kevin Richards
2001			Dan Quinn	Kevin Richards
2002			Dan Quinn	Kevin Richards
2003			Dan Quinn	Kevin Richards

	Hawai`i Thistle Band *Scott Tartan*		Marine Corps Pipe Bank *US Marine Corps Tartan*	
	Pipe Major	Drum Major	Pipe Major	Drum Major
2000	Jacob Kaio, Jr..		Lt. Justin Stodghill	
2001	Jacob Kaio, Jr..		Lt. Justin Stodghill	
2002	Jacob Kaio, Jr..		Lt. Justin Stodghill	
2003	Mark Read		Lt. Justin Stodghill	

	Maui Celtic Pipes & Drums *Mixed Tartans*	
	Pipe Major	Drum Major
2002	John Grant	
2003	John Grant	

Appendix 4

Tune Used by J. F. Farquharson for Alfred, Duke of Edinburgh

`Upoho Uka Nui `O Kekokia — 343

This tune was found in J. F. Farquharson's journal of his voyage around the world with Prince Alfred in 1869.

`Upoho Uka Nui `O Kekokia – 345

Is There a Bagpipe in Your Future?